Poetry of
the Age of Chaucer

Poetry of
the Age of Chaucer

Edited by
A. C. and J. E. Spearing

Edward Arnold

First published 1974
by Edward Arnold (Publishers) Ltd
25 Hill Street, London W1X 8LL

ISBN: 0 7131 5744 5   boards edition
      0 7131 5745 3   paper edition

Printed in Great Britain by
Butler & Tanner Ltd, Frome and London

Contents

Acknowledgements

The publishers' thanks are due to the following for permission to reproduce copyright material: Faber & Faber Ltd and Harcourt Brace Jovanovich, Inc. for an extract from T. S. Eliot's 'Little Gidding' (*Collected poems 1909–1962*); Faber & Faber Ltd and Random House, Inc. for an extract from W. H. Auden's 'To a Writer on His Birthday' (*Collected shorter poems 1930–1944*).

General Introduction

The poetry of Chaucer's age

Chaucer is the only medieval English poet who has been read continuously from his own time down to ours, and the only medieval English poet who is at all widely read, by students and by general readers, today. There are good reasons for this. The best reason is his greatness: he is the greatest poet of his age, and one of the half-dozen greatest who have ever written in English. Another reason is the accidental fact that Chaucer happened to write in the dialect of medieval English from which standard modern English is derived, so that his work is more easily understood by modern readers than that of medieval poets, however distinguished, who wrote in other dialects.

But the effect of this overwhelming predominance of Chaucer has been to distort our picture of medieval English poetry generally, and to deprive us of much enjoyment, by throwing his contemporaries into the shade. It is true that Chaucer was immensely influential on the poetry of the age which succeeded his own, the fifteenth century; but in his own time the picture was quite different. The second half of the fourteenth century is an age of great poets, who, like the writers of any literary period, can be seen to have much in common, and who may have known each other's work and influenced each other, but who also possessed distinct individual talents. It is an age fully comparable for its magnitude and variety of poetic talent with the Romantic period (Wordsworth, Coleridge, Byron, Shelley, Keats) or, if we set aside the supreme achievement of Shakespeare, with that from Spenser to Milton. It is indeed the first such age in English poetry: the first age in which poetry moves away from formulaic anonymity into recognizable individuality. The earlier kind of poetry, and one whose methods were still influential on Chaucer and his contemporaries, is represented in this volume by *Sir Orfeo* and by some of the short poems: poems whose authors we do not know and do not need to know, because their aim was not to express an individual view of life through an individual literary style, but to pass on a traditional story or theme by means of a traditional art. It must be emphasized from the beginning that we do not see this more archaic kind of medieval poetry as necessarily inferior to the more 'modern' kind which is found in the later fourteenth century. It often has a direct appeal to the unbiased reader, although to appreciate it more fully, he may need to learn to look for different qualities from those he is accustomed to expect in literature. More will be said about this later.

The first aim of this volume, then, is to encourage a wider reading of fourteenth-century poetry, which will we hope lead to a fuller appreciation of the variety the period has to offer. In the end, the reader may still find Chaucer the supreme poet of his time; but even if he does, he will then be able to see Chaucer not as a solitary giant, in the artificial perspective of 'prescribed texts', but as a great writer among talented contemporaries, by some of whom he may have been significantly influenced. Chaucer himself is represented in this volume by poems deliberately selected because they are not conventional choices as prescribed texts. *The Friar's Tale*, though it is one of the most characteristically witty and decisively ordered of the comic tales to which he turned late in his career, is perhaps too short ever to have been separately edited before. On its small scale, it is as perfect as anything he ever wrote, and more perfect indeed, more completely balanced and finished, than greater and more comprehensive poems such as *Troilus and Criseyde* or *The Knight's Tale*. Shorter still are the two *balades*, *To Rosemounde* and the *Balade de Bon Conseyl*, which represent a side of his work for which he was famous in his own time. *Rosemounde* is related to the 'ditees and . . . songes glade' with which his friend John Gower, speaking through the mouth of Venus in his poem *Confessio Amantis*, wrote that he had filled all the land; the *Balade de Bon Conseyl* is a more serious and tersely sententious treatment of one of the fundamental values of his poetry and the poetry of his age. Our extract from *Piers Plowman* is a better-known part of the work of this less well-known poet. It is very possible that Chaucer knew Langland's work, and even that the dominant theme of *Piers Plowman*—life as a pilgrimage of all the estates of society towards an elusive goal—may have influenced him in the conception of *The Canterbury Tales*. The confessions of the seven deadly sins show Langland at his best, or at least at one of his kinds of best: widely knowledgeable about the lives of criminals and drop-outs and the multitudinous poor; sharply penetrating into human motive and yet, for all his satirical spirit, deeply compassionate; often difficult in his multi-faceted allegory and allusive language.

Langland wrote in alliterative verse; so did another of Chaucer's contemporaries whose work is included in this book, the anonymous poet who was the author of *Sir Gawain and the Green Knight* and, in all probability, of *Patience*. The *Gawain*-poet's work is far more lavishly decorated than Langland's; like Chaucer's, it is court poetry, and it possesses a good deal of Chaucer's sly humour in its treatment of high human aspirations confronted by forces they cannot control, whether the case in question is that of King Arthur's festive court insulted by a monstrous and magic knight, or of a wilful Hebrew prophet trying vainly to escape from the will of a God who shows both terrible anger and fatherly forgiveness. It is possible that Chaucer knew this poet's work too: there are at least striking similarities between the beginning of his *Squire's Tale* and the section of *Sir Gawain and the Green Knight* included here.

Chaucer, Langland and the *Gawain*-poet were all writing towards the end of the century. The date of *Sir Orfeo* is uncertain, as is the identity of its author, but it is undoubtedly earlier, and it may even go back to the late thirteenth century. It deserves a place in the poetry of the age of Chaucer, however, because it was still being copied and read in Chaucer's time, and because there is some reason to believe that Chaucer himself possessed one of the manuscripts in which it has survived. It is a fine example of the English tradition of poetry whose influence upon him has been somewhat overshadowed by our knowledge of his reading in Latin, French and Italian. Some of the shorter poems which form the final section of this book are also uncertain in date: except for the two by Chaucer, their authors are unknown, and the poems themselves may well be earlier in date than the earliest manuscripts in which they occur. They are intended to give some impression of the range of shorter poems in English about Chaucer's time, and they include religious poetry, love poetry and comic poetry—the last category taking in even a rare but irresistible example of the short alliterative poem.

Each poem or group of poems in this book has its own introduction; but we begin with this general introduction, in which we shall first consider some of the features the various poems have in common, and especially those which may be unfamiliar to modern readers, and then discuss some of the differences among the poems, in dialect, metrical form, genre and social context. Finally we shall write briefly about the language and pronunciation of medieval poetry, as a supplement to the recording of readings of the texts which is available with this volume.

Narrative poetry

Most of the poems in this volume tell a story, and this in itself may well be surprising to twentieth-century readers. Storytelling is no doubt one of the most fundamental impulses of art, and it has a power of enchantment; the storyteller's temporary dominance over the minds of his listeners is a kind of magic. Anyone who has told stories to young children will know how true this is, and how urgently they demand, 'Go on, go on; what happened next?' Or, as the *Gawain*-poet puts it, when the Green Knight rides out of Camelot as abruptly as he had entered, leaving us bursting with curiosity as to the consequence of his challenge and its acceptance, 'What thenne?' (GGK 426).[1] In the sixteenth century, Sir Philip Sidney in his *Apology for Poetry* wrote of the poet that 'with a tale forsooth he cometh unto you, with a tale which holdeth children from play, and old men from the chimney corner'. It would be a great mistake to dismiss this magical art of storytelling as fit only for children, or for our medieval ancestors, whom we may wrongly think of as children. As Sidney went on to say, later in the same paragraph, most men 'are childish in the best things, till they be cradled in their graves'. Yet in our time the function of telling stories has receded from poetry to prose, in the form of the novel and short story, and to other, newer art-forms, such as film and television, which use prose so far as they use words at all. And even in the novel story-telling has been dismissed by influential twentieth-century critics as being beneath the interest of truly adult and mature readers. E. M. Forster, in his *Aspects of the Novel*, when he came to *that* aspect of the novel, remarked wearily,

> Yes—oh dear yes—the novel tells a story. That is the fundamental aspect without which it could not exist. That is the highest factor common to all novels, and I wish that it was not so, that it could be something different—melody, or perception of the truth, not this low atavistic form.

In saying this, he was undervaluing his own mastery of the art of narra-tive in his novels. And F. R. Leavis in *The Great Tradition* has commen-ted adversely on another novelist that

> ... he has, apart from some social history, nothing to offer the reader whose demand goes beyond the 'creation of characters' and so on. His attitudes, and the essential substance of interest, are so limited that (though, of course, he provides incident and plot) for the reader it is merely a matter of going on and on; nothing has been done by the close to justify the space taken—except of course that time has been killed (which seems to be all that even some academic critics demand of a novel).

It is of course possible for a writer to have the storyteller's gift in the absence of the other gifts that make up greatness; but that gift is not in itself to be despised, even though its workings may be mysterious and defy analysis. Storytelling may be a way of passing time, as it is on most occasions when we watch a television play or an instalment of a soap opera, and as it was in the Middle Ages in situations like that which Chaucer describes as the framework of the *Canterbury Tales*—a group

---

[1] In references, the texts included in this book are abbreviated as follows: SO = *Sir Orfeo*; GGK = *Sir Gawain and the Green Knight*; Pat = *Patience*; PP = *Piers Plowman*; FT = *The Friar's Tale*.

of pilgrims need some self-created entertainment to fill in the time taken by their slow horseback journey from Southwark to Canterbury and back, and agree to tell each other stories. But time passed is not necessarily time killed. The art of the storyteller is to shape time, to carve shapes out of time. The fundamental structure of narrative is linear, sequential, moving through time in one direction only, just as our lives do. However impressed we may be by particular scenes or incidents, or by the recurrence and development of certain themes or patterns, it is the shape carved by the whole which forms our main impression of the narrative poem.

In this volume, the purest example of narrative art is the earliest poem, *Sir Orfeo*. Its means are simple: we learn nothing of the story-teller or of any significance that he found in the story; we have simply the story itself, of how Orfeo lost his wife and found her again, and of how his country lost and found its ruler. The tale seems to unfold itself in a void, an act of pure creation as much as God's creation of the world out of nothing. It is a story about magic, the arbitrary power of faery, which has nothing to do with individual character or morality; but the prime magic is that of the story itself. *Sir Gawain and the Green Knight*, another tale of magic, has something of the same arbitrariness in its own being, an *aventure* which takes over its hero, tests him, and then returns him to his society, changed and bewildered, and leaves it to us (though with far more guidance than we get as readers of *Sir Orfeo*) to find a meaning or a moral in the absorbing sequence of events. Throughout the poem we are caught in a web of suspense, urgently longing to know what will come next, how the challenge to a monstrous beheading game will finally be met; and when our longing is at last answered, it is in a way so unexpected that we are forced to look back once more over the whole intricate shape of the narrative, and see it in a quite different perspective. This is already a more complex effect than is aimed at by *Sir Orfeo;* and late fourteenth-century poets generally, without abandoning narrative itself, began to treat it in new ways. The extract we have chosen from *Patience* tells a story, that of the first part of the Book of Jonah in the Bible; but in its context in the whole poem, this story is set in the framework of a definition of the virtue of patience. Jonah's impatience, his unwillingness to submit to the will of God, is met by God's patience, and thus the same story exemplifies at once the negative and the positive. The narrative *exemplum*, the illustration taken from everyday life of an abstract moral conception, was one of the commonest features of medieval preaching, and as such it is one sign of the medieval appetite for storytelling. In *Patience* one does not know whether to be more impressed by the independent life of the narrative or by the subtlety with which it is used to illuminate and realize the moral concept. One is in a similar position when one reads *The Friar's Tale*. It is a superb story in itself, in which we watch with delight as the wicked summoner is enticed into the devil's trap, until at last, in the very stupidity of his avarice and callousness, he hands himself over, bound hand and foot, to eternal damnation. Yet once more, the story in its full context has a frame which makes us see it in a further perspective. It is told by the Friar precisely for the benefit of one particular Summoner among the Canterbury pilgrims. We already know of the personal and professional enmity which exists between these two egregious representatives of the corruption of the late medieval Church; and we are aware with every word of the electrical effect the story has and is designed to have on the pilgrim-Summoner. Our withers are unwrung; all the more pleasurably so, because we recognize how delicately that galled jade is made to wince. *The Friar's Tale* is only one example, of course, of the complex possibilities opened up by Chaucer's plan of attributing stories to specific tellers and making us keep in mind the presence of specific listeners. In *The Canterbury Tales* the art of narrative is given a complete new dimension.

In one sense, our extract from *Piers Plowman* also takes the form of a narrative. Langland's subject is the prevalence of the sins in the everyday life of his time, the need for confession, for the change of heart that can only be brought about by self-criticism and self-recognition, and the possibility of salvation which is then opened up. But he treats this subject not in general terms, but in the form of a story, in which each of the seven sins appears as a character, confessing himself to a character called Repentance. Within this narrative framework, further narratives are included, because in several cases a sin's confession consists of the story of his life, while in the case of Gluttony we are told the exemplary anecdote of how his sin intervened between himself and confession, and he ended not absolved in church on Friday, but in his own bed, and in a drunken stupor, on Sunday evening. Another example, then, of the late fourteenth-century framed narrative; but Langland is not so fully dedicated to narrative as Chaucer and the *Gawain*-poet, and he always shows a tendency to wander bafflingly between story and homily. Thus the overall effect is not one of solidity, though many of the details are convincingly solid, but of a kind of phantasmagoria, in which we cannot be sure that there is any ultimately valid frame of reference. In a word, the effect is that of a dream; and this is appropriate enough, because the outer frame of the poem as a whole (though we see nothing of this in the extract in this volume) is the narration of a series of dreams whose dreamer is William Langland, the author of the poem.

Piers Plowman, then, is a somewhat ambiguous case, but apart from this it is only the short poems in this collection which are not essentially narratives. The genius of English poetry in Chaucer's time was for storytelling, and even moral ideas were imagined by Chaucer and his contemporaries in the forms of sequences of actions. In the twentieth century, many great writers and film-directors have partly or wholly abandoned the framework of narrative, often because they wish to convey a sense of life itself as fragmented, non-sequential, phantasmagoric. We may therefore find it particularly refreshing to turn to medieval masters of the storyteller's art; and it may even be that we are on the verge of a situation in which the artists of our own time will once more take up this fundamental resource. The most recent films of the distinguished Italian director Pasolini have been taken from ancient collections of stories, two of them medieval: *The Thousand and One Nights*, Boccaccio's *Decameron*, and Chaucer's *Canterbury Tales*. Pasolini himself has spoken of the making of these films as 'this experience of entering into the most mysterious workings of artistic creation, this proceeding into the essence of narration', and he adds: 'I find it the most beautiful idea I have ever had, this wish to tell, to recount, for the sheer joy of telling and recounting.'[1] That joy is also conveyed in the work of the narrative poets of the fourteenth century.

Poetry for listeners

A second respect in which fourteenth-century poetry differs from twentieth-century poetry is that it was written for listeners, not readers. In Chaucer's time, before printing had been invented, books were scarce and very expensive. Chaucer himself, an unusually bookish man, is said by one of his characters (the God of Love in the *Prologue* to *The Legend of Good Women*) to possess sixty of them—few enough in our time, but an exceptionally large private collection then. Moreover, partly as a consequence of this, literacy was far from universal, and people generally were used to retaining information taken in through their ears, without expecting to possess a written copy of what they were hearing. The sermon, the university lecture (a strange survival into modern times), the story told aloud, often enough by a minstrel who himself possessed no copy of it: these were the typical experiences of Chaucer's contemporaries, and it may perhaps take an effort for us to imagine ourselves inside those experiences. Perhaps the nearest parallel is the experience of watching a film or a television programme: we do not expect, in most cases, ever to see the script, or even to be able to halt the performance for a moment while we think about it, or go back to an earlier part to compare it with what we have just seen. We experience films and television programmes only as irreversible sequences, even if we have the opportunity to see them a second time; and many of us have developed a considerable skill in taking in the significance of

[1] Interview with Gideon Bachmann, *The Guardian*, 13 August 1973, p. 8.

images which have appeared to us only momentarily, as part of an ever-moving linear progression. A medieval listener was in a similar position, except of course that he was relying on the ear rather than the eye—though the ear was to some extent aided by the eye when a poem was recited or a sermon preached, because dramatic gesture was a regular part of the medieval arts of poetry and preaching.

In this book we are inevitably concerned with poems which have come down from the Middle Ages in written form. Before the invention of the tape-recorder, there was no possibility of recapturing the art of minstrels who composed poems which did not exist in written form at all, but were re-created in a slightly different form each time they were recited. And, as literacy spread in England in the course of the fourteenth century, and books began to be produced and sold on a commercial basis (though still written by hand, of course), it began to be possible for poets to expect their work to circulate in manuscript as well as being recited aloud. *Piers Plowman* exists in over fifty manuscripts, and no doubt found many readers; *The Canterbury Tales* exist in over eighty, though it may be significant that they all date from after Chaucer's death. The normal situation in Chaucer's time was still that which he turns into fiction in *The Canterbury Tales*: a story is told aloud to a group of listeners who are in the teller's presence, whose tastes and interests have to be taken into account in the initial selection of the tale, and who may comment on it at the end, or may even interrupt it if it contains something they dislike (as the Summoner indignantly interrupts the Friar's tale, and has to be silenced by the Host). There are many traces of this situation in the poems in this book, though sometimes in introductory sections which we have not included in our extracts. Indeed, the very existence of such sections is a sign of oral delivery: the storyteller cannot plunge straight into his story, but has to begin by gaining his audience's attention, giving them some indication of what kind of tale is to follow, and allowing latecomers to settle themselves. *Sir Orfeo*, in one of its manuscript versions, begins with a prologue in which the poet talks generally of how the Breton minstrels composed lays about adventures, and addresses his audience directly, with a request for attention, giving them ample opportunity to get settled before he really begins:

> Now, of this aventours that weren yfalle
> I can tell sum, ac nought alle: *but*
> Ac herkneth, lordinges that beth trewe, *who are faithful*
> Ichill you telle Sir Orfewe.   *I will*

He creates in the course of the poem an atmosphere of intimacy with the action which includes intimacy with the audience, as we can see near the end, when he enthusiastically exclaims, 'Lord! ther was grete melody!' (SO 566) at the queen's return, and comments lastly,

> Thus com Sir Orfeo out of his care;
> God graunt us alle welle to fare! (SO 579–80)

Again, in *Sir Gawain and the Green Knight*, before our extract, there are two stanzas in which the poet places his story in the context of the legendary history of Britain, and finally he introduces the story proper with an appeal for attention:

> Forthi an aunter in erde I attle to showe,
> That a selly in sight summe men hit holden,
> And an outtrage aventure of Arthures wonderes.
> If ye will listen this laye bot on littel while,
> I shall telle hit astit. . . .

(And so I intend to disclose an adventure, which some men consider a marvel to behold—an extraordinary adventure from among the wonders associated with Arthur. If you will listen to this poem for only a little while, I shall at once recite it. . . .) At the end of the third section of his poem, by which time some of his listeners may have been getting restive, he once more calls for silence:

> And ye will a while be stille,   *if*
> I shall telle you how they wroght.

Familiarity

Once the story is under way, it has to be told in a style which will be easily followed by a listening audience. Medieval people may have been more practised listeners than we are, but when a poem was read to them for entertainment they could not be expected to give its words the kind of concentrated study that modern poetry often demands from its readers. For one thing, the poet needed to write in a style with which his audience would be largely familiar: a common and traditional style rather than one permeated and appropriated by the poet's individual inventiveness. By the end of the fourteenth century, it is true, we begin to find poets writing in unmistakably personal styles: most of Chaucer's work, for example, bears his signature in its very texture even if we have no other evidence as to its authorship. But originality was not consciously sought for or praised, and indeed there was no English word to name it. Poets claimed no more than to be repeating a story in a form sanctioned and fixed by tradition; they were still near the situation of primitive cultures, in which poetic form is primarily a mnemonic device, to preserve ancient stories and customs in the memories of those who have no other way of keeping them alive. The *Gawain*-poet continues his introduction to his story, quoted above, by saying that he will repeat it as he has heard it among men, fixed in shape by the ancient traditional form of alliterative verse:

> I shall tell hit astit, as I in toun herde,
>> With tonge,
>> As hit is stad and stoken
>> In story stiff and stronge,
>> With lel lettres loken,
>> In londe so has been longe.

(I shall at once recite it aloud as I have heard it among men, as it is firmly set down in a brave story, fastened with true letters, as has long been the custom in this land.) The *Gawain*-poet and Chaucer were in fact more original writers than they cared to claim to be, but, so far as literary style was concerned, there could be no question of any four-teenth-century poet wrenching language to his own purpose as radi-cally as Milton or Hopkins or Ted Hughes. His audience would not have had the means of understanding him if he had done; and even a poet as original and difficult as Langland was doing no more than develop a style within an already existing tradition of alliterative moral allegory; and his style in turn was further imitated and developed by later alliterative writers whose work is often difficult to distinguish from his own.

We may find some of the poetry of Chaucer's age difficult to under-stand, especially if it is in the alliterative style, but this is because it belongs to a tradition which is unfamiliar to us. To its original audiences it is likely to have seemed reassuringly familiar. It was full of phrases worn as smooth as pebbles by constant use, such as alliterative pairs of a type still common in English speech: 'life and limb' (PP 37), 'neither stub nor stone' (SO 322), 'body and bones' (SO 30, and, in a very different context, FT 244; compare also 'Bone and blood' [*Lullaby* 8]), 'words and works' (PP 24 and 308), and many others. Especially within the alliterative tradition, complete lines or half-lines often belong to a common stock available to all poets. To take a single example, compare

> The first word that he warp, 'Wher is,' he said,   *uttered*
> The governour of this ging?'   (GGK 188–9)   *company*

with

> The firste worde that he warpe was, 'Where is the bolle?' (PP 305)

The contexts are different and the poets are different, and there is no reason whatever to suppose that one was influenced by the other; yet they are both content to use a half-line that can be traced as far back as the Anglo-Saxon alliterative poetry of several centuries earlier. If we found something similar in a modern writer, we should use pejorative terms such as 'plagiarism' or 'cliché'; but where it is not assumed that originality of style is the poet's goal, such terms lose their meaning. To take another example, Chaucer's Friar describes the summoner in his story as being as mad as a hare (FT 27), thus using a simile which was familiar in his own time and is still familiar in ours. Chaucer has no wish, usually, to step outside the bounds of common language, and this implies a willingness to put his trust in common experience. (It makes all the difference, of course, that Chaucer and his audience had probably seen hares leaping wildly in the spring, whereas most modern people who use the cliché 'as mad as a March hare' have not had this experience.) Chaucer, like the other English poets of his time, does not claim to be an exceptional person whose exceptional experiences demand an exceptional language for their expression. He is perfectly capable of recognizing and parodying what is merely and deadly conventional in life and in language (as we see in the parody of love-poetry in *To Rosemounde*), but where common experience is still solid and vital he is content with it and with its traditional means of expression.

Diffuseness

Poetry written for listeners needs not only to contain a large element of the familiar, but also to be diffuse rather than concentrated in style. When the poet of *Sir Orfeo* wishes to say that Queen Heurodis was the most beautiful of ladies, he describes her as

> The fairest levedy for the nones   *lady indeed*
> That might gon on body and bones.   (SO 29–30)

We have seen that 'body and bones' was a well-worn phrase; and neither it nor 'for the nones' adds anything significant to the meaning of his description. Both phrases are no more than tags, and such tags are of use to poets, obviously enough, as fillers for their rhyming and metrical schemes. As such, they go back to the time when poetry was orally composed, and poets needed what breathing-spaces they could get in order to think ahead to the next line and the next incident. They are also useful to listeners, as a means of ensuring that they do not have to concentrate on every word in order to take in the poet's meaning. *Sir Gawain and the Green Knight* contains many almost meaningless tags of this kind, often in metrically awkward positions: *on sille* (19), *in daye* (44), *on live* (349), *in stedde* (403). Anyone who has composed a speech or lecture for public delivery will have learned that he cannot afford to follow Keats's advice to Shelley and 'load every rift with ore'; he has to surround the crucial points with less crucial matter, and he has to repeat himself a good deal too. It was the same for medieval poets. Sometimes their repetitions are a matter of repeating the same words, and are connected with the whole tendency of medieval poetry to rely on traditional modes of expression. Thus the *Gawain*-poet repeats the same group of alliterating words at the end of one stanza and the beginning of the next to tell us that Arthur, unlike the other nobles at the New Year feast, was standing upright: 'He stightles stiff in stalle' (GGK 68) (He stands boldly upright) and 'Thus there stondes in stalle the stiff king hisselven' (GGK 71) (Thus the bold king himself is standing up). He does the same in *Patience*, using the same group of words in God's command to Jonah—' "Rys radly," He says, "and rayke forth even"' (Pat 5) ("Rise quickly," he says, "and go forth directly")— as in Jonah's response to that command—'Thenne he rises radly and raykes bilive' (Pat 29) (Then he rises quickly and goes at once). But here, as often in this poet's work, one suspects that the repetition of the formula may not be merely automatic, since, though Jonah is rising quickly and going as God has ordered, he is doing so in the opposite direction to that intended by God. There is a contrast between the action and the purpose, which the use of the same words helps to underline.

We shall see in a moment how other kinds of verbal repetition form part of the artistry of medieval verse. But another kind of repetition which belongs to the characteristic diffuseness of medieval poetry involves using not the same words but different words with the same meaning. This may be done simply for emphasis, to underline a crucial moment in the narrative. When Orfeo, after all his miseries, regains his wife and at once sets off back to his own country, we are told so twice:

> His wif he took by the hond
> And dede him swithe out of that lond,   *went quickly*
> And went him out of that thede.   (SO 449–51)   *country*

Here *dede him* means the same as *went him* and *that lond* the same as *that thede*. In *Sir Gawain and the Green Knight*, when the Green Knight is setting out the conditions of the beheading game, he declines to tell Gawain his name and address before receiving Gawain's axe-stroke, and this point is so significant (because the unknown is mysterious, and presumably if Gawain's blow is effective he will never know these things) that it is put in two ways. It will be sufficient, says the Green Knight,

> If I thee telle truly, when I the tappe have
> And thou me smoothely has smitten, smartly I thee teche
> Of my house and my home and myn owen nome.   (GGK 370–72)

(If I tell you truly when I have received the blow and you have struck me neatly, I am prompt to inform you about my house and my home and my own name.) Line 371 says the same as line 370, but with the elements in reverse order; and here we are surely meant to recognize and enjoy the ingenuity of the variation even as we take in the point being made. It is part of the flamboyance of expression which is characteristic of alliterative rather than metrical verse in Chaucer's time. Another example, from *Patience*, helps to suggest how variation can be used deliberately to create not merely diffuseness and emphasis but elevation of style. The poet intervenes in the story to point out how foolish Jonah was to suppose that he could escape from God's sight; could he not have read in the Psalms that the creator of ears must hear everything, and the creator of eyes see everything?

> O fooles in folk, feeles otherwhile
> And understondes umbestounde, thagh ye be stape foole!   (Pat 61–2)

(O fools among the people, perceive now and then and understand occasionally, though you are quite mad!) Here once more the second line repeats the meaning of the first, but in reverse order; and the repetition, reversal and variation are all derived from Psalm 93, verse 8: 'Understand, ye senseless among the people: and, you fools, be wise at last.'[1] The parallelisms of Hebrew poetry fall very naturally into the style of English alliterative verse; parallelism has been a normal means of creating a formal, elevated style in many different literary traditions. It carries with it suggestions of wealth and leisure: the wealth of available words and phrases, and the leisure of an aristocratic audience which can spare the time to hear them repeated. It is particularly appropriate that God should speak in such a style, and so he does, for example when he is telling Jonah to preach to the Ninevites because of their wickedness:

> For iwisse hit arn so wikke that in that won dowelles,
> And her malis is so much, I may not abide,
> Bot venge me on her vilanye and venim bilive.   (Pat 9–11)

(For indeed those who dwell in that city are so wicked, and their evil is so great, that I cannot endure it, but shall take vengeance on their villainy and venom at once.) *Wikke, malis, vilanye, venim*: after these near-synonyms we cannot fail to note the evil of the Ninevites, or the grandeur with which God denounces it.

Metaphor and simile

A remark of Aristotle's which has been widely quoted and approved in modern discussions of poetry is that metaphor is the greatest distinction of poetry and the only sign of poetic genius. Metaphor has been a key concept in much modern literary criticism, and we have become used

[1] Biblical quotations are taken from the Douay version, the English translation of the Latin Vulgate Bible which medieval poets would have known.

to responding with excitement and delight to the richly metaphoric poetic language of Shakespeare or Keats. And yet metaphor is largely absent from medieval poetry. One reason for this is undoubtedly that metaphors, except for those which form part of the common language and are therefore not the creation of individual poets, are in general too difficult, too concentrated, to be easily taken in by a listener. (This cannot be the only reason, because Shakespeare's strongly metaphorical style was also written for listeners—though they were listeners who were often readers of printed books, and who had the enactment of the story on the stage to help them when they were listening.) Whatever the cause, we may be disappointed at first to find that what may seem to us some of the most exquisite local effects in poetry are simply unknown in the poetry of Chaucer's time. Two lines by Keats may serve as an example, chosen almost at random:

> Those green-rob'd senators of mighty woods,
> Tall oaks, branch-charmed by the earnest stars.

Exquisitely beautiful, in a way which depends on a deep metaphoric texture, but surely quite impossible for those who are *only* listeners to grasp. On the other hand, a major disadvantage of a style as rich as that is that it is quite unsuitable for narrative, because the complex interest of the words will inevitably obscure the events; and, as we have seen, the chief genius of fourteenth-century poetry is for narrative. One ideal of medieval style, represented in a more naive form by *Sir Orfeo* and in a more sophisticated form by *The Friar's Tale*, is that it should be an almost completely transparent medium, through which we observe the flow and patterning of events. The style of alliterative poetry is denser than that of metrical poems such as these, but it is still largely lacking in metaphor.

In place of metaphor we find simile, a more open and diffuse literary figure; but even that is thin-spread, and is largely confined to traditional comparisons and comparisons drawn from everyday experience. *Sir Orfeo* is almost totally lacking even in simile, to such an extent that we may feel tempted to read the whole poem as *implied* simile, or metaphor; a sequence of events and emotions which as a whole has another meaning, concerning the inner world of the human mind. Our extract from *Sir Gawain and the Green Knight* has a few similes, well chosen for a specific purpose. They suggest the paradox that the Green Knight is both a natural phenomenon and a product of civilization. His beard is as big as a bush (GGK 146) and yet together with his hair it is trimmed to the shape of a royal cape, a highly artificial *kinges capados* (150). He and his horse are as green as grass (199), but, no, they are greener than that, like green enamel glowing on gold (200), in one of the elaborate jewels or *joyaux* that were so much loved by the aristocracy in the

Middle Ages. *Patience* too has a small number of striking similes, including that which compares Jonah being swallowed by the whale to a speck of dust entering a cathedral door (Pat 208). There are some fine similes in our extract from *Piers Plowman*, taken from familiar areas of experience, domestic or agricultural (for even Londoners in the Middle Ages were still close to the country), but applied with great inventiveness to human behaviour and appearance. Envy looks like a leek that has been lying too long in the sun (PP 20–21); he lives as unloving and unloved as a bad dog (56); Gluttony's guts begin to rumble like two greedy sows (283); and so on. *The Friar's Tale* has almost as few similes as *Sir Orfeo*, though one of those few has a more complex effect than at first appears. The Friar asserts that his summoner is

> as full of jangles
> As full of venim been thise waryangles,   (FT 107–8)

that is, he is as full of chatter as butcher-birds are full of venom. Now this does not directly compare the summoner with a cruel butcher-bird, but it obviously implies such a comparison, and all the more so because birds are frequently described in Middle English as 'jangling'. It is easy to imagine the Friar's delight in the implied double insult to the real Summoner as both jangling and venomous. It is obvious, however, that this simile is something very special, a small set-piece which we are expected to notice particularly: it is all the more effective because of the very rarity of such devices in the *Tale*.

Description

If imagery, in the sense of metaphor and simile, is rare in medieval poetry, imagery in another sense, pictorial description, is considerably more common. The medieval storyteller is always ready to pause in order to conjure up before the mind's eye of his audience vivid pictures of crucial events, places and persons in his story. As the Middle Ages proceeded, this pictorial element grew to be more and more prominent in literature, until in much fifteenth-century poetry it becomes excessive, swamping the narrative and halting its forward movement. Some would say that signs of this excess can already be found in some of Chaucer's poetry, for example in the elaborate descriptions of the temples and the champions in *The Knight's Tale*; but, however this may be, the poems in this volume generally achieve an admirable balance between story and description. It is normal—and this again makes things easier for an audience of listeners—for descriptions to take the form of self-contained sections of the poem, clearly marked off from the narrative so that we can recognize them for what they are. There is an early example in *Sir Orfeo*, in the description of the underworld country at lines 328–50, which has as its centrepiece the description of the richly-ornamented castle.The content of the description of the country in general is largely traditional: it contains the normal elements of medieval descriptions of paradise—the green meadow, the brilliant jewellery, the unchanging brightness despite the fact that there was no sun—and it leads up naturally to Orfeo's verdict:

> By all thing him think that it is   *it seems to him*
> The proude court of Paradis.   (SO 351–2)

Like the poem's listeners, Orfeo recognizes the traditional features of this poetic landscape and identifies it accordingly (though we are eventually left in doubt as to whether the identification is correct). Our extract from *Piers Plowman* contains several set-piece descriptions of people, such as those of Envy and Avarice. These too are traditional in origin: there was a long tradition of verbal and pictorial representations of the seven deadly sins in allegorical poems, moral treatises, manuscript illuminations, stained glass, carvings in stone and wood. It does not appear that Langland is closely following any specific sources within this general tradition, and many of the details of his descriptions are probably invented. Many of them, too, have at once a physical and a moral significance. For example, Avarice's cheeks lolling 'as a letheren purs' (PP 130) are part of a physically repellent picture of miserly old age, but the reference to a leather purse (that is, a medieval purse, a small bag made of soft leather and shapeless unless it had money in it) also suggests how his obsession with money has permeated even his physical appearance. Again, the 'forsleeves' of Envy's costume are taken from a friar's habit (PP 19); this tells us what they looked like, but it also suggests a connection between the sin and the friars which is part of Langland's general opposition to friars, whom he saw as begging and hypocritical parasites.

The most splendid descriptions of all in this volume are those by the *Gawain*-poet. The description of the Green Knight, his horse and his equipment, occupies over eighty lines, and it is carefully framed by two similar lines marking its beginning and its end: 'There hales in at the halle door an aghlich maister' (GGK 100) (There comes in at the hall door a terrible lord) and 'This hathel heldes him in and the halle entres' (GGK 185) (This knight comes in and enters the hall). Between these two lines the action of the poem is suspended, and yet the description itself is by no means undramatic. The poet's eye moves over the monstrous apparition like that of one of the astonished spectators in the poem, taking in first the general, paradoxical effect of hugeness combined with chivalric elegance, then the details of the knight, next those of his horse and its trappings, and lastly coming to a horrified focus on the forbidding axe. There is nothing random about the ordering of the details; one can sense the poet's enjoyment in producing suspense and astonishment, as he saves the supremely strange fact of the knight's green colour for the very last word of the first stanza of the description, and the almost equal strangeness of the horse's greenness for the end of the second stanza. Lines 160–66 invite us to see the apparition through the eyes of the courtiers, and the hint the last lines here give us of the possibility of blows from him—

> Hit seemed as no man might
> Under his dintes drye   (GGK 165–6)

(It seemed as if no man could survive under blows from him)—is taken up and expanded in the fourth and final stanza with the fascinated, lingering look at the immense (and also green) battle-axe. More than any other poet of the fourteenth century, more even than Chaucer himself, the *Gawain*-poet has the power of entering into the worlds of his poems, seeing events and objects as they would be seen by the inhabitants of those worlds, and thereby confirming their three-dimensional solidity. The effect is strongly cinematic, as the eye of the camera moves into the poem-space, showing crucial details in close-up, and following and entering into the movement of action. Thus we follow the downward sweep of Gawain's axe-blade as it carves gruesomely through the flesh and bones of the Green Knight's neck and finally bites into the ground; then we follow the severed head as it in turn hits the floor and rolls forward, to be kicked nervously away by the onlookers, and finally picked up by its hair by its headless owner.

In *Patience*, too, the elaborately repulsive description of the inside of the whale is presented as seen by Jonah himself, as he enters its jaws like a speck of dust going through a cathedral door, then passes through its gills and intestines till he comes to a jarring halt in its filthy belly, where he searches in vain (in vain until he seeks the aid of prayer) for some resting-place. Here, as much as in *Sir Orfeo* and *Piers Plowman*, the details of the description are not only vividly realistic, but also conform to an established tradition for descriptions of hell.

Sound-effects

One last aspect of this poetry which may seem strange to modern readers, and which is closely connected with the fact that it was written to be heard, is that much of its effect is conveyed through its sound, and therefore is likely to be noticed only if it is read aloud. This is much more striking with alliterative than with metrical poetry. Langland, and still more the *Gawain*-poet, create an exceptionally rich texture of sound in their verse, sometimes directly onomatopoeic and sometimes more generally evocative of sensory experiences. This texture can be better demonstrated, by reading the verse aloud, than it can be discussed, but it may be worth mentioning a few brief examples.

The crunching of the Green Knight's neck-bone by the axe is conveyed directly by the line: 'That the sharp of the shalk shindered the bones' (GGK 388) (So that the blade shattered the bones of the man). The whirling and bubbling of the stormy sea is marvellously captured in the line: 'The pure poplande hourle playes on my heved' (Pat 259) (The boiling sea-surge itself plays on my head). To take a slightly longer example, the conflict and sickening rise and fall of the tempest at sea are evoked precisely in the sound and rhythm of these lines:

> The windes on the wonne water so wrastel togeder
> That the wawes full woode waltered so highe
> And efte bushed to the abym. . . .   (Pat 81–3)

(The winds on the dark water so wrestled together that the mad waves rolled so high and plunged back to the depths. . . .)

Onomatopoeic effects of this kind (which reach their uproarious height in the short poem *Blacksmiths*) are spectacular enough not to remain unappreciated; but what may be less easily noticed and enjoyed are the constant, quieter patternings of sound which pervade metrical as well as alliterative verse. Alliteration itself is very common in the rhyming verse of Chaucer's time:

> In a *t*abernacle of a *t*owre,   *niche*
> As I stoode *m*using on the *m*oone,
> A *c*rowned *q*ueene, most of honoure,
> Apered in gostly *s*ight full *s*oone.   *spiritual vision*
>   (*Quia Amore Langueo* 1–4)

Still more common are a whole range of kinds of verbal and phrasal repetition. Medieval works on the art of poetry, written in Latin, and probably well known to Chaucer and the *Gawain*-poet, devote a great deal of attention to such patterns of repetition, analysing the different types and giving them technical names: repetition of the first word in successive sentences is called *repetitio*, repetition of the last word *conversio*, repetition of the first and last words *conplexio*, and so on. These theoretical works, however, the *artes poeticae*, serve only to formulate the practice of the poets, and we need not concern ourselves here with the details of their categorization. Practical examples can easily be found. In *Sir Orfeo*, the passage contrasting Orfeo's wretched condition in the wilderness with the luxury in which he had lived as a king consists of a series of sentences, each beginning 'He that hadde . . .', and each going on to repeat 'Now . . .'. The repetition is not merely decorative but functional: it underlines the painful contrast between past and present:

> *He that hadde* ywerd the fowe and griis,   *variegated and grey fur*
> And on the bed the purper biis,   *purple linen*
> *Now* on hard hethe he lith,

With leves and gresse he him writh.   *covers himself*
He that hadde had castels and tours,
River, forest, frith with flours,   *woodland*
Now, thei it comenci to snewe and freese,   *though it begins*
This king mot make his bed in mese.   *must   moss*
He that had yhad knightes of pris   *value*
Bifor him kneeland, and levedys,   *ladies*
Now seeth he nothing that him liketh,   *pleases him*
Bot wilde wormes by him striketh.   *serpents   glide*
He that had yhad plenté
Of mete and drink, of ich dainté,
Now may he all day digge and wrote   *grub*
Er he finde his fille of roote. (SO 217–32)

There is a similar set piece of repetition later in *Sir Orfeo*, in the passage describing the supposedly dead people found by Orfeo in the underworld, where they have been carried off by the fairies; in this, seven successive lines begin with the phrase 'And sum . . .' (SO 368-74).

In Chaucer's work, and especially in late poems such as *The Friar's Tale*, whose art is partly to suggest a casual ease and naturalness, patterns of repetition are less ostentatious, but they are still present throughout, affecting the listeners without their necessarily being conscious of it. One might note the fairly obvious repetitions of the list of matters with which the archdeacon was judicially concerned at the beginning of the tale, where each item is introduced by an *of*, but where also repetition is combined with variation in the different connectives by which the items are marshalled into pairs. Thus we have successively *of*, *of . . . and eek of*, *of . . . and*, *of . . . and of* (twice), and *of . . . and of . . . also*:

In punishinge of fornicacioun,
Of wicchecraft, and eek of bawderye,   *procuring*
Of diffamacioun, and avowtrye,   *adultery*
Of chirche reves, and of testaments   *church robberies*
Of contractes and of lakke of sacraments,
Of usure, and of simonye also. (FT 4–9)

Or there is the functionally unnecessary but rhetorically highly effective triple repetition of the word *theef* in the following lines:

And right as Judas hadde purses smalle,
And was a *theef*, right swich a *theef* was he;
His maister hadde but half his duetee. *what was due to him*
He was, if I shall yeven him his laude,   *due praise*
A *theef*, and eek a somnour, and a bawde. (FT 50–54)

In calling attention to such devices, one inevitably distorts their effect, for they are intended to work below the level of consciousness, under-lining meaning and emotion, and providing constant small charges of pleasure. It is possible, by reading medieval verse aloud, and hearing it read, to develop a far greater sensitivity towards auditory patterning than modern readers normally possess; and if one does so, one's pleasure in medieval literature will be considerably enhanced.

Variety and difference: dialect and literary tradition

So far we have chiefly been concerned with things the different poems in this book have in common; but we began by emphasizing the variety which is one of the most attractive features of the literature of Chaucer's age. It is by no means monolithic, and the time has now come for us to say something more about the differences which exist among the dif-ferent poems included here, and the causes of those differences. Perhaps the difference which will be most obvious is that some of the poems are considerably easier to understand than others without the help of glosses and translations, and Chaucer's work is perhaps the easiest of all. The reason for this is not that what Chaucer wrote is intrinsically easier in content or in mode of expression, nor that it was more easily under-stood by all fourteenth-century readers; it is that different poets of the fourteenth century wrote in different dialects.

We all know how difficult it can be, even nowadays, to understand what ordinary people are saying, especially perhaps country people, if one visits a part of Britain where one has never been before. Yorkshire shepherds and Cornish fishermen and London coalmen speak such different versions of English that they sound almost like different languages the first time one hears them. In Chaucer's time, before the standardizing effects of printing, rapid communications, newspapers, radio, and television had occurred, there were still more striking dif-ferences among the dialects spoken in different parts of the country. John of Trevisa, a Cornishman, said of the speech of Yorkshiremen that it was 'so harsh, piercing, grating and formless that we Southern men can hardly understand that language'; and no doubt Yorkshire-men would have been equally rude about his dialect. Nearly a century after Chaucer's time, Caxton tells a story of how some southerners wished to buy eggs in the north of England, and were almost defeated by the fact that their word for 'eggs' was *eyren* while the northern word was *egges*.

But in Chaucer's time, unlike our own, serious literature was still being written in several of these dialects. In our time, there is a single form of standard English, which is used by all writers, whichever part of the country they come from, and however far their own speech may diverge from the standard. It so happens that the dialect of Middle English from which modern standard English is derived is that in which Chaucer himself wrote—the dialect of the London area, which even then was beginning to become predominant, through being the country's largest city and commercial centre, and the normal home of the king and his court. It is for this reason that we now find Chaucer's work comparatively easy to understand. The poet of *Sir Orfeo* probably wrote in the dialect of the Westminster–Middlesex area, which is much the same as Chaucer's; but *Sir Orfeo* may be a little more difficult to understand, because it was written earlier.

The *Gawain*-poet, on the other hand, wrote in the dialect of the north-west Midlands (more specifically, perhaps, in south-east Cheshire or north-east Staffordshire), a dialect from which standard modern English is not derived, and this is one reason why so many of his words are unfamiliar to us. He has a very rich vocabulary, including not only English elements, but many French words (which is also true of Chaucer), and also many words derived from Norse, because he came from the part of the country which had been under Scandinavian rule before the Norman conquest. Words such as *cayred* (GGK 7), *glaum* (10), *samen* (14), *nayted* (29), *graythed* (38), *glent* (46), and many others, are of Scandinavian origin, and have not descended into modern English. But the difficulty of the *Gawain*-poet's work is not only a matter of the area in which he wrote but also of the literary tradition in which he wrote. Alliterative verse had been the only kind of verse written by the Anglo-Saxons, and it had formed the basis of a major literature, of which the epic poem *Beowulf* is the finest example. After the Norman Conquest we find far more written evidence of rhyming metrical verse on the French model, though this often includes alliterative phrases. But about the middle of the fourteenth century there appears to have been a revival in the writing of alliterative poetry, centred in the west Midlands, and much of the greatest poetry of Chaucer's age, including the work of Langland and the *Gawain*-poet, is in fact alliterative. There must have been an unbroken tradition linking this fourteenth-century alliterative poetry with that written before the Conquest, though it may be that this tradition was largely orally transmitted, and that it was only in the fourteenth century, with the revival of an interest in the English language and English literature generally after centuries of the dominance of French and Latin, that it was once more commissioned by noble patrons and written down in permanent form. In any case, one important aspect of the alliterative style is its use of a special poetic diction, including many words and constructions which appear not to have been a normal part of the spoken language of the west Midlands, but to have been reserved for the formality of verse. The best-known example of this diction consists of a group of ten words, all meaning 'man' or 'warrior', with little ascertainable difference in meaning among them, and nearly always used to bear alliteration. These are: *burne, freke, gome, hathel, lede, renk, segge, shalk, tulk* and *wye*. Nearly all of these words were used for similar purposes in pre-Conquest alliterative poetry; only one of them (*tulk*) is of Scandinavian origin; and none of them is found in Chaucer's work or in modern standard English. It will be noticed that each of the ten words begins with a different sound, and it will be obvious how useful it would be to a composer of alliterative verse to have this range of near-synonyms available to provide alliterative words which will fit into almost any line (particularly when he could add to them normal words, such as *man* and *knight*). Thus when he wishes to write of the *k*ing *c*oming with men he will use the words '*k*nights' (GGK 26); when he wishes to speak of the *b*est men sitting a*b*ove he will use '*b*urne' (GGK 37); when he wishes to speak of men venturing *l*ife for *l*ife he will use '*l*ede' (GGK 62); and so on. There is a similar group of near-synonyms all bearing the sense 'go' or 'move', such as *cayre* (7), *cheve* (27), *hale* (100), *founde* (231), and several others. There are several synonyms used for such a central concept in *Sir Gawain and the Green Knight* as 'game': *layk* (226), *gomen* (237), *game* (328), *play* (not in our extract). This rich poetic diction certainly adds greatly to the difficulty of the *Gawain*-poet's work for the modern reader, until he has learnt what all the synonyms mean; but it also helps to produce an incomparably fluent, expressive and elevated poetic style. We must not allow the modern prejudice against special poetic language (a feature which has been found in the early poetry of most great literatures) to influence us against the work of one of England's greatest poets.

To return for a moment to the question of dialect: Langland also wrote in alliterative verse, and he too probably came from the west Midlands, though not from the north-west but the south-west—his poem begins with the Dreamer falling asleep on the Malvern Hills. There are west Midland elements in the dialect in which he wrote, but he lived most of his life, probably, in London, and this influenced the language of his poetry and helped to make it easier for modern readers to understand. He also used very little of the alliterative poetic diction; indeed, in this he is almost unique among the poets of the fourteenth-century Alliterative Revival; and this too makes his work less difficult. It is one reason, no doubt, why his poem survives in over fifty manuscripts, and was printed in the sixteenth century and went on being read by at least some readers down to our own time, while the *Gawain*-poet's work survives in only one manuscript, and appears to have been completely unknown after the age of Chaucer until it was first printed in the nineteenth century.

Alliterative verse

This will be a convenient place to say a little more about alliterative verse and its differences from metrical verse in the medieval period. The most immediately obvious feature of alliterative verse is its alliteration; but this is not its fundamental basis. Alliterative verse is basically accentual; that is, it depends for its structure on an arrangement of stressed or accented syllables. The alliterative line of the fourteenth century is made up of two half-lines, each of which contains at least two syllables bearing a heavy stress; and the stressed syllables may be surrounded by almost any number of unstressed or lightly-stressed syllables. It may well be the case that the two-stress phrase which makes an alliterative half-line is a fundamental unit of English speech itself. It is worth considering, for example, what a high proportion of the titles of English novels consist of two-stress phrases, some alliterating, some not: *Príde and Préjudice, Sóns and Lóvers, The Píckwick Pápers, Róderick Rándom, Vánity Fáir, Bléak Hóuse, The Pórtrait of a Lády, The Máyor of Cásterbridge*. These titles will serve to illustrate something of the rhythmic variety that is possible within the half-line framework, ranging from the sombre simplicity of *Bleak House*, which has no unstressed syllables, to more complex patterns such as *The Portrait of a Lady*, with five unstressed syllables. Much twentieth-century verse has been written in lines whose rhythmic basis is just the same as that of medieval alliterative verse: four main stresses to the line, with occasionally an extra stress, and an unfixed number of unstressed syllables. Thus:

> Midwinter spring is its own season
> Sempiternal though sodden towards sundown,
> Suspended in time, between pole and tropic,
> When the short day is brightest, with frost and fire,
> The brief sun flames the ice, on pond and ditches,
> In windless cold that is the heart's heat,
> Reflecting in a watery mirror
> A glare that is blindness in the early afternoon.
>
> (T. S. Eliot, from Little Gidding)

Or:

> August for the people and their favourite islands.
> Daily the steamers sidle up to meet
> The effusive welcome of the pier, and soon
> The luxuriant life of the steep stone valleys,
> The sallow oval faces of the city
> Begot in passion or good-natured habit,
> Are caught by waiting coaches, or laid bare
> Beside the undiscriminating sea.
>
> (W. H. Auden, from To a Writer on his Birthday)

It will be noticed that several lines in the above examples do in fact alliterate; and modern English contains countless alliterative phrases such as 'life and limb', 'house and home', 'kith and kin', 'through thick and thin', 'from rags to riches', many of them descended from the medieval period or earlier. In medieval alliterative verse, the alliteration normally falls on stressed syllables. At least one stressed syllable in the first half of a line must alliterate with at least one (normally the first) in the second half. It is normal for both stressed syllables in the first half to alliterate, and in many cases other syllables, whether stressed or unstressed, bear alliteration too. In most cases the alliteration is on consonants, but any vowel may alliterate with any other vowel. It is not unusual for alliteration to be on pairs of consonants, such as *gl*, *kn*, or *st*. It must be remembered that the stressed syllable, which bears the alliteration, is not necessarily the first syllable of a word; thus in the following line the alliteration is on *b*: 'De*b*ated *b*usily a*b*oute tho giftes' (GGK 32).

We have probably said enough now about the theory of alliterative verse. It was meant, of course, for the ear, and it was a traditional craft handed on by practice: there are no medieval theoretical treatises on how to write this verse, though alliteration is recognized by the *artes poeticae* as one of the many possible kinds of auditory patterning. Alliterative verse can be forceful, muscular, and onomatopoeic; it can also be marvellously fluent and delicate, varying constantly in rhythm from one line to another, and yet never losing touch with the firm beat of stressed syllables. The reader may like to contrast, for example, the style in which Gawain speaks, with its courteous and sinuous complexity (especially in his first long speech, requesting to be allowed to take up the challenge, at lines 307–25), with the style in which the Green Knight speaks, blunt, commanding, contemptuous. It may be helpful, finally, if we print a passage from *Patience*, marking the caesuras (i.e. the divisions between half-lines) by /, syllables bearing the main stress by ' and those bearing a less marked stress by \, and italicizing the alliterations:

'Oure *S*ire *s*ittes,' he *s*ays, / 'on *s*ege so highe
In His *gl*owande *gl*orye, / and *gl*oumbes full littel
Thagh I be *n*ummen in *N*inive / and *n*aked dispoiled,
On *r*oode *r*uly torent / with *r*ibaudes mony.'
Thus he *p*asses to that *p*ort / his *p*assage to seeche,
*F*indes he a *f*air ship / to the *f*are redy,
*M*aches him with the *m*arineres, / *m*akes her paye
For to *t*owe him into *T*arce / as *t*id as they might.   (Pat 33–40)

Metrical verse

Medieval metrical verse is constructed on a different basis from alliterative verse. It derives from French, a language in which stress is far less prominent in speech than it is in English, and its theoretical basis there is the number of syllables in the line. For example, in the decasyllabic French verse from which the verse-form of *The Friar's Tale* is derived, there are ten syllables in every line, and the lines rhyme in couplets. But stress is so important in English speech that it is scarcely possible to write pure syllabic verse in English, and so the decasyllabic line becomes one of five feet, in each of which an unstressed syllable is followed by a stressed syllable, and there may be an extra syllable after the final stress. This is the normal English line, often called the iambic pentameter, in the rhyming verse of poets such as Pope or Keats, or the blank verse of Shakespeare or Milton, and we need probably say little more about it. It allows a great deal of variation, for example by reversing feet (so that the first syllable of a foot is stressed instead of the second), by allowing the stress to fall on a syllable which would normally be lightly stressed, and by adding extra unstressed syllables. One licence which is common in Chaucer, but not in more recent English verse of this type, is the omission of the first unstressed syllable of a line. The effect of all this variability in practice is that we find Chaucer writing couplets in which the main element of regularity is that each line has five stressed syllables; and where, as is often the case, one of these five is only lightly stressed, and there is a marked caesura, his verse is not so very different from alliterative verse. There is often a very delicate play of the English stress-pattern against the French syllabic pattern. Such effects can be sensed by the listener far more easily than they can be discussed and defined, and we must refer readers at this point to the tape accompanying this volume; but it may be of some use if we print a few lines from *The Friar's Tale*, marking stresses and secondary stresses, as before, with / and \ respectively, and also unstressed syllables with ×. It will be noticed that it is generally assumed that a final -*e* (which would be silent in modern English) is pronounced except where the next word begins with a vowel (or an *h-*, which was sounded only very lightly, if at all). Such elisions are marked by ⌢.

> / ×   × \   / × ⌢× \ × /
> Whilom ther was dwellinge in my contree
> × / × / × × / × /   × /
> An erchedeken, a man of heigh degree,
> × / × \ × ⌢ /× / × /
> That boldely dide execucioun
> × / × \ ⌢× / × / × /
> In punishinge of fornicacioun,
> × / × / × / × × /×
> Of wicchecraft, and eek of bawderye,

Of diffamacioun, and avowtrye,
Of chirche reves, and of testaments,
Of contractes and of lakke of sacraments,
Of usure, and of simonye also.
But certes, lechours dide he grettest wo—
They sholde singen if that they were hent—
And smalle titheres weren foule yshent,
If any persoun wolde upon hem plaine.   (FT 1–14)

Sir Orfeo is written in the English verse-form which corresponds to French octosyllabic couplets; this was a common form for English metrical narratives before Chaucer introduced the longer line based on decasyllabic couplets. In the case of *Sir Orfeo*, the syllabic basis has been even more completely resolved into a stress-rhythm than in Chaucer, and in practice what we find are lines with three or four stresses and an unfixed number of unstressed syllables. They often seem somewhat rough, but this may be partly a result of the fact that we have to rely on a rather careless manuscript version of the poem. The short poems in the final section of this volume are written in a variety of metres, ranging from the purely alliterative verse of *Blacksmiths* to the fairly regular stressed decasyllabics of the two poems by Chaucer. Most of the other short poems are based on stress, frequently supported by alliteration.

Literary genre

Having considered some of the differences among our poems brought about by dialect and metrical form, we now turn to another kind of difference, that of literary kind, or genre. The sense of genre was probably more important as an influence on writers in the Middle Ages than it is today, though it cannot be said that the genre 'romance' was any more clearly definable then than that of 'novel' is now. The importance of genre is one part of the importance of tradition in medieval literature, with the corresponding unimportance (at least on the conscious level) of originality and individuality. But in the twentieth-century cinema, to take that as a parallel, the 'Western', the 'thriller', the 'Ealing comedy', and the 'historical epic' have all been recognizable genres, with their own distinctive conventions and methods of procedure, arousing and fulfilling certain specific expectations in the audiences who went to see them, even though there might be many films that did not fall precisely into any such category, or that combined one category with another. One major medieval literary genre, represented in this volume by *Sir Orfeo* and *Sir Gawain and the Green Knight*, is the romance. Medieval romances were stories of adventure, whose heroes were normally people of the highest social classes—kings, princes, knights. One large sub-class of medieval romances (generally called the 'Matter of Britain') are set in the court of King Arthur, that idealized projection into legend of medieval conceptions of aristocratic life. Idealization is a crucial element in medieval romances: everything in them belongs to an extreme, and usually an admirable extreme, characteristically expressed in superlatives. Thus Orfeo's queen was

> The fairest levedy for the nones   *at that time*
> That might gon on body and bones,
> Full of love and of godenisse;
> Ac no man may telle hir fairnisse.   (SO 29–32)   *but*
>
> The fairest levedy that ever was bore   (SO 186)   *born*

and what happens to her arouses extreme emotions:

> Men wist never wher she was bicome.   *gone*
> Tho was ther crying, weepe and wo;
> The king into his chaumber is go,
> And oft swooned opon the ston,
> And made swiche diol and swiche mon   *sorrow   lamentation*
> That neighe his lif was yspent.   (SO 170–76)

Similarly, in *Sir Gawain and the Green Knight*, Arthur's whole court consists of

> The most kyd knightes under Cristes selven,   *famous*
> And the lovelokkest ladies that ever lif hadden,   *loveliest*
> And he the comlokkest king that the court holdes.   *comeliest*
>   (GGK 15–17)

The *Gawain*-poet goes on to assert that 'Hit were now gret nye to neven / So hardy a here on hille' (GGK 22–3) (It would now be difficult to name such a bold army on hillside), and this contrast between the idealized world of the poem, frequently set in the distant past or in a remote place, and the inferior present, is also common in romance. Clearly, medieval audiences did not turn to romance with the expectation of an overall realism, and neither should we. In holding up a mirror to the aspirations and longings of their audiences, medieval romances shared some of the functions of modern 'gracious living' magazines. But this is not to say that the world of romance is merely one of escapism or wish-fulfilment. In it, characteristically, the hero is confronted with, or chooses to confront, some challenge which will test his physical, moral and spiritual qualities to the utmost. He is required

B

to be a courageous warrior, but also, usually, to show his devotion and loyalty to some chosen lady: he must possess and display all the qualities involved in the medieval codes of chivalry and courtliness. It is of the essence of his test that it should be undertaken voluntarily, not because he is himself in danger but because it is impossible for him to refuse it without betraying the whole system of values by which he lives. Orfeo is not compelled to go into exile and into the underworld; it is his love for his wife that leads him there. Gawain is not compelled to take up the Green Knight's apparently absurd challenge; but what would become of the reputation of Camelot, and of his own reputation as the most courteous and one of the most famous of Arthur's knights, if he failed to do so?

In the course of his adventures, the hero is often led into situations in which the ideals by which he lives seem to contradict one another. This does not happen to Orfeo, but it does happen to Gawain (at a later point in the poem than the extract included here), when courtesy towards ladies, chastity, and loyalty towards his host pull him in different directions. The outcome of such testing is normally a happy ending, in which the hero is restored to his lady or to King Arthur's court, but only after a searching exploration of his system of values and a kind of self-discovery, sometimes of a disillusioning nature. Romance was the literary genre in which the medieval ruling class ruthlessly probed and tested in imaginary actions its own highest values. There is nothing escapist about this; and, moreover, though the imaginary action often included elements of fantasy, such as the Green Knight, or elements that modern readers would see as fantastic or mythical, such as the underworld which Orfeo visits, these elements can often be felt to have a profound symbolic significance, somewhat as the fantasies of our dreams may reflect important elements in our real lives. Again, the idealization and the imaginary quality of the whole are often combined with much local realism. One sees this particularly in *Sir Gawain and the Green Knight*, with the bristling detail of its descriptions of court life, and the poet's slyly-intimated scepticism about human motive: when the Green Knight enters the hall, everyone remains silent, and the poet comments, 'I deeme hit not all for doute, / Bot sum for courtaisye' (GGK 210–11) (Not all out of fear, I judge, but some out of courtesy)— a strong hint that most of them really were afraid, and that for them, unlike Gawain, courtesy was only an excuse. The *Gawain*-poet is exceptional in the extent to which he blends subtle comedy and a realistic depiction of human weaknesses such as irritation, embarrassment and self-deception, into the idealizing and imaginative mode of romance; but romance was always capable of absorbing such complexities.

Another medieval genre represented in this volume, and one at the opposite extreme to romance, is the *fabliau*, or comic tale, as seen in *The Friar's Tale*. Broadly speaking, *fabliaux* are short stories in verse, intended to arouse laughter. They tend towards farce rather than more subtle kinds of comedy, and they deal commonly with two topics that are taboo in romance—the excretory functions, and sex (as opposed to love). These have been the subject-matter of dirty stories in all ages; but in Chaucer's time the distinction between lowbrow and highbrow, or between the dirty story and art-literature, scarcely existed, and it was perfectly possible for Chaucer to treat the *fabliau* with as much skill and elaboration as he treated the romance. It is essential to the *fabliau* that it should take a low, unidealizing view of human life, seeing human beings as consumed by animal passions such as greed and lust, and seeing their intelligence, if they possess any, only as animal cunning. *The Friar's Tale* is unusual among Chaucer's *fabliaux* in its lack of sexual and lavatory humour, and in the exquisite delicacy with which it shows the rapacious, stupid and unscrupulous summoner putting himself in the power of the witty and scrupulous devil. The devil distinguishes between *sleighte* and *violence* as means by which he gains his ends (FT 131); in this tale he uses *sleighte*, and so does Chaucer. Where the *Tale* is not unusual for Chaucer, however, is in the learning and intelligence brought to bear on a low theme: for example, in the crucial part played by the theological doctrine of intention in bringing about the summoner's downfall. Chaucer's *fabliaux* owe much of their distinctive relish to the paradoxical bringing together of literary and theological learning with grossness and animality.

A third literary genre represented in this book is that of the dream-allegory, in *Piers Plowman*. There was a long tradition, stretching back to Scriptural and classical times, of visionary writings, in which the writer was carried in a dream to the other world, whether heaven or hell, or was shown visions of distant places or times, as in the Revelation of St John. In imitation of this, in the Middle Ages, there were written secular visions of earthly paradises, often paradises of love, as in the French *Roman de la Rose*. Chaucer translated at least part of the *Roman de la Rose*, and also wrote several such poems himself, including *The Book of the Duchess* and *The Parliament of Fowls*. Another branch of the tradition, and one which was especially found in the alliterative poetry of the west Midlands, consisted of dreams in which the poet saw not another world, but the real world of his own time, only in a new perspective. Examples of this include *Winner and Waster*, *The Parliament of the Three Ages*, and *Piers Plowman* itself. Such dream-poems were not always allegories, but they very frequently were, making use of symbols because real dreams have usually been thought to have symbolic significances, and of personifications partly because such clarifying abstractions as Love, Learning, Old Age, Generosity, Nature or

Gluttony could not be met with in the waking world and might there-
fore be thought to demand a poet's vision as their setting. Personifica-
tion allegory is one of the commonest medieval literary schemes, and it
is important to recognize that it was so popular not merely as a decora-
tive device, or as a way of hiding the poet's meaning, but as a way of
thinking imaginatively about life, of perceiving its underlying patterns
and tendencies, and of presenting them with the greatest possible vivid-
ness, in energetic action, not as dead concepts. The main allegory of the
part of *Piers Plowman* included here is extremely simple: human sinful-
ness is divided into seven traditional categories, and each of these seven
deadly sins is conceived as a person, confessing himself to another
personified abstraction called Repentance, being sharply questioned if
necessary, and finally, if truly repentant, receiving absolution. Each sin
is imagined as a sinner of a particular kind, and in most cases we learn
of his life-story. In this way Langland is able to give a lively and detailed
account of the operation of human sinfulness in the everyday life of his
time, within a framework which ensures theoretical completeness and
comprehensiveness.

In many cases the allegory is developed further. Envy explains how
he has dwelt among London tradesmen, and has employed Backbiting
as an agent to cast aspersions on the quality of his competitors' goods.
Anger has been a gardener in a religious house, and has grafted lies onto
certain friars, and these have borne successively leaves of flattery of
lords, blossoms of hearing private confessions in the lords' families, and
fruit of other people's unwillingness to confess (as they ought) to their
parish priests. In such cases we are meant to admire not only the witty
and imaginative ingenuity of the expression but also the social and
psychological penetration Langland shows in demonstrating how sin
works in the real world—what motive really underlies the tradesman's
devaluation of 'Brand X', or how the special, flattering relationship
which friars try to gain with influential men can undermine the whole
brotherhood of the Church, and lead to angry antagonism between
parish priests (who were provided with a living by their parishes) and
friars (who were supposed to beg for their communal living). That was
a fact of life in Langland's time, not a mere poet's dream. There are
many other influences on *Piers Plowman* besides the dream-allegory;
indeed, it is one of the most complex and wide-ranging works of its
time. Medieval preaching, for example, also made much use of alle-
gorical illustrations, and was often as outspokenly critical of the evils
of the time, and of the Church's own corruption, as Langland ever
was.

Preaching was also an influence on another of our poems, *Patience*.
This poem as a whole takes the form of a celebration and definition of
the virtue of patience or longsuffering—a favourite virtue of medieval

times, if less so now. (It may well be that the disfavour into which this quality has fallen belongs to the comparatively brief period, from the Renaissance to the mid-twentieth century, when it appeared that, by *not* being patient, but imposing his own desires on the natural world, man could continuously change his situation for the better. In our own time it seems likely that this period of optimism is coming to an end, because man's attempts to dominate his environment have reached their limit, have become counter-productive, and may even have led him to the brink of disaster—in which case we can expect to start feeling the value and necessity of patience again quite soon, as Jonah does in the poem, confronted with the destructive power of nature.) The poem is thus in principle a kind of poetic sermon on the text, 'Blessed are they that suffer persecution for justice' sake; for theirs is the kingdom of heaven' (Matthew 5.10). The key word of the text is 'suffer', which implies longsuffering, and of which the Latin is *patiuntur*, from the same root as our 'patience'. The story of Jonah then exemplifies impatience, for he is one who is unwilling to suffer persecution for justice' sake (by preaching God's word among the Ninevites), and who learns by his suffering in the whale's belly the necessity for longsuffering, or submission to the will of God. And God's actions, in first saving Jonah from destruction in the whale, and then (in the second part of the story, not included here) not carrying out his threat to destroy Nineveh, show *his* patience.

We have remarked earlier, however, that if this is a sermon it is one in which the narrative *exemplum* has come to dominate the whole; and the treatment of the story of Jonah relates *Patience* to yet another medieval genre, that of the scriptural narrative. The text of the Bible itself was not available in English before the unauthorized Wycliffite translation at the end of the fourteenth century, but there were several examples of English poems which told stories from the Bible, sometimes in a summary form which was intended to make clear the great shape of God's purpose in human history, as in the encyclopaedic poem, *Cursor Mundi*. There were also first produced in the lifetime of Chaucer and the *Gawain*-poet the great cycles of mystery plays, most of whose scenes dramatized specific incidents from Scripture and related them (as *Patience* obliquely does) to subsequent events of which they were considered to be symbolic types. Thus dramatic representations of the story of Abraham and Isaac not only re-told the story 'in modern dress', as one of contemporary life, but also showed that it was a type of God's sacrifice of his son on the cross. Similarly, allusions in the text of *Patience* show that it assumes the typological identification of Jonah with Christ, and his three days in the whale's belly with the three days between the crucifixion and the resurrection during which Christ harrowed Hell. *Patience* would thus have been a more familiar kind of work to its medieval audience than it is likely to be to us. There is also a parallel with the mystery cycles (for example in their handling of characters such as Mrs Noah and the Shepherds) in the way that *Patience* treats Jonah as a figure of realistic comedy—almost indeed a *fabliau* character, whose cunning is foolishly transparent (to God), and who grumbles, snores, slobbers, and gets his clothes filthy in a most undignified way. The *Gawain*-poet here re-creates the Scriptural narrative as completely as he re-creates the romance in *Sir Gawain and the Green Knight*.

We are left with the short poems; and these too belong to a variety of recognized genres, rather than being the spontaneous expressions of personal feeling that we may expect to find in the short poem in our own time. *Quia Amore Langueo* is one of many religious poems in which the reader (and in this field, for once, we should probably think of readers as much as listeners) is directly addressed either by Christ or by the Blessed Virgin, with an appeal for love, pity, and hence spiritual reform. The strongly emotional religion of the later Middle Ages is also found in *Lullaby*, the earliest example of a lullaby in English, but one in which the conventional form is given an unusual twist, because the baby is not comforted but is reminded of how much cause it has to weep in the world of sin into which it has been born. *Lenten is Come* is a charming example of another convention, the poem in which the joy of nature in the spring is associated with the pangs of love. Once again, there is no reason to suppose any personal reference in the poem; its 'I' is not truly autobiographical (in the way Shelley's, say, almost invariably is), and its mixture of joy, sorrow and a touch of ironic detachment is probably a poetic invention rather than a reflection of a real love-affair. Even the splendidly vituperative *Blacksmiths* is probably an exercise on a congenial theme rather than a complaint against the neighbours. The poem in praise or dispraise of some class of people is another medieval genre, and one to which the agreeably unpretentious *For Women* also belongs. Many such poems are attacks on women as a sex, expressions of the habitual misogyny of a period in which men were socially dominant and a celibate priesthood was intellectually dominant. But alongside this misogyny lies an almost equally powerful tradition of woman-worship, whether secular and directed towards an idealized courtly lady, or religious and focusing in the Blessed Virgin, who made good the sin of Eve. *For Women* is an answer to misogyny in a lower and more realistic key. Of the two *balades* by Chaucer, that to Rosemounde is a parody of the many poems in praise of a distant and standoffish courtly lady, while the *Balade de Bon Conseyl* is a poem addressing a general moral message (the favourite medieval contempt of the world in favour of heaven) to a particular person, and is an early example of a tradition represented later by some of the poems of Jonson and Pope. The doctrine is familiar; the poet's task is to express it with telling compression and exactness.

Social context

Yet another cause of differences among these poems lies in the varying social contexts in which they were written and the audiences they were written for. The medieval poet was not 'a nightingale, who sits in darkness and sings to cheer its own solitude', as Shelley put it; he was a member of his society, who wrote to serve the social purposes of entertainment, devotion or instruction, sometimes in answer to the command of some noble patron. (Gower, for example, tells us that he wrote his *Confessio Amantis* on the orders of King Richard II, while an illumination in one of the manuscripts of Chaucer's *Troilus and Criseyde* shows the poet reading his work aloud to Richard II's court.) One reason for the many differences between *Sir Orfeo* and *Sir Gawain and the Green Knight*, despite the fact that they are both romances, is that *Sir Gawain* was written for a courtly audience, while *Sir Orfeo* probably originated lower down the social scale, though exactly where is not certain. The *Gawain*-poet probably wrote at the court of some great lord in the north-west Midlands; we know that an earlier alliterative romance of a somewhat similar type, *William of Palerne*, was translated from the French under the patronage of another west Midland nobleman, Humphrey de Bohun. In *Sir Gawain and the Green Knight* the poet shows a detailed knowledge of aristocratic pursuits such as hunting and feasting, and an exceptionally subtle grasp of courtly and chivalric values—*courtaisye* especially, with its wide range of connotations, including politeness, eloquent speech, modesty, deference to ladies, and skill in elegant conversation about love. For the poet of *Sir Orfeo*, kings and noblemen are figures of myth (as they are in fairy stories) rather than everyday reality, and it seems unlikely that he was writing for aristocratic listeners. Chaucer also wrote in the first place for a court circle. He did not aim at a wide audience, though his work probably circulated in manuscript among the wealthy bourgeoisie as well as the aristocracy. We must certainly not imagine *The Canterbury Tales* in its own time as being addressed to a public of the wide social range represented by the Canterbury pilgrims.

We have only to compare Chaucer with Langland to recognize the difference between a courtly and a popular writer. *Piers Plowman* seems to have reached a very varied audience. A reference to it in one of the pieces of propaganda associated with the Peasants' Revolt of 1381, John Ball's letter to the peasants of Essex, appears to indicate that it reached the great mass of the illiterate working population, and Langland throughout his work certainly shows a more detailed knowledge of the life of the poor than Chaucer does, and also a much less generalized and idealized compassion for their lot. But there are also indications that *Piers Plowman* was read by the clergy, and, given its close connections with medieval preaching, it is even possible that in some cases parts of it were read aloud by parish priests to their congregations. It must not be supposed that the distinction between 'courtly' and 'popular' can be identified with one between 'learned' and 'unlearned', or even that 'learned' literature in English forms a completely separate category from the other two. Much of *Piers Plowman* is difficult and allusive, and assumes for a full understanding a detailed knowledge of the Latin Bible and of standard commentaries on it. As with many medieval authors, Langland's learned allusions do not always indicate that he had read the whole work of the author alluded to—there was much reliance on anthologies of extracts—but he was undoubtedly what would now be called an 'intellectual'. On the other hand, if he had not been aiming at a wider audience, he would presumably have written in Latin rather than English. The *Gawain*-poet, in *Patience*, is less ostentatious in his learning, but he too assumes an audience that knew the text of the Bible, and was capable of picking up slight allusions to the typological identity of Jonah with Christ and the whale with Hell or the devil. Theological learning, of a serious though not necessarily technical kind, is the common property of the great English poets of the late fourteenth century, and their work implies a lay audience, whether courtly, bourgeois or popular, with a good knowledge of theological concepts and issues.

Spelling and pronunciation

We have emphasized that medieval poetry was written for listeners, and that much of its effect is conveyed through sound. If modern readers are to appreciate it fully, they will need to learn to read it aloud. Here there is the difficulty that our knowledge of medieval pronunciation is far from complete, particularly in such difficult but important areas as stress and pitch. But all the same, a modern reader can easily learn to achieve a good approximation of what scholars believe the different dialects of Middle English to have sounded like; and it is in order to encourage readers of this book to add to their enjoyment of medieval poetry in this way that the publishers have made available a tape-recording of readings of the poems in it, and that we include in our introduction some simple instructions about the spelling and pronunciation of the texts.

Since spelling is the chief guide we have to pronunciation in the medieval period, we begin with some remarks about that. Medieval spelling was probably nearer to being phonetic than modern English spelling is, but it was less standardized (so that different scribes, and frequently enough the same scribe, would spell the same word in different ways), and it included various conventional elements which are far from being phonetic. For example, in the one manuscript in which *Sir Gawain and the Green Knight* and *Patience* have come down to us, the final sound of words such as *has* and *was* (which, in the fourteenth-century north-west Midlands was almost certainly not a voiced *s*, as in the modern 'has' and 'was', but an unvoiced *s*, as in the modern 'hiss') is spelt *tȝ*. The symbol ȝ, called 'yogh', was used to stand for a number of different sounds: the voiced and unvoiced fricatives (i.e. the unvoiced sound represented by the *ch* in Scottish 'loch' and its voiced equivalent), the sounds now represented by *y* and *w*, and, through confusion with the letter *z*, for that sound too. Another symbol widely used by fourteenth-century scribes but no longer current is þ ('thorn'), for the *th* sound. In this edition, in order to make easier the reading of texts, some of which have a large number of unfamiliar words, we have regularized the spelling, and to a small extent modernized it. This has involved removing ȝ and þ and replacing them by appropriate modern equivalents, with ȝ becoming *gh*, regardless of its medieval pronunciation, in cases where the modern equivalent of a medieval word is spelt with a *gh*. We have also adjusted single or double consonants and vowels so that they correspond to modern spelling usage, since the doubling of a consonant is not necessarily phonetically significant in medieval script, and in many circumstances a single vowel can indicate a long sound as well as a short one. Where different spellings were commonly used to indicate the same sound (as *ai*, *ei*, *ay*, *ey* were all used to represent approximately the sound of the modern 'eye', or as *sh* and *sch* were both pronounced as *sh*), we have chosen whichever spelling would enable a modern reader to recognize the word most easily. Where, as was often the case, a medieval scribe spelt the same word in several different ways, we have always chosen that which is closest to modern spelling. We have also made a number of other small adjustments, in a pragmatic rather than a systematic spirit, and the result, we believe, is that almost every word of the texts in this edition is spelt in a way which is authentic, in the sense that it was or could have been used by a scribe writing in the relevant medieval dialect, but that the texts generally look less intimidatingly different from modern English than they do in most modern editions of medieval literature. Modern editors of Chaucer have frequently gone a long way in the direction of normalizing the spelling of his medieval scribes, but the texts of other medieval poets have generally had a more frightening look. We would emphasize that we have altered only spellings, never the actual words; and we hope that once readers of this book have gained a certain familiarity with medieval poetry, they will go on to make use of other, more scholarly editions, in which they will find reproduced the spelling of specific medieval manuscripts.

The punctuation of these texts is our own; and this is true of all editions of medieval literature that use modern punctuation, because medieval scribes either did not punctuate what they wrote at all, or else they used symbols which are quite different from modern ones. This point is worth making, because we have noticed that ordinary modern readers of medieval texts often suppose the punctuation to be as authoritative as the words. It cannot be; but we have done our best to punctuate these texts in such a way as to bring out what the authors meant to say.

Pronunciation

VOWELS

Vowels can be either short or long; in either case, they are generally purer in sound than in modern English, in which most of the sounds we call vowels and spell as such are pronounced as diphthongs. Middle English vowels are more like the vowels of modern German.

ă represents the sound now written *u*, as in 'but'
ā roughly as in modern 'rather'
ĕ as in modern 'bet'
ē (open) roughly as in modern 'there'
ē (close) as *é* in French 'bébé', but longer
ĭ or ў as in modern 'bit'
ī or ȳ as in 'machine' (*not* as in 'site', 'ripe', etc.)
ŏ as in modern 'pot'
ō (open) represents the sound now written *aw* or *au*, as in 'dawn' or 'pause'
ō (close) as *au* in French 'gauche'
ŭ as in modern 'put' (*not* as in 'but')
ū (often spelt *ou* or *ow*) as in 'flute' (but in words taken from French, as *cure*, ū was pronounced either as in modern 'cure' or as *u* in French *tu* or *ü* in German *Tür*)

As indicated, ē and ō can be either open or close in sound. In deciding which, modern spelling and pronunciation of the equivalent word can usually be taken as a guide. In a word where ē is now spelt *e* or *ee* (as in 'he' or 'see') it should usually be pronounced close; where it is spelt *ea* (as in 'team') it should usually be pronounced open. In a word where ō is now pronounced like the *o* or *oo* in 'mother', 'food', or 'good', it should be pronounced close; where it is now pronounced like the *o* or *oa* in 'rode' or 'road', it should be pronounced open. But medieval spelling does not usually indicate any distinction between open and close vowels, and it is not certain how far the distinction was still noticeable in fourteenth-century pronunciation. The modern reader can probably get along well enough without troubling about it.

Final -*e* presents a difficult problem, about which there is much scholarly controversy. It would be generally agreed that in the speech of Chaucer's time -*e* was ceasing to be pronounced; in modern English, of course, it is normally silent. But it appears that in Chaucer's verse it was normally still pronounced, as a neutral vowel (like the *e* in 'delight'), except where the following word began with a vowel or an *h*. In texts from further north, such as the works of the *Gawain*-poet, it may not have been pronounced, except perhaps optionally in particular places, as for emphasis, or before a pause, or in certain archaic rhymes. Medieval scribes seem frequently to have added or omitted -*e* somewhat randomly in spelling, and we must often proceed by guesswork in reconstructing its pronunciation.

DIPHTHONGS

ai, ay, ei, ey all roughly represent the long sound now written *i* or *y*, as in 'lie' or 'dye'

au and *aw* represent the sound now written *ou* or *ow*, as in 'ounce' or 'now'

ou and *ow* are interchangeable, but have two pronunciations. If in the modern equivalent word these sounds are pronounced as in 'house' or 'through', the medieval pronunciation was as in 'through'. If in the modern equivalent word they are pronounced as in 'know' or 'bought', the medieval pronunciation was similar to that of the *au* or *aw* diphthong.

SPELLING OF VOWELS

We have not regularized the spelling of all vowels, partly because to do so would have produced spellings never actually used by medieval scribes, and partly because it would have made many words more difficult for the modern reader to recognize. One common variant of which the reader should be warned is that the *ŭ* sound is sometimes represented by an *o*, as in Middle English *yong* ('young'), *bot* ('but'), or *word*.

CONSONANTS

These are generally much the same as in modern English, though (for reasons explained above) *gh*, which is usually silent in modern English, can stand for the sounds represented by *ch* in Scottish 'loch', the voiced equivalent of that sound, and *y* or *w*. A further important difference is that many other consonants which are sometimes silent in modern English were still always pronounced in the fourteenth century. Thus:

k was pronounced before *n* (hence the alliteration of GGK 192: 'To *k*nightes he *c*est his yye').

r was trilled more strongly than in modern English, so as to produce an effect more like Scottish pronunciation. It was still pronounced after a vowel where in modern English (as in 'hair' or 'horse') it is usually silent.

l was still pronounced before *f*, *k* and *m*, where in modern English (as in 'half', 'folk', or 'calm') it is silent.

Initial *h*- seems to have been pronounced rather lightly, or even not at all, especially in words derived from French.

Finally, we are anxious to make it quite clear that there is still much uncertainty in medieval pronunciation, and that the modern reader does not have to learn a complicated and exact set of rules before he can read medieval poems aloud. The experts in this field, if they could be transported in a time-machine to the fourteenth century, might still find communication difficult, and Chaucer might well think their pronunciation archaic, rural, or foreign-sounding. This being so, it is far better for the average modern reader to read medieval poetry aloud with gusto, even if inaccurately, than for him to be inhibited from reading it aloud at all. Those who wish for more detailed information could begin by consulting Helge Kökeritz, *A Guide to Chaucer's Pronunciation* (Stockholm, Almqvist and Wiksell, 1954).

Grammar and vocabulary

The various dialects of Middle English represented in this book differ among themselves and from modern English in certain grammatical respects. In most cases, these will not give much difficulty to the modern reader, and we do not propose to offer any systematic description of medieval grammar. In any case, we think it best to begin by reading actual poems, and to learn the grammar of the language from them, with the help, where necessary, of the notes. We do wish to mention, however, two points of difference from modern English, failure to notice which has sometimes misled modern readers. One is that the subjunctive mood is used more commonly than in modern English, to express hypotheses, conditional statements and suppositions. This is most noticeable in the third person singular, as in

> he wolde never ete
> Upon such a dere day er him devised *were*
> Of sum aventurous thing an uncouthe tale   (GGK 55-7)

(He would never eat upon such a festive day before there *was* told him a strange tale of some adventurous matter), where modern English would have the indicative 'was' in place of the subjunctive 'were'. The other is that the second person singular, which in modern English is used only in religious language, was still normally used in Middle English for addressing close friends and inferiors. Thus a king could properly address any of his subjects as 'thou', but would expect them to address him as 'you' or 'ye', as Gawain addresses Arthur in *Sir Gawain and the Green Knight*. When the Green Knight addresses Arthur as 'thou' (as in GGK 222 ff.) it is part of his generally insolent attitude; and when in the same speech he uses the plural 'ye' (as in line 229) it is probably because he has turned from the king to address the court at large.

In this edition, we have not included a glossary as a separate section, but have glossed all words we thought likely to give difficulty along with the notes on the pages facing the text. The omission of a glossary has the disadvantage that readers will not be able to see brought together the different uses, meanings and forms of the same word; but we believe that this disadvantage will be greatly outweighed by the advantage of not having to be constantly turning from the text to another section of the book. Clearly, it would not be possible or necessary for us to gloss every word which differs only in spelling from its modern equivalent; and where a strange word occurs many times in the course of a text we have usually glossed it only on the first few occasions, or if it occurs in isolation after a long gap. We have not usually glossed the following common short words, in order to save the pages facing the text from becoming too cluttered, and we recommend that the reader should learn any of them that he does not know before starting to use the book.

ac   but
but if   unless, except
eek, eke   also
er   before
fro   from
full   very (or can be used to intensify almost any adjective, adverb or verb)
hem   them
her   their (as well as 'her')
hit   it
mo   more
ne   not, neither, nor
other   or (as well as 'other')
sithen, sethen   then, since
swithe   very (or can be used to intensify almost any adjective, adverb or verb)

tho   then
wot   knows
yive, yeve   give

Suggestions for further reading

W. F. Bolton (ed.), *The Middle Ages* (London, Sphere Books, Sphere History of Literature in the English Language, 1970), vol. 1

D. S. Brewer, *Chaucer in His Time* (London, Longman, 1963)

J. A. Burrow, *Ricardian Poetry* (London, Routledge and Kegan Paul, 1971)

Dorothy Everett, *Essays on Middle English Literature* (Oxford, Clarendon Press, 1955)

Maurice Hussey, *Chaucer's World: A Pictorial Companion* (Cambridge University Press, 1967)

Gervase Mathew, *The Court of Richard II* (London, John Murray, 1968)

Charles Muscatine, *Poetry and Crisis in the Age of Chaucer* (Notre Dame, Indiana, University of Notre Dame Press, 1972)

A. C. Spearing, *Criticism and Medieval Poetry* (London, Edward Arnold, 2nd edn, 1972)

Sir Orfeo

Introduction

This anonymous poem dates from the late thirteenth or early fourteenth century, and survives in three manuscript versions. Two of these are late and corrupt, but the third, in the Auchinleck Manuscript, which dates from about 1330, is much better. *Sir Orfeo* claims to be a 'Breton lay', and this manuscript also contains two other such lays in English, *Lay le Freyne* (that is, 'the lay of the ash tree') and *Sir Degaré*. One of Chaucer's poems, *The Franklin's Tale*, is also offered as a Breton lay; and since the information it gives about Breton lays could all have been gained from the poems in the Auchinleck Manuscript, and there is no evidence that Chaucer had any other source of information about them, it has been plausibly suggested that he once owned this very manuscript. *Sir Orfeo* was probably written in the Westminster–Middlesex dialect area.

In its plot, *Sir Orfeo* is basically a retelling of the classical legend of Orpheus and Eurydice. Orfeo is Orpheus, Heurodis is Eurydice; but the medieval poet has abandoned the tragic ending of the story as it is told by Virgil, Ovid and Boethius. According to them, Eurydice was stolen away from Orpheus by Pluto, the king of the underworld, and when Orpheus went in search of her he was told that he could have her back on condition that he did not look round to see if she was following him on his return journey. But just before the end of the journey he could not resist taking a single backward glance, and at the last moment she was snatched away from him again, this time for ever. A tragic ending of this kind was not to medieval taste; indeed, tragedy as we understand it is not at all common in the literature of the Middle Ages. The medieval poet gave the story a happy ending instead, and also attached to it a theme familiar in folktales, of the king who disappears from his kingdom, but returns secretly to test the behaviour of the person he has left behind as his substitute. (That theme is found later in, for example, Shakespeare's *Measure for Measure*.) *Sir Orfeo* shows a concern for good rule and political loyalty which is strongly characteristic of medieval English romances of the more popular kind. Moreover, the author of *Sir Orfeo* has considerably modified the classical legend in other ways by giving it a Celtic colouring. Much of the supernatural and fantastic material of medieval romance in France and

England derived from Celtic sources, and in *Sir Orfeo* the classical Pluto becomes the king of the fairies, and the underworld to which he carries off Eurydice is not the dark world of the dead but a brightly shining and apparently paradisal fairyland. The fairy hunt which Orfeo sees in the wilderness is common in Celtic legend, and there are Celtic stories of heroes taking to the woods in grief and madness. The Celtic element in the poem is explicitly indicated in the text, in the closing lines, in which we are told that the story was put into circulation by Breton harpers who made a lay of it; and it is emphasized still more strongly in a prologue (not included in our text), which is missing from the Auchinleck version of *Sir Orfeo*, though found in the other two manuscript versions and also in the Auchinleck version of *Lay le Freyne*. (Lines 9–22 of our text are also missing from the Auchinleck version.) It is probable that to medieval audiences the Breton lay would have been a familiar literary genre, within the general class of romance, and that it would have aroused certain definite expectations; we must therefore say a little more about the lays in general.

We do not know of any lays which are actually in the Breton language; the first known collection of lays was made in French in the twelfth century by a very gifted poet, Marie de France. Her lays are quite short, ranging in length from 100 to 1200 lines; they are all narratives of the romance type, usually concerned with love and often with magic, but rarely with war. Unlike most later medieval romances, and especially courtly romances, they include very little interpretation by the author of the meaning of her story. She leaves the story to speak for itself, through dramatic moments and evocative symbols, giving a superficial effect of simplicity and purity, but underneath that an extremely potent and complex range of implications. If one puts together the various references to lays in Marie's poems, one gathers that the original Breton lays were essentially musical performances, in which the words expressed the emotions appropriate to some dramatic moment in a story (like an operatic aria), and were accompanied by the harp or a violin-like instrument, the rote. These true lays, especially if they were sung in the Breton language outside Brittany, would have needed to be accompanied by narratives which explained the stories from which they arose; and Marie's lays appear to have been based on such narratives. But the Breton lays in French and in English never completely lost their original associations with music, and we shall suggest later that it is of great importance that the hero of *Sir Orfeo* is himself a musician as well as a king. There are several references in medieval romances to the existence of a Breton lay of Orpheus, presumably in French, and in each case the reference implies music rather than words. No such French lay survives, however. There are several Breton lays in English, including some (such as *Lay le Freyne*) translated from Marie de France; indeed *Sir Orfeo* is the only Middle English Breton lay for which no French source is known, though it seems likely that such a source once existed.

Sir Orfeo is written in the accentual equivalent of the French octosyllabic couplets in which Marie wrote her lays. This was one of the commonest Middle English metrical forms up to Chaucer's time; in *Sir Orfeo* it is somewhat clumsy compared with Marie's exquisitely-shaped verses. Perhaps it was written for chanting to the harp or rote; it was certainly composed for performance, where the accomplished minstrel could instinctively supply emphases or rests to create a satisfying rhythmical effect, and it may well be that even the best of the manuscript versions does not quite accurately represent what a medieval performer would have said or sung. For all that, the verse is by no means insensitive. Because its accentual nature allows great freedom of rhythm, it can sometimes seem to act out most effectively the events it is describing. For example, when Orfeo in the wilderness sees the fairy knights and ladies dancing, the rhythm changes to suggest that of a dance, whose repeated figures are enacted by the four-times-repeated sound of the rhyme, and the repetition of the word *quaint*:

> Knightes and levedys com dauncing
> In quaint attire, gisely,
> Quaint pas and softly,
> Tabours and trumpes yede hem by,
> And all manner minstracy.   (SO 274–8)

In complete contrast to the mysterious slowness of the movement here is the dramatic moment when Orfeo returns and the steward recognizes who he is. He overturns the table in his eagerness to throw himself at the king's feet, and the verse-movement conveys the excitement and confusion:

> Over and over the bord he threwe,
> And fell adown to his feet.   (SO 554–5)

What is true of the poem's rhythm is true of its style as a whole: it is not exquisitely controlled, but it has moments of surprising power. We have seen in the General Introduction how poetry meant for listeners tends to be somewhat diffuse and to make repeated use of traditional tags or formulas, and there are many signs of this in *Sir Orfeo*. To take a single example, there is a strong similarity between the lines describing the knights Orfeo sent to protect his wife from being carried off—

> . . . welle ten hundred knightes with him,
> Ich y-armed, stout and grim,   (SO 159–60)

—and those describing the fairy knights he sees in the wilderness—

> Welle atourned, ten hundred knightes,
> Ich y-armed to his rightes. (SO 267–8)

But there is probably no special significance in this similarity; it occurs because the poet's idiom automatically supplied him with a certain cluster of expressions to convey the general idea 'many armed knights'. In apparent contrast to this, one moment of remarkable verbal power comes (like so many of the poem's most memorable moments) in another of its descriptions of the fairies. This is the first time Orfeo sees them, when he is in the wilderness:

> He might see him bisides
> Oft in hot undertides
> The king o fairy with his rout
> Come to hunt him all about
> With dim cry and blowing,
> And houndes also with him berking;
> Ac no beest they no nome,
> No never he nist whider they bicome. (SO 257–63)

Some of the power there is a matter of the rhythmic variation between short lines where almost every syllable is stressed, such as 'With dim cry and blowing' and 'Ac no beest they no nome', and lines with the tripping movement produced by extra unstressed syllables, such as 'And houndes also with him berking' and 'No never he nist whider they bicome'. Some of the power, too, comes from the reticence of the line 'Ac no beest they no nome': with no help from the poet, we are left to make what we can of the fact that this ghostly hunt never harms its prey. It is as though the fairies live in a different dimension from human beings in a world which overlaps that of flesh and blood, especially in wastes and wildernesses, but which is separated from it by a subtle barrier There is one great verbal felicity in this passage, in the line 'With dim cry and blowing'. The word *dim*, so unusually applied to sound rather than sight, is full of mysterious suggestions for the modern reader. Even here, though, we must be cautious. As has been pointed out by C. S. Lewis,[1] this is an essentially modern reaction. In the poet's time, the word 'dim' was applied, just as 'faint' is now, to audible as well as to visible things; and so it seems likely that he was not using language with the originality we so much prize here more than anywhere else.

It is in the deployment of all that is seen through the language that the medieval poet's true art lies. There is, for example, the use of suspense. When Heurodis awakens from her sleep and behaves with such frightening unnaturalness, tearing her clothes, scratching her face

[1] *Studies in Medieval and Renaissance Literature* (Cambridge University Press, 1966), p. 5.

until it bleeds, and, worst of all, looking at her husband as if he were her enemy, we do not know, any more than her ladies or Orfeo do, what has caused this apparent total change in her personality. It is not until she has partly recovered, and has told her husband pathetically that, though they have never been angry with each other since they were married, now they must part for ever, that we learn what happened to her in her sleep. There is a different kind of suspense near the end of the poem, when *we* know that it is Orfeo who has come back to Winchester in the guise of a poor minstrel, but are made to wait anxiously for the moment when the steward will also grasp this. His overturning of the table comes as a thoroughly satisfying ending of the suspense. What is left out by the poet often shows his skill as much as what he puts in. At one superb moment in the poem, it is the absence of words that is the source of power. When Heurodis and Orfeo see each other in the wilderness, neither can speak, and the only sign of emotion is that 'The teres fell out of her eye' (SO 303) to see her husband, who was once a king, now reduced to wretchedness—only it is not called wretchedness but, reticently, *missais*, discomfort. At other times, the poet shows equal skill in leaving out details of the action. We are told about the preparations Orfeo makes to protect his wife against being carried off by the fairies, in a detailed way that corresponds to the elaborateness of the preparations themselves; but her disappearance despite all these preparations, at the very moment when the ten hundred knights are saying that they will die rather than let her go, is narrated briefly and simply, with neither explanation nor exclamation:

> Ac yete amiddes hem full right
> The queen was oway ytwight,
> With fairy forth ynome:
> Men wist never wher she was bicome.   (SO 167–70)

Again, after we have been told in great detail of how Orfeo persuaded the fairy king to release Heurodis, the return of the pair from the underworld to Winchester is over in a few lines. This is quite unlike the versions of Ovid or Virgil, where the crucial event of the story occurs on the journey back, but in its own way it is highly effective. We feel as if a spell had been broken, to produce an almost instantaneous return to the normal and customary:

> His wif he took by the hond
> And dede him swithe out of that lond,
> And went him out of that thede;
> Right as he come the way he yede.
> So long he hath the way ynome,
> To Winchester he is ycome,
> That was his owen cité.   (SO 449–55)

Much of what we have been praising in the rhythm, style and narrative method of *Sir Orfeo* has to do with the fairy element in the poem; and probably most readers would agree that this is one of the most successful of all Middle English poems in its dealing with the supernatural. It happens often enough in medieval romances that supernatural events are made commonplace, often by being too completely realized and rationalized. For example, in another of the Breton lays, *Sir Launfal*, a mortal gains a fairy mistress, and the English poet inserts such details as that her hair shone like gold wire and that she gave her lover ten packhorses laden with gold and silver. There are many more such details, all showing a solid bourgeois concern with material values. We have seen how in *Sir Orfeo* the fairies are surrounded with mystery and insubstantiality; and yet at the same time they are perfectly real creatures once you are able to approach them. Orfeo's final exchange with the fairy king is convincingly lifelike. The king has said that the beautiful Heurodis and the ragged Orfeo would make a loathly sight as a pair, and Orfeo has answered sharply that it would be a still fouler thing to hear of a king going back on his promise, when the fairy king finally gives way with grudging ill grace, saying, in effect, 'Good riddance, and I wish you joy of her!'—

> The king said, 'Sethen it is so,
> Take her by the hond and go:
> Of her ichill thatow be blithe!'   (SO 445–7)

This is surely just what a real king might say, if outwitted by a disreputable beggar in the presence of his whole court. The poet achieves a remarkably convincing mixture of the mysterious and the realistic in his treatment of the fairies. Of course, with some of the details of the fairy world, we cannot tell how far what we are admiring is attributable to the poet, and how far to his sources, whether written or folkloric. One of the most chilling moments in the poem is when Orfeo is admitted to the fairy palace, and sees the ghastly collection of those who were thought to be dead but who had really been 'taken' by the fairies. They are all in the attitudes in which they were taken: presumably in states of special vulnerability, either through extreme pain or tension, or, as in Heurodis's case, through extreme relaxation—some headless, some wounded, some mad, some strangled, some drowned, some burned, some in childbirth, all as if asleep. In origin these are no doubt remnants of the classical conception of the underworld as the world of the dead, but in context the horrible thing is that they are not dead. For Orfeo they form, as John Speirs has suggested, 'a kind of Madame Tussaud's or Bluebeard's Chamber of Horrors',[1] which acts as a final

---

[1] *Medieval English Poetry: The Non-Chaucerian Tradition* (London, Faber and Faber, 1957), p. 147.

test of the hero's courage: if he can make his way unflinching through these apparitions, then he will achieve the goal of his quest. In fact, what might have reduced him to despair, the sight of his beloved Heurodis among them—'By her clothes he knewe that it was he' (SO 384)—only serves to urge him forward, and he pushes his way into the fairy king's hall. All this is admirably done; but there is no way of telling how much of the underlying conception belongs to the individual poet or his sources, and how much to the folk imagination in general. A medieval audience would not have been interested in these distinctions, and would not even have wanted to know the poet's name; it is the story itself that matters, not its creator or reteller.

Finally, we come to the question of the meaning of *Sir Orfeo*. We have mentioned that a peculiarity of the Breton lay among the various kinds of medieval romance was that it usually included very little interpretation of the story on the part of the author. A Breton lay is usually unlike a chivalric romance such as *Sir Gawain and the Green Knight* in that it does not contain within itself clear indications of the concepts in terms of which it is to be interpreted; we are simply left to make what we can of the story as it acts freely on our imaginations. *Sir Orfeo* is certainly a poem of this kind; and, like all the greatest stories, it possesses not so much a single meaning as a power to generate meanings, which may legitimately be different for different readers and different generations. In proposing one such meaning, we do not at all wish to imply that it is the only possible meaning or that it corresponds to the poet's intention: if he had any intention other than to tell a good story, he has concealed it. The poem implies a minstrel performance, and it is also a story *about* minstrelsy. The hero is a minstrel-king, and his one weapon is his harp, the one thing he takes with him when he goes into the wilderness. Obviously, one advantage of this story for the performer is that it gives opportunity for the glorification of his own art. It is a story of the triumph of minstrelsy over seemingly insuperable obstacles, and one in which the great test of a man's worth is whether he enjoys minstrelsy and is generous to minstrels, as the faithful steward is. The story can be expected to suggest to the audience that they too should be generous to the minstrel who is performing it. But, beyond this, minstrelsy seems to have an important symbolic function in the poem. It is presented as a magical harmonizing and civilizing power, which enables Orfeo, like the classical Orpheus, to enchant even wild beasts; and it is even associated with heaven. We are told at the very beginning that everyone who heard Orfeo's harping

> . . . shuld thinke that he were
> In on of the joyes of Paradis,
> Suche melody in his harping is.   (SO 20–22)

The association between music and heavenly order is thoroughly traditional, going back indeed to Plato. In the medieval drama, music and musical instruments are regularly associated with appearances of God; and, to take a single example from Chaucer, the Dreamer in *The Parliament of Fowls* tells us that in the heavenly landscape of his dream,

> Of instruments of stringes in accord
> Herde I so playe a ravishing sweetnesse
> That God, that makere is of all and lord,
> Ne herde nevere better, as I gesse.

But against what is this heavenly power directed in *Sir Orfeo*? Not against death, as in the classical legend. The underworld of the poem is not the classical world of the dead, but of those who are supposed to be dead but are really in the power of the fairies. As the barons tell the steward, there is no remedy against death (SO 527); but Heurodis is not dead. Among the supposed dead in the underworld are mentioned (twice) those who were taken in madness; and there is a constant association in this poem between the fairy world and psychological derangement or disintegration. Heurodis first sees the fairies in her sleep, that is, when her mind is not fully under rational control; she then behaves as if she were mad, and her two maidens tell the court 'That her queen awede wold' (SO 63)—that their queen was going to go mad. No-one else sees the fairies; that is, to a modern way of thinking they might be merely subjective phenomena. But after Orfeo too has behaved as if he had gone mad, and has taken to the wilderness (a kind of objective correlative to the wildness of the mind, as the heath and the storm are correlatives to King Lear's madness), then he too sees them. Thus, for the twentieth-century reader, *Sir Orfeo* can be understood as a poem about psychological disintegration and about how it can be overcome by the healing power symbolized by music. The association of music with healing, especially the healing of mental disorders, is also traditional, and can be found later in, for example, *King Lear*, where Cordelia and the Doctor hope to cure the King's 'untun'd and jarring senses' by means of music, or in *The Tempest*, where Prospero describes what the stage-direction calls 'solemn music' as 'the best comforter / To an unsettled fancy'. The underworld of the poem can be seen as the dark side of the human mind, that 'half-world' of night that Macbeth speaks of, where 'Nature seems dead, and wicked dreams abuse / The curtain'd sleep'. The intangible dark powers within the mind may assert themselves inexplicably at any moment, in tension or in relaxation, setting a barrier between the sufferer and normality, absorbing him or her into an alternative world, glittering dangerously beneath the apparently solid ground. Cure is possible;

but what the poem is suggesting is that it is possible only if the healer has the love and the courage to be willing to go through madness himself, to commit himself, naked and unarmed, to the wilderness and to the underworld and its central citadel. It is ultimately an optimistic poem, for Orfeo has the endurance and skill, both activated by love, to rescue Heurodis and to restore them both to a normality which seems no less secure than before.

We must conclude by repeating that we do not see this as the poem's single 'right' meaning. It could well be seen in quite different terms: for example, Orfeo as king and harper could be seen as parallel to King David, whose musical skill was sometimes interpreted in the Middle Ages as an ability to build a harmony out of the different classes of society; and in this case minstrelsy would be seen as symbolic of his political abilities. *Sir Orfeo* is a poem capable of generating many meanings; this is an important part of its lasting fascination.

Suggestions for further reading

Edition of the complete poem by A. J. Bliss (Oxford, Clarendon Press, 2nd edn, 1966). *Sir Orfeo* and two other Breton lays can also be found in Donald B. Sands (ed.), *Middle English Verse Romances* (New York, Holt, Rinehart and Winston, 1966). All the English lays are collected, with an interesting introduction, by T. C. Rumble, *The Breton Lays in Middle English* (Detroit, Wayne State University Press, 1967).

There has been little extended comment on the poem in book form, but there are valuable brief discussions in Dieter Mehl, *The Middle English Verse Romances of the Thirteenth and Fourteenth Centuries* (London, Routledge and Kegan Paul, 1969) and John Stevens, *Medieval Romance* (London, Hutchinson, 1973).

Sir Orfeo

Orfeo was a king,
In Inglond an heighe lording,
A stalworth man and hardy bo;
Large and curteys he was also.
His fader was comen of King Pluto,   5
And his moder of King Juno,
That sumtime were as goddes yhold
For aventours that they dede and told.
    Orfeo most of any thing
Lovede the glee of harping;   10
Siker was every goode harpour
Of him to have moche honour.
Himself loved for to harpe,
And laide theron his wittes sharpe;
He lerned so, ther nothing was   15
A better harpour in no plas.
In the world was never man born
That ones Orfeo sat biforn,
And he might of his harping here,
Bot he shuld thinke that he were   20
In on of the joyes of Paradis,
Suche melody in his harping is.
    This king sojournd in Traciens,
That was a city of noble defens;
For Winchester was cleped tho   25
Traciens, withouten no.
The king hadde a queen of pris
That was ycleped Dame Heurodis,
The fairest levedy for the nones
That might gon on body and bones,   30
Full of love and of godenisse;
Ac no man may telle hir fairnisse.
    Bifell so in the comessing of May
(When mirry and hot is the day,
And oway beth winter shours,   35
And every feld is full of flours,
And blosme breme on every bough

2   *Inglond* England   *heighe lording* great lord
3   *stalworth* stalwart   *bo* too
4   *Large* generous
       curteys courteous (but medieval courtesy implies not just politeness but the whole range of cultivated feelings and behaviour appropriate to courtly life.)
5   *comen of* descended from   *Pluto* the god of the underworld (Classical mythology has been garbled in the transmission of the story: this ought really to be the name of the fairy king whom Orfeo meets later.)
6   *King Juno* More garbled mythology: Juno was really queen of the gods.
7   *yhold* considered
8   *dede* performed
10   *glee* music, revelry
11   *Siker* certain
14   *laide theron* applied to it
15   *nothing* not at all
15–16   *nothing . . . no* In ME negatives do not cancel each other out, but can be multiplied for emphasis.
18–21   *That ones . . . In on* who once sat in Orfeo's presence, if he could hear some of his harping, who would not think that he was experiencing one
24   *defens* fortifications
25   *cleped tho* called then
26   *no* denial (Perhaps even the poet feels a little embarrassed by the quite unauthorized identification of Thrace with Winchester, and is attempting to overrule objections in advance.)
27   *of pris* precious, excellent
28   *ycleped* called
29   *levedy* lady
       for the nones at that time (an almost meaningless tag)
30   Another tag, meaning literally 'who could walk around alive'
31   *godenisse* goodness
32   *fairnisse* beauty
33   *Bifell so* it so happened   *comessing* beginning
34   *mirry* pleasant
37   *breme* bright

Overal wexeth mirry anough)
This ich queen, Dame Heurodis,
Took two maidens of pris,   40
And went in an undrentide
To play by an orchardside,
To see the floures sprede and spring,
And to here the fowles sing.
They set hem down all three   45
Under a fair ympe-tree,
And well soone this fair queene
Fell on sleepe opon the greene.
The maidens durst her nought awake,
Bot lete her ligge and rest take.   50
So she slepe till after noone,
That undertide was all ydone.
Ac, as soone as she gan awake,
She cride, and lothly bere gan make:
She froted her honden and her feet,   55
And crached her visage—it bled wete;
Her riche robe hye all torett,
And was reveyd out of her wit.
The two maidens her biside
No durst with her no leng abide,   60
Bot urn to the palays full right
And told bothe squier and knight
That her queen awede wold,
And bad hem go and her athold.
Knightes urn and levedis also,   65
Damisels sexty and mo.
In the orchard to the queene hye come,
And her up in her armes nome,
And brought her to bed atte last,
And held her there fine fast;   70
Ac ever she held in o cry,
And wold up and owy.
   When Orfeo herd that tiding,
Never him nas wers for nothing.
He come with knightes tene   75
To chaumber, right bifor the queene,
And biheld, and said with grete pité,
'O lef lif, what is te,

38	Grows very pleasantly everywhere (*anough* is here used as an under-statement)
39	*ich* same
41	*undrentide* morning
42	*play* enjoy themselves
45	*set hem* seated themselves
46	*ympe-tree* grafted tree
50	*ligge* lie
51	*slepe* slept
52	*ydone* finished
53	*gan awake* (*Gan*, meaning literally 'began', is often used in ME as an auxiliary verb to indicate the past tense.)
54	*lothly bere* hideous outcry
55	*froted* rubbed
56	*crached* scratched *bled wete* ran with blood
57	*hye* she *torett* tore to pieces
58	*reveyd* driven (but *reveyd* is a highly unusual word, and editors have suggested emendations such as *reveysed*, 'ravished'.)
60	*leng* longer
61	*urn* ran *full right* directly
63	*awede wold* was going to go mad
64	*athold* restrain
66	Sixty girls and more (but 'sixty' is used to indicate any large number.)
67	*hye come* they came
68	*nome* took
70	*fine fast* very firmly
71	*held* persisted
72	*o cry* (literally 'one cry') continuous crying
	wold up and owy wanted to (get) up and (run) away (In ME verbs of motion can be omitted when, as here, their meaning is obvious.)
74	He was never so distressed at anything (a triple negative!)
75	*tene* ten
76	*chaumber* private room
78	O my dear life, what is the matter with you

That ever yete hast been so stille,
And now gredest wonder shille? 80
Thy body, that was so white ycore,
With thine nailes is all totore.
Allas! thy rode, that was so red,
Is all wan, as thou were ded;
And also thine fingres smale 85
Beth all bloody and all pale.
Allas! thy lovesom eyen two
Looketh so man doth on his fo!
A! dame, ich biseeche mercy:
Lete been all this reweful cry, 90
And tell me what thee is, and how,
And what thing may help thee now.'
    Tho lay she stille atte last,
And gan to weepe swithe fast,
And said thus the king to, 95
'Allas, my lord Sir Orfeo!
Sethen we first togider were
Ones wroth never we nere,
Bot ever ich have yloved thee
As my lif, and so thou me; 100
Ac now we mot delen atwo;
Do thy best, for I mot go!'
    'Allas!' quath he, 'Forlorn ich am!
Whider wiltow go, and to wham?
Whider thou gost ichill with thee, 105
And whider I go thou shalt with me.'
'Nay, nay, sir, that nought nis!
Ichill thee telle all how it is.
As ich lay this undertide
And sleepe under our orchardside, 110
Ther come to me two fair knightes,
Wele y-armed all to rightes,
And bad me comen an heighing
And speke with her lord the king;
And ich answerd at wordes bold, 115
I no durst nought, no I nold.
They priked oyain as they might drive.
Tho come her king, also blive,
With an hundred knightes and mo,

79	*That* who *stille* quiet
80	*gredest* criest out *wonder shille* remarkably shrilly
81	*white ycore* excellently white
82	*totore* torn to pieces
83	*rode* complexion
85	*smale* slender
87	*lovesom* lovely
88	Gaze like someone looking at his enemy
90	*Lete been* give up *reweful* pitiful
91	*what ... how* what is the matter with you (cf. *what is te* in line 78), and how it happened
97	*Sethen* since
98	We were never once angry (with each other)
101	*mot delen atwo* must separate
103	*Forlorn* forsaken
104	*wiltow* wilt thou *wham* whom
105	*ichill with thee* I will (go) with thee
107	*nought nis* is of no help
112	Armed well and exactly as they ought to be
113	*an heighing* in haste
114	*her* their
115	*at* with
116	I neither dared nor wished (to do so)
117	They spurred away, hurrying as (fast as) they could
118	*also blive* equally quickly

And damisels an hundred also,   120
All on snowe-white steedes;
As white as milke were her weedes.
I no seighe never yete bifore
So fair creaturs ycore.
The king hadde a crown on hed;   125
It nas of silver, no of gold red,
Ac it was of a precious ston;
As bright as the sonne it shon.
And, as soon as he to me cam,
Wold ich, nold ich, he me nam   130
And made me with him ride
Opon a palfray by his side,
And brought me to his palays,
Wele atird in ich ways,
And shewed me castels and tours,   135
Rivers, forestes, frith with flours,
And his riche steedes ichon;
And sethen me brought oyain hom
Into our owen orchard,
And said to me thus afterward: 140
'Looke, dame, tomorwe thatow be
Right here under this ympe-tre,
And than thou shalt with us go,
And live with us evermo;
And yif thou makest us ylet,   145
Whar thou be, though worst yfet,
And totore thine limes all,
That nothing help thee no shall;
And thei thou beest so totorn,
Yete thou worst with us yborn.'   150
    When King Orfeo herd this cas,
'O we!' quath he, 'allas, allas!
Lever me were to lete my lif
Than thus to lese the queen my wif!'
He asked conseil at ich man,   155
Ac no man him help no can.
Amorwe the undertide is come,
And Orfeo hath his armes ynome,
And welle ten hundred knightes with him,
Ich y-armed, stout and grim;   160

122	*weedes* clothes		
123	*seighe* saw		
124	*ycore* excellent(ly)		
126	*nas* was not		
130	He seized me, whether I would or not		
132	*palfray* palfrey (small saddle-horse)		
134	Well appointed in every respect		
136	*frith* woodland		
137	*riche* noble	*ichon* every one	
138	*sethen* then	*oyain hom* back home	
141	Lady, take care that tomorrow you are		
145	*makest us ylet* cause us any hindrance		
146	*Whar* wherever	*worst yfet* will be fetched	
147	*totore* torn to pieces	*limes* limbs	
148	*That* so that		
149	*thei* though		
150	You will still be carried off by us		
151	*cas* (story of) what had happened		
152	*we* woe		
153	I would rather give up my life		
154	*lese* lose		
155	*conseil* advice	*at ich man* from every man	
157	*Amorwe* the next day		
158	*his armes ynome* taken his weapons		
159	*welle* fully		
160	*stout* fierce		

And with the queen wenten he
Right unto that ympe-tree.
They made sheltrom in ich a side,
And said they wold there abide
And die there everichon,   165
Er the queen shuld fram hem gon;
Ac yete amiddes hem full right
The queen was oway ytwight,
With fairy forth ynome:
Men wist never wher she was bicome.   170
Tho was ther crying, weepe and wo;
The king into his chaumber is go,
And oft swooned opon the ston,
And made swiche diol and swiche mon
That neighe his lif was yspent—   175
Ther was non amendement.
He cleped togider his barouns,
Erls, lordes of renouns,
And when they all ycomen were,
'Lordinges,' he said, 'bifor you here   180
Ich ordainy min heighe steward
To wite my kingdom afterward;
In my stede been he shall
To keepe my londes overal,
For now ichave my queen ylore,   185
The fairest levedy that ever was bore,
Never eft I nill no woman see.
Into wilderness ichill te,
And live ther evermore
With wilde bestes in holtes hore;   190
And when ye understond that I be spent,
Make you than a parlement,
And chese you a newe king.
Now doth your best with all my thinge.'
   Tho was ther weeping in the halle,   195
And grete cry among hem alle:
Unnethe might old or yong
For weeping speke a word with tong.
They kneeled adown all yfere
And prayd him, yif his wille were,   200
That he no shuld nought fram hem go.

161	*wenten he* they went
163	They formed a rank of armed men on every side
165	*everichon* every one
167	*amiddes ... right* from the very midst of them
168	*oway ytwight* snatched away
169	Taken away by magic
170	It was never known what had become of her
172	*is go* went (perfect tense to give a greater sense of immediacy)
173	*ston* stone (floor)
174	*swiche diol* such sorrow *mon* lamentation
175	*neighe* nearly
176	*amendement* remedy
177	*cleped* called
178	*renouns* fame
181	*ordainy* appoint
182	*wite* rule *afterward* henceforward
183	*stede* place
184	*keepe* look after *overal* everywhere, in every respect
185	*ichave* I have *ylore* lost
186	*levedy* lady *bore* born
187	*eft* again *nill* will not
188	*ichill te* I will go
190	*holtes hore* grey (i.e. ancient, desolate) woods (an alliterative formula)
191	*understond* i.e. receive news *spent* finished (i.e. dead)
193	*chese you* choose yourselves
194	*thinge* affairs
197	*Unnethe* hardly
199	*yfere* together

'Do way!' quath he, 'it shall be so!'
All his kingdom he forsooke;
Bot a sclavin on him he tooke—
He no hadde kirtel ne hoode,   205
Shert, no no nother goode;
Bot his harp he took algate,
And dede him barfoot out atte yate;
No man most with him go.
O, way, what ther was weepe and wo   210
When he, that hadde been king with crown,
Went so poverlich out of town!
Thurth woode and over heth
Into the wilderness he geth.
Nothing he fint that him is ais,   215
Bot ever he liveth in gret malais.
He that hadde ywerd the fowe and griis,
And on bed the purper biis,
Now on hard hethe he lith,
With leves and gresse he him writh.   220
He that hadde had castels and tours,
River, forest, frith with flours,
Now, thei it comenci to snewe and freese,
This king mot make his bed in mese.
He that had yhad knightes of pris   225
Bifor him kneeland, and levedys,
Now seeth he nothing that him liketh,
Bot wilde wormes by him striketh.
He that had yhad plenté
Of mete and drink, of ich dainté,   230
Now may he all day digge and wrote
Er he finde his fille of roote.
In somer he liveth by wild frut,
And berien bot goode lite;
In winter may he nothing finde   235
Bot roote, grasses, and the rinde.
All his body was oway dwine
For missais, and all tochine.
Lord! who may telle the sore
This king sufferd ten yere and more?   240
His here of his berd, blak and rowe,
To his girdelstede was growe.

202	*Do way!* enough!		
204	*Bot a sclavin* only a pilgrim's mantle		
205	*kirtel* short coat		
206	*no no nother goode* nor any other possessions		
207	*algate* at any rate		
208	*dede him* went	*atte yate* at the gate	
210	*way* alas		
212	*so poverlich* in such poverty		
	out of town away from human habitation (*town* can have a more genera l sense than in modern English.)		
213	*thurth* through		
214	*geth* goes		
215	*fint* finds	*him is ais* is comfort to him	
216	*malais* discomfort		
217	*ywerd* worn		
	fowe and griis (literally) variegated and grey fur (a common formula to indicate luxurious aristocratic dress)		
218	*purper biis* fine purple linen (purple is the colour symbolic of royalty.)		
219	*lith* lies		
220	*gresse* grass	*him writh* covers himself	
223	*thei* though	*comenci* begin	*snewe* snow
224	*mot* must	*mese* moss	
226	*kneeland* kneeling.		
227	*him liketh* pleases him		
228	*wormes* serpents	*striketh* glide	
230	*mete* food		
231	*wrote* grub		
232	*Er he finde* before he may find		
234	*berien ... lite* berries of but little value (the rhyme *frut/lite* was at one time satisfactory, because the vowel in both words was pronounced like that in French *tu*)		
236	*rinde* husks, bark		
237	*oway dwine* wasted away		
238	*missais* discomfort	*tochine* scarred	
239	*sore* sorrow		
241	*rowe* rough		
242	*girdelstede* waist		

His harp, whereon was all his glee,
He hidde in an holwe tree;
And when the weder was clere and bright   245
He tooke his harp to him well right
And harped at his owen wille.
Into alle the woode the soun gan shille,
That alle the wilde beestes that ther beeth
For joye abouten him they teeth,   250
And alle the fowles that ther were
Come and sete on ich a brere
To here his harping afine,
So miche melody was therin;
And when he his harping lete wold,   255
No beest by him abide nold.
　　He might see him bisides
Oft in hot undertides
The king o fairy with his rout
Come to hunt him all about   260
With dim cry and blowing,
And houndes also with him berking;
Ac no beest they no nome,
No never he nist whider they bicome.
And other while he might him see   265
As a greet ost by him tee,
Welle atourned, ten hundred knightes,
Ich y-armed to his rightes,
Of cuntenaunce stout and fers,
With many desplayd banners,   270
And ich his swerd ydrawe hold;
Ac never he nist whider they wold.
And other while he seighe other thing:
Knightes and levedys com dauncing
In quaint attire, gisely,   275
Quaint pas and softly;
Tabours and trumpes yede hem by,
And all manner minstracy.
　　And on a day he seighe him biside
Sexty levedys on hors ride,   280
Gentil and jolif as brid on ris;
Nought o man amonges hem ther nis;
And ich a faucoun on hond bere,

243	*whereon ... glee* in which ... delight (but *glee* also means more specifically music and the pleasure it gives, as in line 10.)
246	*well right* immediately
248	*soun gan shille* noise resounded
250	*teeth* come (cf. *te* in line 188)
252	*sete ... brere* sat on every twig
253	*afine* to the end
255	*lete wold* gave up
256	*nold* would not
257	*him bisides* near him
259	*rout* company
261	*dim ... blowing* faint shouts and blowing of horns
263	*nome* caught
264	Nor did he ever know what became of them
265	*other while* at other times *him* (redundant)
266	*ost* army
267	*atourned* equipped
268	Cf. line 112
269	*fers* fierce
270	*desplayd* unfurled
272	*nist* did not know
275	*quaint* elegant *gisely* skilfully
276	*quaint pas* with elegant steps
277	Drums and trumpets accompanied them
281	As charming and gay as a bird on a bough
282	*nis* is not (historic present)
283	*faucoun* falcon *bere* bore

And riden on hawkin by o rivere.
Of game they founde well goode haunt,   285
Maulardes, hayroun and cormeraunt;
The fowles of the water ariseth,
The faucouns hem welle deviseth;
Ich faucoun his prey slough.
That seighe Orfeo, and lough: 290
'Parfay!' quath he, 'Ther is fair game;
Thider ichill, by Godes name!
Ich was ywon swiche werk to see.'
He aros, and thider gan tee.
To a levedy he was ycome,   295
Biheld, and hath welle undernome
And seeth by all thing that it is
His owen queen, Dame Heurodis.
Yern he biheld her, and she him eke,
Ac noither to other a word no speke.   300
For missais that she on him seighe,
That had been so riche and so heighe,
The teres fell out of her eye.
The other levedys this yseighe
And maked her oway to ride: 305
She most with him no lenger abide.
'Allas!' quath he, 'now me is wo!
Why nill deth now me slo?
Allas, wroche, that I no might
Die now after this sight!   310
Allas! too long last my lif,
When I no dar nought with my wif,
No hye to me, o word speke.
Allas! why nill min hert breke?
Parfay!' quath he, 'tide what bitide,   315
Whiderso this levedys ride,
The selve way ichill streche;
Of lif no deth me no reche.'
His sclavin he dede on also spak
And henge his harp opon his bak,   320
And had well goode will to gon;
He no spard nother stub no ston.
In at a roche the levedys rideth,
And he after, and nought abideth.

284 And they rode a-hawking by a river-bank (a favourite place for hunting river-birds with hawks)

285 *well goode haunt* very great plenty

286 *Maulardes* mallards   *hayroun* heron

288 *hem welle deviseth* take good aim at them

289 *slough* slew

290 *lough* laughed

291 *Parfay!* indeed! (literally, 'by faith!')

292 *Thider ichill* I will (go) there

293 I was accustomed to see such activities

296–7 Beheld her, and clearly perceived and saw by all the evidence that it was.

299 *Yern* willingly

301 Because of the discomfort that she saw in him

302 *That* who   *riche* powerful

304 *yseighe* saw

308 *nill* will not   *slo* slay

309 Alas, wretch that I am, that I may not

313 Speak a single word, nor she to me

315 *tide what bitide* happen what may

316 *Whiderso this* wheresoever these

317–18 I will go the same way; I do not care whether I live or die

319 *dede ... spak* put on as quickly (as he could)

321 *well goode will* a very strong desire

322 He did not spare either tree-trunk or stone (i.e. he galloped off without caring about obstacles)

323 *roche* rock, cliff

When he was in the roche ygo   325
Welle three mile, other mo,
He come into a fair cuntray,
As bright so sonne on somers day,
Smoothe and plain and all greene;
Hille no dale nas ther non yseene.   330
Amidde the lond a castel he seighe,
Riche and real and wonder heighe:
All the utmast wall
Was clere and shine as cristal;
An hundred towrs ther were about,   335
Degiselich and bataild stout;
The buttrass com out of the diche
Of rede gold y-arched riche;
The vousour was avowed all
Of ich manner divers aumal.   340
Within ther wer wide wones,
All of precious stones;
The werst piller on to biholde
Was all of burnist gold.
All that lond was ever light,   345
For when it shuld be therk and night
The riche stones light gonne
As bright as doth at noone the sonne.
No man may telle, no thenche in thought,
The riche werk that ther was wrought: 350
By all thing him think that it is
The proude court of Paradis.
In this castel the levedys alight;
He wold in after, yif he might.
Orfeo knocketh atte gate;   355
The porter was redy therate,
And asked what he wold have ydo.
'Parfay!' quath he, 'Icham a minstrel, lo!
To solas thy lord with my glee,
Yif his sweete wille be!'   360
The porter undede the yate anon
And lete him into the castel gon.
   Than he gan bihold about all
And seighe liggeand within the wall
Of folk that were thider ybrought,   365

326	*welle* fully
329	*plain* flat
330	Neither hill nor valley was visible
332	*Riche and real* splendid and royal
333	*utmast* outermost
334	*shine* bright
336	Wonderful and strongly crenellated
337	*diche* moat
339–40	The vaulting was all adorned with every kind of enamel in all its variety
341	*wide wones* spacious dwellings
343	The worst pillar to be seen
344	*burnist* burnished
346	*therk* dark
347	*light gonne* began to shine (or possibly 'shone', with *gonne* used as an auxiliary)
349	*no thenche in thought* nor imagine in his mind
351	*him think* it seems to him (this is a different verb from *thenche* meaning 'think' or 'imagine', as in line 349, but the two were beginning to become confused)
352	Orfeo recognizes the landscape, with its precious stones and brilliant light, as being in keeping with medieval descriptions of paradise.
357	*wold have ydo* wished to have done
359	*solas* entertain
361	*yate* This and *gate*, as in line 355, are variant forms of the same word.
	anon at once
364	*liggeand* lying
365	*Of folk* some people

And thought dede, and nare nought.
Sum stoode withouten hade,
And sum non armes nade,
And sum thurth the body hadde wounde,
And sum lay wode, ybounde,   370
And sum armed on hors sete,
And sum astrangled as they ete;
And sum were in water adreynt,
And sum with fire all forshreynt.
Wives ther lay on childbedde,   375
Sum dede and sum awedde,
And wonder fele ther lay bisides,
Right as they slepe her undertides;
Eche was thus in this warld ynome,
With fairy thider ycome.   380
Ther he seighe his owen wif,
Dame Heurodis, his lef lif,
Sleepe under an ympe-tree:
By her clothes he knewe that it was he.
    And when he hadde bihold this mervails alle   385
He went into the kinges halle.
Than seighe he ther a seemly sight,
A tabernacle blisseful and bright.
Therin her maister king sete,
And her queen, fair and sweete: 390
Her crownes, her clothes shine so bright
That unnethe bihold he hem might.
When he had biholden all that thing
He kneeled adown bifor the king:
'O lord,' he said, 'yif it thy wille were,   395
My minstracy thou shust yhere.'
The king answerd: 'What man artow
That art hider ycomen now?
Ich, no non that is with me,
No sent never after thee.   400
Sethen that ich here regni gan
I no fond never so foolehardy man
That hider to us durst wende,
Bot that ichim wald ofsende.'
'Lord,' quath he, 'trowe full well,   405
I nam bot a pover minstrel;

366	And were supposed to be dead, but are not
367	*hade* head
368	*nade* had not
370	*wode, ybounde* mad and tied up
372	*astrangled* choked
373	*adreynt* drowned
374	*forshreynt* shrivelled
376	*awedde* gone mad (cf. *wode* in line 370)
377	*wonder fele* remarkably many
378	Just as if they were sleeping their mornings away (we are meant to be reminded of Heurodis when the fairies first approached her)
379–80	Each of them had thus been seized in this world (i.e. the world above ground), and had come there (i.e. into the underworld) by magic.
382	*lef lif* dear life (cf. line 78)
383	*sleepe* sleeping
384	*it was he* it was she (Old English *he,* 'he', *heo,* 'she', and *hie,* 'they', can all become *he* in Middle English. The context usually makes clear which meaning is intended.)
385	*this* these
387	*seemly* pleasant
388	*tabernacle* canopied dais *blisseful* pleasant
389	In it sat the king their lord
391	*her* their
392	That he could hardly look at them
395–6	*yif ... yhere* if it should be your will, you shall hear my minstrelsy
399	*Ich, no non* neither I nor anyone
401	*regni* reign
403	*wende* come
404	Unless I should summon him
405	*trowe* believe
406	*nam bot* am only *pover* poor

And, sir, it is the manner of us
To seche many a lordes hous:
Thei we nought welcom no be,
Yete we mot proferi forth our glee.'   410
  Bifor the king he sat adown
And took his harp so mirry of soun,
And tempreth his harp as he welle can,
And blisseful notes he ther gan,
That al that in the palays were   415
Com to him forto here,
And liggeth adown to his feete,
Hem thenketh his melody so sweete.
The king herkneth and sitt full stille;
To here his glee he hath goode wille.   420
Goode bourde he hadde of his glee;
The riche queen also hadde he.
When he hadde stint his harping,
Than said to him the king:
'Minstrel, me liketh well thy glee.   425
Now aske of me what it be,
Largelich ichill thee pay:
Now speke, and tow might assay.'
'Sir,' he said, 'ich biseeche thee
Thatow woldest yive me   430
That ich levedy, bright on ble,
That sleepeth under the ympe-tree.'
'Nay!' quath the king, 'that nought nere!
A sorry couple of you it were,
For thou art lene, rowe and blak,   435
And she is lovesom, withouten lak:
A lothlich thing it were, forthy,
To seen her in thy compayny.'
'O, sir,' he said, 'gentil king,
Yete were it a welle fouler thing   440
To here a lesing of thy mouthe:
So sir, as ye said nowthe,
What ich wold asky, have I shold;
And needes thou most thy word hold.'
The king said, 'Sethen it is so,   445
Take her by the hond and go:
Of her ichill thatow be blithe!'

408	*seche*	seek out	
409–10	Though we may not be welcome, yet we must offer our music		
412	*mirry*	pleasant	
413	*tempreth*	tunes	
417	*liggeth*	they lie	
418	*Hem thenketh*	seems to them	
421	*bourde*	enjoyment	
422	So did the noble queen		
423	*stint*	ceased	
425	Minstrel, your music pleases me well		
426	*what it be*	whatever it may be (i.e. anything you like)	
427	*Largelich*	generously	*ichill* I will
428	*and . . . assay*	and thou mayst find out	
430	*Thatow*	that thou	
431	*bright on ble*	fair of face (an alliterative formula)	
433	*nought nere*	would not be fitting	
434	You would make an ill-matched pair		
435	*rowe*	rough	
436	*lak*	blemish	
437	*lothlich*	repulsive	*forthy* therefore
439	*gentil*	noble	
440	*welle fouler*	much uglier	
441	*lesing*	lie	
442	*nowthe*	(just) now	
443	That I should have whatever I might ask		
444	*needes*	necessarily	
447	I wish you joy of her!		

He kneeled adown and thonked him swithe.
His wif he took by the hond
And dede him swithe out of that lond,   450
And went him out of that thede;
Right as he come the way he yede.
  So long he hath the way ynome
To Winchester he is ycome,
That was his owen cité;   455
Ac no man knewe that it was he.
No forther than the townes ende
For knoweleche no durst he wende,
Bot with a begger, ybilt full narwe,
Ther he took his herbarwe,   460
To him and to his owen wif,
As a minstrel of pover lif,
And asked tidinges of that lond,
And who the kingdom held in hond.
The pover begger in his cote   465
Told him everich a grote:
How her queen was stole owy,
Ten yer gon, with fairy,
And how her king en exile yede,
Bot no man nist in wiche thede,   470
And how the steward the lond gan hold,
And other many thinges him told.
  Amorwe, oyain noonetide,
He maked his wif ther abide;
The beggers clothes he borwed anon   475
And heng his harp his rigge opon,
And went him into that cité
That men might him bihold and see.
Erls and barouns bold,
Burjays and levedys him gun bihold: 480
'Lo!' they said, 'swiche a man!
How long the here hongeth him opan!
Lo, how his berd hongeth to his knee!
He is yclongen also a tree!'
And as he yede in the streete,   485
With his steward he gan meete,
And loude he set on him a cry:
'Sir steward! he said, 'merci!

448	*swithe* heartily
450	*dede him swithe* went quickly
451	*him* (redundant) *thede* country
452–3	He went back just the way he had come. He followed the way for so long (that)
458	Did he dare to go for fear of recognition
459	*ybilt full narrow* housed very meanly
460	*herbarwe* lodging
461	For himself and for his wife
464	*held in hond* was ruling
465	*cote* cottage
466	*everich a grote* every detail
467	*her* their
468	*gon* ago
469	*en exile yede* went into exile
470	But no-one knew into which country
471	*gan hold* ruled
473	Next day, towards the time of noon
476	. *his rigge opon* upon his back
480	*burjays* citizens
481	*swiche* such, what
483	(The increased length of his beard since line 242 marks the passage of time.)
484	*yclongen also* shrivelled like

Icham an harpour of hethenisse:
Help me now in this destresse!'   490
The steward said: 'Come with me, come!
Of that ichave thou shalt have some.
Everich goode harpour is welcom me to
For my lordes love, Sir Orfeo.'
  In the castel the steward sat atte mete,   495
And many lording was by him sete.
Ther were trompours and tabourers,
Harpours fele, and crouders:
Miche melody they maked alle,
And Orfeo sat stille in the halle   500
And herkneth; when they been all stille
He tooke his harp and tempred shille.
The blissefullest notes he harped there
That ever any man yherd with ere:
Ich man liked welle his glee.   505
The steward biheld, and gan ysee,
And knewe the harp als blive:
'Minstrel!' he said, 'so mot thou thrive,
Where haddestow this harp, and how?
I pray that thou me telle now.'   510
'Lord,' quath he, 'in uncouthe thede,
Thurth a wilderness as I yede,
Ther I founde in a dale
With liouns a man totorn smalle,
And wolves him frete with teeth so sharp;   515
By him I fond this ich harp,
Welle ten yere it is ygo.'
'O,' quath the steward, 'now me is wo!
That was my lord, Sir Orfeo!
Alas! wreche, what shall I do,   520
That have swiche a lord ylore?
A, way! that ich was ybore,
That him was so hard grace y-yarked,
And so vile deth ymarked!'
Adown he fell aswoon to grounde: 525
His barouns him took up in that stounde
And telleth him how it geth:
It is no bot of mannes deth.
  King Orfeo knewe welle by than

489	I am a harper from foreign parts
492	Thou shalt have some of what I have
495	As in a film, the action is not always continuous; we pass directly from a shot of the steward and Orfeo in the street to one showing them eating in the castle. The same montage technique is frequently used in ballads, such as *Sir Patrick Spens*.
	atte mete at his food
497	*trompours* trumpeters *tabourers* drummers
498	*fele* many *crouders* fiddlers
502	*tempred shille* tuned it shrilly
506	*gan ysee* saw
507	And immediately recognized the harp
508	*so . . . thrive* as you may prosper (answer this question)
509	Where did you get this harp, and how?
511	*uncouthe thede* an unknown country
514	*totorn smalle* torn into little pieces
515	*frete* eating
521	*ylore* lost
522–4	O, alas that I was born, that such a hard fate was appointed for him, and such a miserable death allotted to him!
525	*aswoon* fainting
526	*stounde* time, moment
527–8	And remind him how things stand: there is no remedy for man's death
529	*than* then

His steward was a trewe man   530
And loved him as he ought to do,
And stont up, and said thus: 'Lo!
Steward, herkne now this thing:
Yif ich were Orfeo the king,
And hadde ysuffred full yore   535
In wildernisse miche sore,
And hadde ywon my queen owy
Out of the lond of fairy,
And hadde ybrought the levedy hende
Right here to the townes ende,   540
And with a begger her in ynome,
And were myself hider ycome
Poverlich to thee, thus stille,
For to assay thy goode wille,
And ich founde thee thus trewe,   545
Thou no shust it never rewe.
Sikerlich, for love or ay,
Thou shust be king after my day;
And yif thou of my deth haddest been blithe
Thou shust have voided also swithe.'   550
    Tho all tho that therin sete
That it was King Orfeo underyete,
And the steward him welle knewe:
Over and over the bord he threwe,
And fell adown to his feet;   555
So dede everich lord that ther sete,
And all they said at o crying:
'Ye beeth our lord, sir, and our king!'
Glad they were of his live;
To chaumber they ladde him als bilive   560
And bathed him, and shaved his berd,
And tired him as a king apert;
And sethen, with gret processioun,
They brought the queen into the town,
With all manner minstracy.   565
Lord! ther was grete melody!
For joye they weepe with her eye
That hem so sound ycomen seighe.
Now King Orfeo newe coround is,
And his queen, Dame Heurodis,   570

532	*stont* he stands
535	*full yore* very long ago
536	*miche sore* great misery
537	*ywon ... owy* regained
539	*hende* gracious
541	And taken her into a beggar's house
543	*stille* quietly (i.e. secretly)
544	*assay* test
546–7	You should never regret it. Certainly, despite (the influence of) love or fear
550	You should have departed (i.e. been thrown out) immediately
551	*Tho all tho* then all those
552	*underyete* realized
554	*bord* table (probably on trestles and therefore easily overturned; medieval dining-tables were not usually permanently set up)
557	*at o crying* in a single shout
559	*of his live* that he was alive
560	*als bilive* immediately
562	And clothed him openly as a king
567–8	Those who saw them returned so safely wept tears of joy with their eyes

And lived long afterward,
And sethen was king the steward.
Harpours in Bretaine after than
Herd how this mervaile bigan,
And made herof a lay of goode liking,   575
And nempned it after the king.
That lay 'Orfeo' is yhote:
Goode is the lay, sweete is the note.
Thus com Sir Orfeo out of his care:
God graunt us alle welle to fare!   580

573   *Bretaine* Brittany   *after than* afterwards
575   And made it into a highly enjoyable lay
576   *nempned* named
577   *yhote* called
579   *com* came

Sir Gawain and the Green Knight

Introduction

Sir Gawain and the Green Knight was written in the north-west Midlands, probably in the last quarter of the fourteenth century. The name of its author is unknown, but there are many reasons for supposing that he wrote three other poems which are also found in the same manuscript as *Sir Gawain*, none of the four being found in any other manuscript. These poems are *Patience* (an extract from which is included in this volume), *Purity* or *Cleanness*, and *Pearl*. *Purity* is a study of this virtue, taken in its widest sense, through examples of God's punishment of its opposite, as in the cases of the Flood, the destruction of Sodom and Gomorrah, and Belshazzar's feast. *Pearl* is an intricately-wrought vision-poem, in which the narrator dreams that he meets his dead small daughter in the other world, and is eventually brought under her guidance to a fleeting glimpse of the New Jerusalem and the Lamb of God. The poet, whoever he was, was a man of learning, a superb craftsman with a delight in the world of the senses, and a man with a keen and subtle sense of humour. Except in the scale and range of his surviving work, he is fully the equal of Chaucer as a poet, and it is perhaps only the difficulty of the dialect in which he wrote that has prevented him from being as widely read.

    Sir Gawain and the Green Knight is a poem of 2530 lines, divided into 101 stanzas (it may not be by accident that *Pearl* also has 101 stanzas: the poet seems to have had a strong interest in numbers and their symbolic significances). The form of the stanzas is unique among medieval alliterative poems: they consist of an irregular number of unrhymed alliterative lines, but each concludes with a five-line rhyming section, called the 'bob and wheel'. Though the stanza-lengths are uneven, the division into stanzas is by no means random, and in the extract included here the reader will notice many examples of the use of stanza-divisions to create effects of tension and climax. The complete poem is divided into four sections or 'fitts', and the first of these sections is printed here complete, except for the first two stanzas, which set the story told by the poem in the wider context of the legendary history of Britain. In this first section, a huge green knight enters King Arthur's court on New Year's Day and insultingly requests a boon: that some knight should agree to exchange blows with him, each to give the other a single stroke with an enormous axe. The Green Knight is to receive his opponent's blow immediately, and to give the return blow at his own home, the Green Chapel, the following New Year. Sir Gawain takes up the challenge, and delivers a blow which cuts off the Green Knight's head; but the Green Knight picks it up in his hand and rides off. In the second section, the year passes until it is time for Gawain to set off to fulfil his bargain. Fully armed, he rides north through bitter weather, and on Christmas Eve comes to a beautiful castle in a forest. There he is made welcome, and the genial lord of the castle tells him that the Green Chapel is nearby. After the Christmas feast, the lord proposes that Gawain should stay at the castle and recuperate himself in the care of the lord's beautiful young wife and her ugly old chaperone, while the lord goes out hunting each day; and at the end of each day, they should exchange whatever they have gained. Gawain agrees. In the third section, this agreement is carried out on three successive days. Each day the beautiful wife comes to Gawain's bedroom and attempts to seduce him, but Gawain, firmly dedicated to chastity and to loyalty to his host, politely fends her off. On the first day he receives one kiss from her, and exchanges it for the deer that the lord has slaughtered. On the second day he receives two kisses, and exchanges them for a boar. On the third day he succumbs so far as to accept from the lady not only three kisses but a magic green girdle, which she says will protect him from being harmed when he goes to the Green Chapel, and which she gives him only on condition that he should conceal it from her husband. Gawain therefore gives the lord only the kisses in exchange for a fox. In the fourth section, Gawain rides off to the Green Chapel, accompanied by a guide who tempts him to flee, with the promise that he will conceal his cowardice. Gawain resists this temptation, and once more faces the Green Knight. The Knight strikes an axe-blow, but Gawain flinches away from it. He strikes a second blow, but this time withholds it before it has touched Gawain. Lastly he strikes a third blow, which only slightly cuts Gawain's neck. As Gawain is rejoicing at his unexpected survival, the Green Knight explains that he was himself the lord of the castle, that the three blows correspond to the three days of Gawain's temptation, and that the slight cut is his punishment for his slight failure in accepting and concealing the girdle. Gawain is bitterly ashamed, despite the Knight's praise of his courage, and he refuses his offer of further hospitality and rides back to Camelot, vowing to wear the green girdle for ever as a sign of his falsehood. There he tells his story; and though he sees it as one of failure, the court see it as one of success, and they agree that they will all wear green girdles in honour of Gawain's adventure.

No single source is known for this splendidly enigmatic story. Each of the two main elements of which it is made up, the Beheading Game and the Temptation, is found in earlier Celtic and French works, and it is possible that the English poet was translating from a French romance which has not yet been identified. It is also possible that the interweaving of the stories was his own work; and, though he and his audience were obviously familiar with the courtly romances which flourished in France from the twelfth century onwards, and with their characteristic conventions and attitudes, he has created a fully integrated and original work of art, in which every detail plays its part in the overall effect. Another element in the romance of which the poet could assume a prior knowledge in his audience, but which he handled in an entirely new way, was the character of its hero. Many of the best-known knights of Arthurian legend had their own reputations, which were kept up by different writers from one romance to another. Lancelot, for example, was always a tragic lover, torn between his loyalty to Arthur and his adulterous love for Arthur's wife, Guinevere; Kay was always churlish and insulting; and Gawain had a firm reputation as the knight of courtesy. This implied exquisite manners, especially in polite conversation; but it also usually implied skill in flirtation—the traditional Gawain was very much a ladies' man. This is the reputation Gawain has in the English poem; when he arrives at the castle in the forest, and discloses who he is, the courtiers there are excited by the hope that they will learn about 'love-talking' from him. It is also a reputation that the beautiful wife can use as a weapon against him: her usual approach is to murmur that surely *Gawain* (if that is who he really is?) could teach something worth knowing to a 'young thing' like her; surely he wouldn't need teaching how to beg for kisses; and so on. But in this poet's Gawain, the reputation does not fully correspond to the inner reality. Certainly, his Gawain is anxious enough to keep up his reputation for courtesy towards all, and especially towards ladies, but inwardly he is dedicated to chastity, and to the Blessed Virgin, whose image he bears on the inner side of his shield. The contradiction adds an emotional piquancy, a persistent comedy of embarrassment and cross-purpose, and a subtle treatment of the whole concept of reputation, to the poet's handling of the story.

We have described the story as enigmatic, and the most obvious question it raises, in the section printed here, concerns the nature and purpose of the Green Knight. Who is this monstrous figure, who rides insolently into the festivities at Camelot, in which an aristocratic society celebrates with religious sanction its own community of order and

plenty? Why has he 'displaced the mirth, broke the good meeting /
With most admired disorder' (to quote from *Macbeth*)? Several sugges-
tions are made in the poem as to his identity. The courtiers, stunned by
his extraordinary appearance, judge it to be a matter of 'fantoum and
fairie' (GGK 204); and it is true that green is frequently the colour of
the fairies in ancient legends. The suggestion of magic is taken up
again towards the end of the poem, when, in answer to Gawain's
question, the Green Knight explains that he is really Sir Bertilak de
Hautdesert, the lord of the castle, and that he was sent to Camelot by
Morgan la Fay, Arthur's half-sister and a famous witch, who hoped
thereby to have terrified and even killed Guinevere. It was Morgan
who appeared earlier as the beautiful wife's ugly chaperone; and while
this explanation has the merit of tying up a loose end in the plot, it
simply deflects our attention away from the story itself and from the
substantial presence of the Green Knight, who is so elaborately de-
scribed in the first fitt. Another explanation which the poem itself
suggests is that the Green Knight is a devil. When Gawain eventually
approaches the Green Chapel, which is no more than a desolate mound,
he fears that it will prove to be a place where the devil says matins at
midnight. We know from *The Friar's Tale* that devils were thought to
have the power to shift from one external shape to another. Moreover,
the devil there was first met dressed in green (except for the black
fringe on his hat), and, like the Green Knight, he dwelt 'fer in the north
contree' (FT 113). Yet the Green Knight professes to be pleased that
Gawain has *not* fallen into the trap set for him, and he even speaks of
his adventure in terms belonging to Christian confession: he has com-
mitted a fault, but he has acknowledged it, has received penance (in
the form of the cut in his neck), and is now offered absolution. Is the
Green Knight then a devil or a priest, a spokesman for false or true
values, when he assures Gawain that his fault, though real, is only
small compared with his many knightly virtues? Yet another possibility
about the Green Knight is hinted at by Arthur at the end of our extract,
when he assures Guinevere (who is frightened, though not to death),
that 'Well bicommes such craft upon Cristmasse' (GGK 435). It seems
likely enough that the medieval feast of Christmas and New Year,
which marked among other things the movement of the year past its
shortest day and back to the promise of spring, did sometimes include
masques or 'interludes' (GGK 436) in which there appeared a figure
clad in green, and representing the new year or the spring. Such
figures are common enough in folk ceremonies marking the passage of
the seasons, and they may have been imitated in courtly ceremonies.
The Green Knight seems in many ways to be connected with the
greenness of the natural world of vegetation: he and his horse are as
green as grass (GGK 199), his beard is as big as a bush (145), and he

carries in one hand a branch of holly, 'That is grattest in greene when greves are bare' (171)—an emblem, it might be, of the survival of nature's green vitality through the winter. Yet here too we are met with paradox. In the description of the Green Knight, as much emphasis is laid on art as on nature. He is no naked or skin-clad wild man or 'wodwose' such as Gawain encounters on his journey north; his clothing and equipment and his horse's trappings are ingenious products of human skill. The very hair of his horse is entwined with gold and hung with bells, and his own bushy beard and hair are cut into such a shape that they resemble a hood, a 'kinges capados' (150). No interpretation of the poem that simply contrasts the civilization and artifice of Camelot with the Green Knight's 'natural' qualities will work; and by the end of the poem the seasonal theme, which is emphasized in a beautiful passage describing the sequence of the year at the beginning of Fitt II, has almost been forgotten.

It seems that the Green Knight, for all the fascination he exerts over us, will not fit into any ready-made category; and indeed, it almost looks as though the poet was deliberately trying to make us feel this, expressing from the beginning his own uncertainty as to whether he ought to be called half a giant or the largest of men (GGK 104–5). The figure's power to fascinate and to disturb, to challenge us to see reality in an unaccustomed way, surely depends on our inability to place him, to pin him down. Undoubtedly, this element of uncertainty is an essential part of the test that first Camelot, and then Gawain as its representative, have to face. The challenge the intruder offers is only to a game, but it is a game in which heads are at stake, and the Arthurian court scarcely knows how to respond to such a test. The Green Knight claims that he has come to test Camelot's reputation, their *los* (GGK 223) or *renown* (277). This is a key value in medieval treatments of heroism. In many early societies, such as Homeric Greece or Anglo-Saxon England, what people say about a man *is* what he is, and the thought of what reputation one will gain by one's acts is a crucial motive in decisions about how to act. Even in our own time, most people would find it difficult to say how far their image of themselves can be separated from the way they believe themselves to be reflected in the eyes of others. The challenge to Camelot's name and fame is irresistible; it is the Green Knight's jeer that his own words have overthrown the court's reputation (GGK 273–9) that impels Arthur himself to take it up. When it has been agreed that Gawain should take his place, it is Gawain's reputation too that is at stake. We have seen how the lady in the castle plays on it, telling him that he cannot be Gawain if he does not take part in flirtation; and at the Green Chapel too, when Gawain flinches, the Green Knight asserts, 'Thou art not Gawain.' His reputation and his name, his very identity, it appears, are one and the same thing. And yet, like so many things in the poem, reputation is an ambiguous value. Is a man merely what others think him to be? Gawain himself repudiates this view when he is tempted to flee by the guide, and proudly asserts that, even if the guide kept his promise to tell no-one of his shameful act, he would still be 'a knight coward—I might not be excused'. And yet Gawain's courage in rejecting mere outward appearances as the criterion of human integrity is less complete than it might appear, because at this moment he is wearing the green girdle, which is supposed to offer him magical protection against death. And he has accepted the girdle without apparently feeling any qualm of conscience about breaking his agreement to exchange winnings with his host, presumably because he feels confident that it cannot be in the lady's interest that any one but the two of them should know what he has done. His feeling of acute shame comes at the point when he realizes that he has been found out; it is only then that he sees his agreement to conceal the girdle as a matter of 'villainy and vice', and that he determines to give himself a different reputation, by wearing the green girdle for ever as a badge of shame. Even that wish is frustrated, because what is a badge of shame to him is taken by the court as a badge of honour.

What appears in the first fitt, then, to be a macabre but simple test of a reputation for courage and truth to one's word, is eventually revealed to be far more complicated. In this, the shaping of the narrative itself is of great importance. Once Gawain has stepped forward to become the hero of the poem, we see its events chiefly through his eyes. As it appears to him, what happens during his stay in the castle in the second and third fitts is no more than an episode, an interlude filling the time pleasantly enough before he meets his final test at the Green Chapel. But when he does arrive at what he has expected to be the climax of his adventure, it turns out to be a carefully-contrived anticlimax. The completion of the Beheading Game is only a symbolic reflection of his temptation in the castle; the real test he has had to face has not been that of pitting himself against a monster, but a test of the values of his normal life—courtesy, fidelity, chastity—in a setting as civilized as Camelot; and this test he has already failed. In him, Camelot has failed; the complex value-system implied so confidently and gaily in the Christmas festivities has been shown to be ultimately unstable, and if Camelot does not recognize this when Gawain returns, that only goes to confirm its failure. The end of the poem is less cheerful than its beginning, even though Gawain unexpectedly comes through his adventure alive.

And yet the poet's praise and enjoyment of the scene in Camelot is not, cannot be, simply cancelled out by the poem's end. It is true that, even in the extract we print, a certain irony is implied by the poet's

many superlatives. They were the most famous knights, the loveliest
ladies, the comeliest of kings, and

> Hit were now gret nye to neven
> So hardy a here on hille.   (GGK 22–3)

Yet we cannot fail to notice that they are not, in accordance with the
heroic formula he uses, a hardy army on hillside, but a cheerful indoor
company, very much taken aback when confronted with a dangerous
challenge. The poet uses a number of phrases suggesting that there is
something childishly innocent about them: 'For all was this faire folk
in her first age' (GGK 18), and Arthur himself is not the aged king of
some romances, but is active, changeable, 'sumwhat childgered' (50).
There is something engagingly boyish about the nervousness with
which the courtiers kick away the severed head as it rolls on the floor,
and which is shown by Arthur and Gawain when, in their relief at the
knight's departure, they laugh and grin. But there can be no doubt
about the poet's enjoyment of the life he depicts at Camelot: the bustling
activity, the ample feasting, the brilliant colours (as in the green and
gold of the knight and the contrasting red of his eyes and his blood),
and, perhaps above all, the loud and various sounds. He enters fully
into the sensory world of Camelot, and delights especially in clanging
noise—

> Wilde werbles and wight wakned lote,
> That mony hert full highe hef at her touches   (GGK 83–4)

—and in contrasting silence:

> And all stunned at his steven and ston-still seten
> In a swoghe silence thurgh the salle riche;
> As all were slipped upon sleepe so slaked her lotes.   (206–8)

In our extract, before Gawain is embarked on an adventure that will
lead him through moral blindness to bitter self-knowledge, the poet
offers an incomparable evocation of the civilization of his time, idealized
no doubt, but realized with splendid solidity. If there is a touch of
childishness in Camelot, it is perhaps a concomitant of the resilience
children possess and which a civilization needs if it is not to succumb
to gloomy self-criticism when it encounters setbacks. The poet does not
take his characters with entire seriousness, and he does not intend that
we should do so; there is nothing naive about him, he does not believe
in Green Knights in any literal way, and he does not expect us to be as
frightened by this one as the courtiers are. We are meant to enjoy the
ingenuity with which he contrives for Camelot and for Gawain games
which they cannot avoid playing and which they are bound to lose.

The courage shown by Arthur and Gawain is at once admirable and slightly ridiculous; the poet's affection for them, with their aspirations and their inevitable human faults, is unmistakable.

Suggestions for further reading

Editions of the complete poem: those of J. A. Burrow (Harmondsworth, Penguin, 1972) and of R. A. Waldron (London, Edward Arnold, York Medieval Texts, 1970) are likely to be most helpful to those reading the poem for the first time.

Larry D. Benson, *Art and Tradition in Sir Gawain and the Green Knight* (New Brunswick, Rutgers University Press, 1965)

J. A. Burrow, *A Reading of Sir Gawain and the Green Knight* (London, Routledge and Kegan Paul, 1965)

A. C. Spearing, *The Gawain-Poet: A Critical Study* (Cambridge University Press, 1970)

Sir Gawain and the Green Knight

This king lay at Camelot upon Cristmasse
With mony lovelich lorde, ledes of the best,
Rekenly of the Rounde Table alle tho rich brether,
With rich revel oright and rechless mirthes.
There tournayed tulkes by times full mony,   5
Jousted full jollily these gentile knightes,
Sithen cayred to the court caroles to make.
For there the fest was iliche full fifteen dayes,
With all the mete and the mirthe that men couthe avise;
Such glaum and glee glorious to here,   10
Dere din upon day, dauncing on nightes,
All was hap upon highe in halles and chambres
With lordes and ladies, as levest hem thoght.
With all the wele of the worlde they woned there samen,
The most kyd knightes under Cristes selven,   15
And the lovelokkest ladies that ever lif hadden,
And he the comlokkest king that the court holdes;
For all was this faire folk in her first age,
     on sille,
    The hapnest under heven,   20
    King highest man of wille;
    Hit were now gret nye to neven
    So hardy a here on hille.

While New Yere was so yep that hit was new cummen,
That day double on the des was the douth served.   25
Fro the king was comen with knightes into the halle,
The chauntry of the chapel cheved to an ende,
Loude crye was there cest of clerkes and other,
Nowel nayted onewe, nevened full ofte;
And sithen riche forth runnen to reche hondeselle,   30
Yeyed yeres-yiftes on high, yelde hem by hand,
Debated busily aboute tho giftes;
Ladies laghed full loude, thogh they lost hadden,
And he that wan was not wrothe, that may ye well trowe.
Alle this mirthe they maden to the mete time;   35
When they had washen worthily they wenten to sete,

1	*This king* i.e. Arthur, introduced in the preceding stanza as the noblest of the kings of Britain.
	lay was staying (medieval kings were in the habit of travelling from one castle or palace to another; Arthur was supposed to hold court on the five Christmas festivals of Easter, Ascension, Pentecost, All Saints and Christmas)
	Camelot Medieval writers did not agree about the location of Arthur's capital; this poet imagined it as being, like London, in southern England.
2	*lovelich lorde* gracious lords *ledes* knights
3	All the noble brethren, as was fit, of the Round Table
4	*oright* fittingly *rechless mirthes* carefree pleasures
5	At times there were tournaments in which many knights took part
6	*jollily* gaily *gentile* noble
7	*Sithen cayred* then went *caroles* ring-dances with song
8	*fest* festivity *iliche* (at) the same (pitch)
9	*mete* food *couthe avise* could devise
10	*glaum* revelry *glee* merriment
11	*Dere din* gay noise
12	*hap upon highe* happiness in the highest degree
	halles and chaumbres large and small rooms
13	*With* among *levest hem thoght* pleased them best
14	*wele of* joy in *woned* dwelt *samen* together
15	*kyd* famous *under Cristes selven* i.e. beneath heaven (literally, 'Christ himself')
16	*lovelokkest* loveliest *lif hadden* were alive
17	And he who was holding the court was the fairest of kings
18	*in her first age* in the springtime of life
19	*on sille* on earth (a tag with little meaning)
20	*hapnest* most fortunate people
21–3	And their king was the noblest of temperament; it would now be very difficult to name so bold a company on earth
24	While New Year was so fresh that it had newly arrived (an elaborate way of saying 'on New Year's Day')
25	*double* double (helpings) *des* dais (where the high table was placed, as in an Oxford or Cambridge college) *douth* company
26	*Fro* when
27	*The chauntry ... cheved* the singing of Mass in the chapel having come
28–31	Loud shouts were raised by clerics and laymen, and 'Noel' was repeated again, and called out many times; and then the nobles rushed forward to give presents; they cried aloud 'New Year's gifts!', gave them by hand
32	*Debated ... aboute* eagerly discussed
33–4	Probably these are games in which kisses are forfeits
34	*wan* won *wrothe* angry *trowe* believe
35	*to the mete time* until it was time to eat

The best burne ay above, as hit best seemed,
Queene Gwenore, full gay, graythed in the middes,
Dressed on the dere des, dubbed all aboute,
Small sendal bisides, a celure her over   40
Of tried tolouse, of tars tapites innoghe,
That were enbrawded and beten with the best gemmes
That might be preved of pris with pennies to bye,
      in daye.
    The comlokkest to discrye   45
    There glent with yyen grey;
    A semlokker that ever he syye
    Soth might no man say.

Bot Arthur wolde not ete till all were served,
He was so jolly of his joifness, and sumwhat childgered: 50
His lif liked him light, he loved the lasse
Auther to longe lie or to longe sitte,
So busied him his yonge blood and his brain wilde.
And also another manner meved him eke
That he thurgh nobelay had nomen; he wolde never ete   55
Upon such a dere day er him devised were
Of sum aventurous thing an uncouthe tale,
Of sum main mervaile, that he might trowe,
Of alderes, of armes, of other aventures,
Other sum segge him bisoght of sum siker knight   60
To joine with him in jousting, in jopardé to lay,
Lede, lif for lif, leve uchon other,
As fortune wolde fulsun hem, the fairer to have.
This was the kinges countenaunce where he in court were,
At uch farand fest among his free meny   65
      in halle.
    Therfore of face so fere
    He stightles stiff in stalle,
    Full yep in that New Yere
    Much mirthe he mas with alle.   70

Thus there stondes in stalle the stiff king hisselven,
Talkande bifore the highe table of trifles full hende.
There goode Gawan was graythed Gwenore biside,
And Agravain-à-la-dure-main on that other side sittes,
Bothe the kinges sistersunes and full siker knightes;   75

37	With the noblest men always at the upper end, as was most fitting
38	*Gwenore* Guinevere, Arthur's wife *graythed* set
39	Placed on the fine dais, with adornments all round her
40	*Small sendal bisides* fine silk (curtains) alongside her *celure* canopy
41	Of choice material, and plenty of Turkestan silk carpets
42	*enbrawded* embroidered *beten* set
43–4	That money could purchase at any time
45	The loveliest lady to behold (i.e. Guinevere)
46	*glent* glanced about *yyen grey* (Medieval beauties are usually described as having grey eyes.)
47–8	Truly no man could say that he had ever seen anyone fairer
50	*jolly of his joifness* gay because of his youth *childgered* boyish in behaviour
51–2	It pleased him to have a gay life, he little liked either to lie or to sit for too long
53	*busied* stirred
54	*manner* custom *meved* influenced
55	*thurgh nobelay* as a matter of honour *nomen* taken up
56	*dere* festive *devised* related
57	*aventurous* perilous *uncouthe* strange
58	*main* great
59	*alderes* princes
60–63	Or until some warrior had begged him for a trusty knight to join with him in a joust, a man who would stake his life against another, each of them letting the other have the victory according as fortune should favour them.
64	*countenaunce* custom *where ... were* wherever he might hold court
65	*uch farand* every splendid *free meny* courtly company
67–70	Therefore, with proud face, he stands boldly upright; most eagerly he makes merry with everyone in that New Year.
71	*stondes in stalle* is standing up *stiff* bold (This line recapitulates line 68, linking the end of one stanza with the beginning of the next, a common device in this poem.)
72	*talkande ... of trifles* making small talk *hende* graciously
73	*There* i.e. at the high table, of which we now get a seating plan; the Round Table is evidently not being used. *graythed* placed Guinevere is on Arthur's left, and Gawain is on her left; Arthur is in the middle of the long side of the table facing the hall.
74	*à-la-dure-main* 'hardhand'; Agravain, Gawain's brother, is on his left.
75	*sistersunes* nephews *siker* reliable

D

Bishop Baudewin above biginnes the table,
And Ywain, Urien son, ette with himselven.
These were dight on the des and derworthly served,
And sithen mony siker segge at the sidbordes.
Then the first course come with crakking of trumpes,   80
With mony banner full bright that therby henged;
New nakren noise, with the noble pipes,
Wilde werbles and wight wakned lote,
That mony hert full highe hef at her touches.
Dainties driven therwith of full dere metes,   85
Foisoun of the freshe, and on so fele dishes
That pine to finde the place the peple biforne
For to sette the silveren that sere sewes holden
        on clothe.
    Iche lede as he loved himselve   90
    There laght withouten lothe;
    Ay two had dishes twelve,
    Good beer and bright wyn bothe.

Now will I of her service say you no more,
For uch wye may well wit no wont that there were.   95
Another noise full newe neghed bilive,
That the lude might have leve liflode to cach;
For unethe was the noise not a while cesed,
And the first course in the court kindely served,
There hales in at the halle door an aghlich maister,   100
On the most on the molde on mesure highe;
Fro the swire to the swange so sware and so thik,
And his lindes and his limes so longe and so grete,
Half etain in erde I hope that he were,
Bot man most I algate minn him to beene,   105
And that the mirriest in his muckel that might ride;
For of back and of brest all were his body sturne,
Both his wombe and his wast were worthily small,
And alle his fetures folwande, in forme that he hadde,
        full clene;   110
    For wonder of his hue men hadde,
    Set in his semblaunt seene;
    He ferde as freke were fade,
    And overall enker-greene.

76 Bishop Baldwin (sits) further along in the place of honour (i.e. on Arthur's right)

77 *with himselven* i.e. beside Baldwin (on his right)

78 *dight* placed *derworthly* sumptuously

79 *sithen* then *segge* men, knights *sidbordes* side-tables

80 *crakking* blaring

81 *therby henged* hung from the trumpets

82 *New nakren noise* a sudden noise of kettledrums (*nakren* is genitive pl.)

83 Wild and shrill warblings aroused the echoes

84 *full highe hef* were greatly uplifted *touches* bursts of music

85 With that, there came in delicacies of rare foodstuffs

86 *Foisoun of the freshe* abundance of fresh meat (a great luxury in winter, when usually only salted meat was available)
   fele many

87 *pine* (it was) difficult

88 *silveren* silver dishes *sere sewes* various broths

90–91 Each person took ungrudged what he himself desired

92 *Ay two* every pair

95 Everyone might well know that there was no lack (of anything) (*were* is subjunctive)

96–7 Another very sudden noise quickly approached, so that the prince might have leave to take his food. (The arrival of the Green Knight is going to satisfy Arthur's demand for a marvel.)

98 *unethe* hardly *not* (redundant)

99 *kindely* duly

100 *There hales* (when) there comes *aghlich maister* terrible lord

101 One (who was) the largest in the world so far as height was concerned

102 *swire* neck *swange* waist *sware* squarely built

103 *lindes* loins *limes* limbs

104 *etain* giant *in erde* on earth *hope* suppose

105–6 But at any rate I can assert that he was the biggest of men, and at the same time in his stature the shapeliest man who could ride a horse

107 *all* although *sturne* forbidding

108 *wombe* stomach *worthily small* becomingly slender

109 *folwande* to match *forme . . . hadde* his own way

110 *clene* elegant

112 *semblaunt seene* appearance, plain to see

113–14 He behaved like a man who would be hostile, and (was) bright green all over. (The exact meaning of *fade* is uncertain.)

And all graythed in greene this gome and his weedes: 115
A straite cote full streght, that stek on his sides,
A merry mantle above, mensked withinne
With pelure pured apert, the pane full clene
With blithe blaunner full bright, and his hood bothe,
That was laght fro his lokkes and laide on his shulderes;   120
Heme well-haled hose of that same,
That spenet on his sparlyr, and clene spurres under
Of bright golde, upon silk bordes barred full riche,
And sholess under shankes there the shalk rides;
And alle his vesture verayly was clene verdure,   125
Bothe the barres of his belt and other blithe stones,
That were richely railed in his array clene
Aboute himself and his saddel, upon silk werkes.
That were too tor for to telle of trifles the half
That were enbrawded above, with briddes and flies,   130
With gay gaudy of greene, the golde ay inmiddes.
The pendauntes of his paitrure, the proude croppure,
His molaines, and alle the metail anamaild was thenne,
The stirropes that he stood on stained of the same,
And his arsouns all after and his athel skirtes,   135
That ever glemmered and glent all of greene stones;
The fole that he ferkes on fyn of that ilke,
            certain,
    A greene horse gret and thick,
    A steede full stiff to straine,   140
    In brawden bridel quick—
    To the gome he was full gain.

Well gay was this gome gered in greene,
And the here of his hed of his horse sute.
Faire fannand fax umbefoldes his shulderes;   145
A much berd as a busk over his brest henges,
That with his highlich here that of his hed reches
Was evesed all umbetorne above his elbowes,
That half his armes therunder were halched in the wise
Of a kinges capados that closes his swire;   150
The mane of that main horse much to hit like,
Well cresped and cemmed, with knottes full mony
Folden in with fildore aboute the faire greene,
Ay a herle of the here, another of golde;

115   *graythed* arrayed   *gome* man   *weedes* clothes
116   A straight narrow coat that fitted closely at the waist
117   *merry* fair   *mensked withinne* adorned inside
118   With fur trimmed (to one colour) plain to see, and the facing very elegant
119   *blithe blaunner* gay ermine   *bothe* as well
120   *laght fro his lokkes* thrown back from his locks (of hair)
121   *heme well-haled* neat, well pulled-up   *same* same (green)
122   Which clung to his calf, and below that fine spurs
123   *upon . . . riche* on top of richly striped silk embroidered strips
124   *sholess under shankes* with no shoes on his feet (because, as he explains later, he has come in peace)   *shalk* man, knight
125   *vesture* clothing
126   *stones* gems
127   *railed in* set on
128   *werkes* embroidery
129   *That . . . tor* it would be too difficult   *trifles* details
130   *enbrawded above* embroidered on it   *flies* butterflies
131   *gaudy* ornamentation   *ay inmiddes* always worked into it
132   The hangings of his horse's breast-trappings, the superb crupper (i.e. the strap which keeps the saddle from slipping forwards)
133   *molaines* studs on the horse's bit   *anamailed* enamelled
134   *stained* coloured
135   And his saddlebows (were) all to match, and (so were) his noble saddle-skirts
137   The horse that he rides (is) completely of the same (colour)
138   *certain* yes indeed! (This word perhaps anticipates incredulity among the audience.)
140   *stiff to straine* difficult to manage
141–2 Restive in its embroidered bridle; it was well suited to the man (who was riding it)
144   *of his horse sute* to match his horse
145   *fannand fax umbefoldes* waving hair enfolds
146   *much berd as a busk* beard as big as a bush
147   *with . . . here* together with the splendid hair   *reches* extends
148   *evesed all umbetorne* clipped all round
149   *halched* enclosed
150   *capados* cape and hood   *closes* encloses
151   *main* powerful
152   *cresped* curled   *cemmed* combed
153   *Folden . . . aboute* plaited with gold thread in among
154   First a strand of hair, then one of gold

The tail and his topping twinen of a sute,   155
And bounden bothe with a bande of a bright greene,
Dubbed with full dere stones, as the dock lasted,
Sithen thrawen with a thwong, a thwarle knot alofte,
Ther mony belles full bright of brende golde rungen.
Such a fole upon folde, ne freke that him rides,   160
Was never seene in that salle with sight er that time,
      with yye.
    He looked as lait so light,
    So said all that him sye;
    Hit seemed as no man might   165
    Under his dintes drye.

Whether hadde he no helme ne haubergh nawther,
Ne no pisan ne no plate that pented to armes,
Ne no shafte ne no shelde to shove ne to smite,
Bot in his on hande he hadde a hollyn bobbe,   170
That is grattest in greene when greves are bare,
And an axe in his other, a hoge and unmete,
A spetous sparthe to expoun in spelle, whoso might.
The lengthe of an elnyerde the large hede hadde,
The grain all of greene steele and of golde hewen,   175
The bit burnist bright, with a brod egge
As well shapen to shere as sharp razores.
The stele of a stiff staff the sturne hit by gripte,
That was wounden with irn to the wandes ende,
And all bigraven with greene in gracious werkes;   180
A lace lapped aboute, that louked at the hede,
And so after the halme halched full ofte,
With tried tasseles therto tached innoghe
On botouns of the bright greene braiden full riche.
This hathel heldes him in and the halle entres,   185
Drivande to the highe des, dout he no wothe,
Hailsed he never one, bot highe over looked.
The first word that he warp, 'Wher is,' he said,
'The governour of this ging? Gladly I wolde
See that segge in sight, and with himself speke   190
      resoun.'
    To knightes he cest his yye,
    And reeled hem up and down;
    He stemmed, and con studie
    Who walt ther most renown.   195

155	*topping ... sute* forelock (were) twined to match
157	*dubbed* adorned *as ... lasted* the full length of the tail
158	And furthermore an intricate knot above bound tight with a thong
159	*brende* burnished
160	*folde* earth *freke* man
161	*salle* hall
162	(redundant, repeating *with sight* in line 161)
163	His glances were as bright as lightning
164	*sye* saw
166	Survive under blows from him
167	However, he had neither helmet nor mail-tunic
168	*pisan* neck-armour *plate* armour *pented* belonged
169	*shafte* spear *shove* thrust
170	*on* one *hollyn bobbe* cluster of holly
171	*grattest* most *greves* groves, thickets
172	*unmete* immense
173	A cruel battle-axe to describe in words, if anyone could
174	*elnyerde* ell (45 in. or 1 m. 15) measuring-rod
175	*grain* blade *hewen* hammered
176	*bit* cutting-edge
177	*shapen to shere* devised for cutting
178	The grim (knight) gripped it by the shaft (which was) made of a stout staff
179	*wounden* bound *wandes* staff's
180	*bigraven* carved *gracious werkes* elegant designs
181–3	A thong (was) wrapped round (it), which (was) fastened at the head, and then looped very frequently along the shaft (*halme*), attached to it with plenty of (*innoghe*) fine tassels
184	*botouns* bosses *braiden* embroidered
185	*hathel* knight *heldes him* makes his way
186	*Drivande to* making for *dout ... wothe* he feared no danger
187	*Hailsed* greeted
188	*warp* uttered
189	*governour ... ging* lord of this company. (The words are probably not as rude as they sound to modern ears. Moreover, because Arthur has not sat down in his place, the knight may really not know where he is.)
190	*segge* man *in sight* (redundant)
191	*resoun* speech (redundant after *speke*)
192	*cest his yye* cast his eyes
193	*reeled hem* rolled them (his eyes)
194–5	He halted, and looked carefully to see who (among those) there possessed greatest fame

There was looking on lengthe the lude to beholde,
For uch man had mervaile what hit mene might
That a hathel and a horse might such a hue lach,
As growe greene as the gress and greener hit seemed,
Then greene aumail on golde glowande brighter.   200
All studied that there stood, and stalked him nerre
With all the wonder of the worlde what he worch shulde.
For fele sellies had they seen, bot such never are;
Forthy for fantoum and fairie the folk there hit deemed.
Therfore to answare was arwe mony athel freke,   205
And all stunned at his steven and ston-still seten
In a swoghe silence thurgh the salle riche;
As all were slipped upon sleepe so slaked her lotes
        in highe;
    I deeme hit not all for doute,   210
    Bot sum for courtaisye:
    Bot let him that all shulde loute
    Cast unto that wye.

Then Arthur bifore the high des that aventure biholdes,
And rekenly him reverenced, for rad was he never,   215
And saide, 'Wye, welcum iwis to this place;
The hede of this ostel Arthur I hat;
Light lovelich adown and lenge, I thee praye,
And whatso thy wille is we shall wit after.'
'Nay, as help me,' quoth the hathel, 'He that on highe sittes,
To wone any while in this won, hit was not myn erende;
Bot for the los of thee, lede, is lift up so highe,
And thy burgh and thy burnes best are holden,
Stiffest under steel-gere on steedes to ride,
The wightest and the worthiest of the worldes kinde,   225
Preve for to play with in other pure laykes,
And here is kydde courtaisye, as I have herd carp,
And that has wained me hider, iwis, at this time.
Ye may be siker by this braunch that I bere here
That I passe as in pece, and no plight seeche;   230
For had I founded in fere in fighting wise,
I have a haubergh at home and a helme bothe,
A shelde and a sharp spere, shinande bright,
And other wepenes to welde, I wene well, als;
Bot for I wolde no were, my weedes are softer.   235

196	*on lengthe* for a long time *lude* man
198	*lach* take on
200	Glowing more brightly than green enamel on gold
201	*All . . . stood* all who stood there watched intently (*Stood* may refer to the servants; or possibly the knights too have risen from their seats in astonishment.) *nerre* nearer (to)
202	*what . . . shulde* (to see) what he would do
203	*sellies* strange things *are* before
204	*fantoum* illusion *fairie* magic *deemed* judged
205	*arwe* afraid *mony athel freke* many a noble knight
206	*stunned at his steven* (were) astonished at his voice (i.e. what he said)
207	*swoghe* dead
208	Their words died away as if they had all fallen asleep
209	*highe* haste
210	*deeme* am sure *doute* fear
212	*that all shulde loute* whom all should reverence (i.e. the king)
213	*cast* speak *wye* man
215	*rekenly* promptly *reverenced* greeted *rad* afraid
216	*Wye* sir *iwis* indeed
217	*hede of this ostel* lord of this dwelling *hat* am called
218	*Light lovelich adown* be so good as to dismount *lenge* stay
219	*wit* learn
220	*He . . . sittes* He who dwells on high (i.e. God)
221	*wone* remain *won* dwelling *erende* business
222	*for* because *los* renown *lede* sir *lift up* extolled
223	*burgh* castle, court *burnes* knights
224	*Stiffest* (the) boldest *under steel-gere* in armour
225	*wightest* most valiant *worthiest* noblest
	of the worldes kinde among men (literally, 'of the offspring of earth')
226	(And) brave (too) as opponents in other (kinds of) noble games
227	*kydde* shown *carp* tell
228	(Here the knight breaks off his previous construction and starts again.) *wained* brought
229	*siker* sure
230	*passe . . . pece* come in peace (because the holly-branch is a token of peace, an English equivalent to the olive-branch) *no . . . seeche* seek no hostility
231	*founded* journeyed *in fere* (probably) in force
232	*haubergh* mail-coat
234	*welde* wield *wene well* know
235	*wolde no were* desire no fighting *softer* more peaceful

Bot if thou be so bold as alle burnes tellen,
Thou will grant me goodly the gomen that I ask
    by right.'
     Arthur con answare,
     And said, 'Sir courtais knight,   240
     If thou crave battail bare,
     Here failes thou not to fight.'

'Nay, frayst I no fight, in faith I thee telle,
Hit arn aboute on this bench bot berdless childer.
If I were hasped in armes on a highe steede,   245
Here is no man me to mach, for mightes so wayke.
Forthy I crave in this court a Cristmas gomen,
For hit is Yol and Newe Yer, and here are yep mony:
If any so hardy in this hous holdes himselven,
Be so bolde in his blood, brain in his hede,   250
That dar stiffly strike a strok for an other,
I shall gif him of my gift this giserne riche,
This axe, that is hevy innogh, to handle as him likes,
And I shall bide the first bur as bare as I sitte.
If any freke be so felle to fonde that I telle,   255
Lepe lightly me to, and lach this wepen
(I quitclaime hit for ever), keepe hit as his owen,
And I shall stonde him a strok, stiff on this flet,
Elles thou will dight me the doom to dele him an other
      barlay,   260
     And yet gif him respite,
     A twelmonith and a day;
     Now hye, and let see tite
     Dar any herinne oght say.'

If he hem stunned upon first, stiller were thanne   265
Alle the heredmen in halle, the high and the lowe.
The renk on his rouncy him ruched in his saddel,
And runishly his rede yyen he reeled aboute,
Bende his bresed browes, blycande greene,
Waived his berde for to waite whoso wolde rise.   270
When non wolde keepe him with carp, he coghed full highe,
And rimed him full richely, and right him to speke:
'What, is this Arthures hous,' quoth the hathel thenne,
'That all the rous rennes of thurgh realmes so mony?

237	*goodly* kindly *gomen* game
238	*by right* as a privilege (of the Christmas season)
241–2	If you wish for unarmed battle, you will not lack for a fight here
243	*frayst* seek
244	There are only beardless children sitting round this table
245	*hasped* buckled
246	There is no man here to equal me, their strengths are so feeble
247	*gomen* game
248	*yep mony* many bold (fellows)
249	*holdes* considers
250–51	*Be ... stiffly* (to) be so bold of mettle, (so) reckless of mind, that (he) dares stoutly
252	*giserne* (halberd, or) battle-axe
254	*bide* endure, receive *bur* stroke *bare* unarmed
255	If any warrior be so fierce as to try out what I suggest
256	*Lepe ... to* let him come quickly to me *lach* seize
257	*quitclaime* renounce (legal term) *keepe* let him keep
258	*stonde him* endure from him *stiff* unflinching *flet* floor
259	So long as you will grant me the right to deal him a second (blow)
260	*barlay* The word *barley* is still used in children's games in some parts of England to mean 'truce' or 'bags I'; here it may mean 'I claim first blow', or 'when I claim my turn'.
262	A year and a day is a normal term in medieval legal agreements.
263–4	Now hurry, and let it be seen at once whether anyone dares take up this challenge
265	*stunned* astounded *stiller* (even) quieter
266	*heredmen* courtiers
267	*renk* knight *rouncy* horse *him ruched* turned himself
268	And he fiercely(?) rolled his red eyes from side to side
269	*bende* arched *bresed* bristling *blycande* brilliant
270	*Waived* wagged *for ... whoso* to see if anyone
271	*keepe ... carp* engage in conversation with him *coghed full highe* cleared his throat loudly
272	*rimed ... richely* drew himself up in a lordly way *right him* proceeded
273	*hathel* knight
274	*That ... rennes of* whose fame is talked of

Where is now your surquidry and your conquestes,   275
Your grindellayk and your greme, and your grete wordes?
Now is the revel and the renown of the Rounde Table
Overwalt with a worde of on wyes speeche,
For all dares for drede withoute dint shewed!'
With this he laghes so loude that the lorde greved;   280
The blood shot for shame into his shyre face
    and lere;
    He wex as wroth as winde,
    So did alle that there were.
    The king as keene by kinde   285
    Then stood that stiff man nere,

And saide, 'Hathel, by heven, thyn asking is nys,
And as thou folly has frayst, finde thee behoves.
I know no gome that is gast of thy grete wordes;
Gif me now thy giserne, upon Godes halve,   290
And I shall baythen thy boone that thou boden habbes.'
Lightly lepes he him to, and laght at his hande.
Then feersly that other freke upon foote lightes.
Now has Arthur his axe, and the halme gripes,
And sturnely stures hit aboute, that strike with hit thoght.   295
The stiff man him bifore stood upon hight,
Herre then any in the hous by the hede and more.
With sturne cheere there he stood he stroked his berde,
And with a countenaunce dryye he drow down his cote,
No more mate ne dismayd for his main dintes   300
Then any burne upon bench hade broght him to drink
    of wine.
    Gawan, that sate by the queene,
    To the king he can encline:
    'I beseeche now with sawes seene   305
    This melly mot be mine.

'Wolde ye, worthilich lorde,' quoth Wawan to the king,
'Bid me bowe fro this benche, and stonde by you there,
That I withoute vilany might voide this table,
And that my lege lady liked not ille,   310
I wolde com to your counsel bifore your court riche.
For me think hit not seemly, as hit is soth knowen,
There such an asking is hevened so highe in your sale,

275	*surquidry* pride
276	*grindellayk* fierceness *greme* wrath *grete wordes* big talk
277	*revel* revelry
278	*Overwalt* overthrown *of on wyes speeche* spoken by a single man
279	*dares* cower *dint shewed* a blow offered
280	*greved* was offended
281	*shyre* bright
282	*lere* cheeks
283	*wex* grew
285	*as . . . kinde* like the bold man he was by nature
286	*that . . . nere* nearer to that fearless man
287	*asking is nys* request is foolish
288	*frayst* asked for *finde thee behoves* (it) is right that you should get (it)
289	*gast* frightened
290	*upon Godes halve* by God
291	*baythen* grant *boone* request *boden habbes* hast asked for
292	*Lightly* swiftly *laght at* seized
293	*freke* man
294	*halme* handle
295	And brandishes it grimly, intending to strike with it
296	*upon hight* upright
297	*Herre* taller
298	*cheere* expression
299	*dryye* unmoved
300	*mate* daunted *main dintes* powerful blows (it is not clear whether this describes the practice strokes referred to in line 295, or to the real blows he was about to strike.)
301	*Then . . . bench* than if any man at the table
304	*can encline* bowed (and said)
305	*with sawes seene* in plain words
306	(That) this contest may fall to me
307	*Wolde ye* if you would *worthilich* honoured *Wawan* A variant form of 'Gawan'.
308	*bowe fro* move from
309	*That* so that *vilany* ill-breeding (the opposite of the *courtaisye* for which Gawain is famed) *voide* leave
310	And if it were not displeasing to my liege lady (i.e. to Guinevere, who is placed next to Gawain)
311	*to your counsel* to advise you *riche* noble
312–14	For it seems to me unbecoming, to tell the truth, when such a request is made so loudly in your hall, to take it upon yourself, even though you should be desirous (of doing so)

Thagh ye yourself be talentyf, to take hit to yourselven,
While mony so bolde you aboute upon bench sitten,   315
That under heven I hope non hawerer of wille,
Ne better bodies on bent there baret is rered.
I am the wakkest, I wot, and of wit feeblest,
And lest lur of my lif, who laytes the soothe—
Bot for as much as ye are myn em I am only to praise,   320
No bounty bot your blood I in my body knowe;
And sithen this note is so nys that noght hit you falles,
And I have frayned hit at you first, foldes hit to me;
And if I carp not comlily, let alle this court riche
      bout blame.'   325
    Riche togeder con roun,
    And sithen they redden alle same
    To rid the king with crown,
    And gif Gawan the game.

Then commaunded the king the knight for to rise;   330
And he full radly upros, and ruched him faire,
Kneeled down bifore the king, and caches that weppen;
And he lovelily hit him laft, and lifte up his hande,
And gef him Godes blessing, and gladly him biddes
That his hert and his hande shulde hardy be bothe.   335
'Keepe thee, cosin,' quoth the king, 'that thou on kyrf sette,
And if thou redes him right, redily I trowe
That thou shall biden the bur that he shall bede after.'
Gawan gos to the gome with giserne in hande,
And he boldly him bides, he bayst never the helder.   340
Then carpes to Sir Gawan the knight in the greene,
'Reforme we oure forwardes, er we fyrre passe.
First I ethe thee, hathel, how that thou hattes
That thou me telle truly, as I trist may.'
'In good faith,' quoth the goode knight, 'Gawan I hatte,   345
That bede thee this buffet, whatso bifalles after,
And at this time twelmonith take at thee an other
With what wepen so thou wilt, and with no wye elles
      on live.'
    That other answares again,   350
    'Sir Gawan, so mot I thrive
    As I am ferly fain
    This dint that thou shall drive.

316	*That* (following from *so bolde*) *hope* think
	hawerer of wille readier of courage
317	Nor more able(-bodied) in the field when battle is joined
318	*wakkest* weakest *wit* intelligence
319	And my life would be the smallest loss, if one wishes to know the truth
320	*Bot* only *em* uncle *to praise* praiseworthy
321	*bounty* worth
322	And since this business is so foolish that it is not fitting for you
323	*frayned hit at* asked it of *foldes hit* it belongs
324	*carp not comlily* speak unsuitably *riche* noble
325	(Be) free from blame (i.e. Gawain is pointing out that the responsibility for what he has said is his alone; he is modestly suggesting that it might have been better to be silent, like the rest of the courtiers.)
326	The nobles whispered together
327	*redden alle same* advised jointly
328	*rid* relieve (of the challenge)
331	*radly* quickly *ruched him faire* went forward politely
332	*caches* receives
333	*lovelily hit him laft* graciously gave it up to him
336	'Take care, nephew,' said the king, 'that you strike one blow'
337	*redes him right* manage him properly *redily* without difficulty
338	*biden* survive *bur* blow *shall bede* is to offer (you)
340	And he (the Green Knight) waited for him boldly, he was not the more dismayed for that
341	*carpes* speaks
342	Let us restate our agreement before we get any further
343	*ethe* beg *how . . . hattes* what thou art called
344	*as . . . may* in such a way that I may believe (you)
346	*That bede* who offer
347	*take . . . other* (agree to) receive a second from thee
348–9	*with no . . live* from no other living man (by making this stipulation Gawain of course hopes to avoid receiving any return blow at all, if his own blow kills the knight; this is what Arthur is hinting at in lines 336–8.)
351	*mot I thrive* may I prosper
352	*ferly fain* extremely glad
353	That it is thou who art to strike this blow

'Bigog,' quoth the greene knight, 'Sir Gawan, me likes
That I shall fange at thy fust that I have frayst here.   355
And thou has redily rehersed, by resoun full true,
Clanly all the covenaunt that I the kinge asked,
Save that thou shall siker me, segge, by thy trawthe,
That thou shall seeche me thyself, whereso thou hopes
I may be founde upon folde, and foch thee such wages   360
As thou deles me today bifore this douthe riche.'
'Where shulde I wale thee,' quoth Gawan, 'where is thy place?
I wot never where thou wonies, by Him that me wroght,
Ne I know not thee, knight, thy court ne thy name.
Bot teche me truly therto, and telle me how thou hattes,   365
And I shall ware alle my wit to winne me thider,
And that I swere thee for soothe, and by my siker trawthe.'
'That is innogh in New Yer, hit needes no more,'
Quoth the gome in the greene to Gawan the hende;
'If I thee telle truly, when I the tappe have   370
And thou me smoothely has smitten, smartly I thee teche
Of my house and my home and myn owen nome,
Then may thou frayst my fare and forwardes holde;
And if I spende no speeche, then speedes thou the better,
For thou may leng in thy londe and layt no fyrre—   375
        bot slokes!
    Ta now thy grimme toole to thee,
    And let see how thou knokes.'
    'Gladly, sir, for soothe,'
    Quoth Gawan; his axe he strokes.   380

The greene knight upon grounde graythely him dresses,
A little lut with the hede, the lere he discoveres,
His longe lovelych lokkes he laid over his crown,
Let the naked neck to the note shewe.
Gawan gripped to his axe, and gederes hit on hight,   385
The kay foot on the folde he before sette,
Let hit down lightly light on the naked,
That the sharp of the shalk shindered the bones,
And shrank thurgh the shyre grese, and shadde hit in twinne,
That the bit of the brown steel bot on the grounde.   390
The faire hede fro the halse hit to the erthe,
That fele hit foined with her feete, there hit forth rolled;
The blood brayd fro the body, that blikked on the greene;

354   *Bigog* by God   *me likes* it pleases me

355   That I shall receive from your fist (i.e. at your hands) what I have asked
      for here

356   *redily rehersed* repeated without hesitation
      by resoun in a statement

357   *Clanly* completely   *covenaunt* agreement

358   *shall siker* must promise   *segge* sir
      trawthe faith, honour

359   *seeche* seek   *whereso thou hopes* wherever thou thinkest

360   *upon folde* on earth   *foch thee* receive   *wages* payment

361   *deles* givest   *douthe riche* noble company

362   *wale* find

363   *wonies* dwellest   *wroght* created

365–6   But direct me there accurately, and tell me what thou art called, and I
      shall apply my whole mind to getting there

367   *for soothe* truly   *siker trawthe* pledged word

368   *hit needes* is necessary (the point being that, at New Year especially,
      the time for resolutions, Gawain's pledged word is a sufficient oath)

369   *hende* gracious

370   *tappe* knock

371   And thou hast struck me neatly—if I am prompt to inform thee (This whole
      line simply repeats the meaning of the previous line in reverse order and in
      different words.)

372   *nome* name (It was often believed that to know a man's name gave
      one power over him.)

373   *frayst my fare* see what I will do (literally, 'try my behaviour')
      forwardes holde keep to the agreement

374   *spende* utter   *speedes ... better* thou wilt be better off

375   *leng* stay   *layt no fyrre* seek no further

376   *slokes!* stop! (i.e. enough talking!)

377   *Ta* take

378   *let see* let it be seen

381   *graythely him dresses* at once takes up his stance

382   With his head a little bent, he uncovers the flesh

384   *to the note* in readiness

385   *gripped to* laid hold of   *gederes* lifts

386   *kay* left   *folde* floor

387   *lightly* swiftly   *light* (to) land
      naked naked neck

388   So that the sharp (blade) severed the man's bones

389   *shrank* penetrated   *shyre grese* bright flesh (literally 'fat')
      shadde cut   *twinne* two

390   *bit* blade   *brown* bright   *bot on* bit into

391   *halse* neck   *hit* fell

392   *That fele* so that many   *foined* thrust at   *there* where, as

393   *brayd fro* spurted out of   *that blikked* and it gleamed

And nawther faltered ne felle the freke never the helder,
Bot stithly he start forth upon stiff shankes,   395
And runishly he raght out, there as renkes stooden,
Laght to his lovely hed, and lift hit up soone;
And sithen bowes to his blonk, the bridle he caches,
Steppes into steelbowe and strides alofte,
And his hede by the here in his hande holdes;   400
And as sadly the segge him in his saddle sette
As non unhap had him ailed, thagh hedless he were
          in stedde.
      He brayde his bulk aboute,
      That ugly body that bledde;   405
      Mony on of him had doute,
      By that his resouns were redde.

For the hede in his hande he holdes up even,
Toward the derrest on the des he dresses the face,
And hit lifte up the yye-liddes and looked full brode,   410
And meled thus much with his mouthe, as ye may now here:
'Looke, Gawan, thou be graythe to go as thou hettes,
And layte as lelly till thou me, lude, finde,
As thou has hette in this halle, herande thise knightes;
To the Greene Chapel thou choose, I charge thee, to fotte   415
Such a dunt as thou has dalt—diserved thou habbes
To be yederly yolden on New Yeres morn.
The knight of the Greene Chapel men knowen me mony;
Forthi me for to finde if thou fraystes, failes thou never.
Therfore com, other recreaunt be calde thee behoves.'   420
With a runish rout the reines he tornes,
Halled out at the hall door, his hed in his hande,
That the fyr of the flint flawe fro fole hooves.
To what kith he becom knew non there,
Never more then they wiste from whethen he was wonnen.   425
          What thenne?
      The king and Gawan thare
      At that greene they laghe and grenne,
      Yet breved was hit full bare
      A mervail among tho menne.   430

Thagh Arthur the hende king at hert had wonder,
He let no semblaunt be seene, bot saide full highe

394	*never the helder* any the more for that (cf. line 340)
395	*stithly* stoutly *stiff shankes* firm legs
396	And he reached out fiercely to where the people were standing
397	*Laght to* seized *lovely* splendid (ironic, of course, but no doubt it was *lovely* to him) *soone* at once
398	*bowes to his blonk* turns towards his horse
399	*steelbowe* stirrup-iron *alofte* i.e. into the saddle
401	*sadly* steadily *him . . . sette* seated himself
402	*As . . . ailed* as if no mishap had disturbed him
403	there (a tag)
404	He twisted his (headless) trunk about
406–7	Many men were afraid of him by the time his words were uttered. (Once more, the most astonishing fact is saved for last: that, after all this, the Green Knight can still speak; and there is irony in the suggestion that it was only after he had spoken that the onlookers were afraid—their nervous thrusting at the severed head as it rolls on the floor indicates otherwise.)
408	*even* actually
409	*derrest* noblest (i.e. the nobles) *dresses* turns
410	*full brode* with staring eyes
411	*meled* said
412	*graythe* ready *hettes* hast promised
413	And search till thou find me, sir, as truly
414	*hette* promised *herande* in the hearing of
415	*thou choose* make thy way *fotte* receive
416	*dunt* blow *has dalt* hast given *habbes* hast
417	*yederly yolden* promptly repaid
418	*men . . . mony* I am known to many (as)
419	*fraystes* askest
420	*thee behoves* thou wilt have to
421	*runish rout* violent jerk
422	*halled* passed
423	So that sparks flew from the stones as his horse's hooves touched them
424	*kith* country *becom* went
425	*wiste* knew *whethen* whence *was wonnen* had come
428	Laughed and grinned at that green (knight) (this is no doubt the nervous laughter that comes with a sudden release of tension)
429–30	Yet among that company it was declared most openly to be a wonder (thus releasing Arthur from his refusal to sit down and eat)
431	*hende* gracious
432	*semblaunt* outward sign *highe* loudly

To the comlych queene with courtais speeche,
'Dere dame, today demay you never;
Well bicommes such craft upon Cristmasse,   435
Layking of enterludes, to laghe and to sing,
Among these kinde caroles of knightes and ladies.
Never the lesse to my mete I may me well dress,
For I have seen a selly, I may not forsake.'
He glent upon Sir Gawan, and gainly he saide,   440
'Now sir, heng up thyn axe, that has innogh hewen;'
And hit was don above the des on doser to henge,
Ther alle men for mervail might on hit looke,
And by true title therof to telle the wonder.
Thenne they bowed to a borde, thise burnes togeder,   445
The king and the goode knight, and keene men hem served
Of alle dainties double, as derrest might falle;
With alle manner of mete and minstralsy bothe,
With wele walt they that day, till worthed an ende
              in londe.   450
     Now thenk well, Sir Gawayn,
     For wothe that thou ne wonde
     This aventure for to frayn
     That thou has tan on honde.

433	*comlych* fair
434	*demay you never* do not be in the least perturbed
435	*Well . . . craft* such doings are very suitable
436	The performance of interludes (i.e. short dramatic pieces) with laughter and singing
437	*kinde caroles* seasonable dances
438	None the less (i.e. all the more) for that may I proceed to my food
439	*selly* marvel *forsake* deny
440	*glent upon* glanced towards *gainly* aptly (The following remark is apt because it gives a literal reference to the metaphor in the proverbial saying, 'Hang up your axe', meaning, 'Have done with the matter'.)
441	*innogh hewen* done enough cutting
442	*don* placed *doser* the wall-tapestry
443	*for mervail* in wonder
444	And give an account of the marvel based on its genuine authority
445	*bowed* turned *borde* table *burnes* warriors
446	*keene* bold
447	With double helpings of all the delicacies, as would be fitting for noblemen
448	*mete* food
449	*With wele* joyfully *walt* spent *worthed* came
450	A tag
452	That thou dost not hesitate for danger
453	*frayn* seek out
454	*tan on honde* undertaken

Patience

Introduction

Patience, as we have seen elsewhere, is one of the poems in the same manuscript as *Sir Gawain and the Green Knight*, and probably written by the same north-west Midland poet, in the last quarter of the fourteenth century. It is a poem of 531 lines, written in unrhymed alliterative verse. Some scholars have believed the alliterative lines to be divided into groups of four; in our view this division is not of great regularity or significance, and we do not reproduce it in our text. The complete poem begins with a prologue of 60 lines, in which the narrator summarizes the Beatitudes (Matthew 5.3–10), giving special emphasis to the first and the last, which concern the heavenly reward promised to poverty and patience. He himself has poverty, he says, and he intends to undertake patience also, because he has no choice, and because patience can lighten one's burdens, while impatience only makes them heavier. It is not known whether this prologue is genuinely autobiographical; if so, it might indicate that the poet was vowed to poverty for religious reasons, or it might simply give a new twist to the complaints of poverty which medieval poets commonly set before their patrons. He proceeds to tell the story of Jonah to illustrate this truth; this is where our extract begins, at line 61 of the complete poem.

The whole story is closely based on the Latin text of the Book of Jonah. In this first part of it, Jonah is ordered by God to preach to the Ninevites and threaten them with vengeance if they do not give up their evil ways; but Jonah, afraid of persecution, is reluctant to do so, and instead tries to escape from God by taking a ship to Tarshish. But when the ship is at sea God sends a great storm, which threatens to destroy it. The sailors decide that they must have someone on board who has offended his god, and they cast lots to settle who it is. Jonah is asleep, but he is awakened, and when the lot falls on him he confesses that he is a Jew who has offended the God of the Jews, the only true God. So they throw him overboard, the storm ceases, and they reach land safely at Tarshish and there confess that Jonah's is indeed the true God. But Jonah is swallowed by a whale, and he stays inside its revolting stomach (which the poet describes in great detail) for three days and nights. While he is there he repents, prays to God to rescue him, and promises that in future he will do his will. The whale spews

Jonah up on the shore of Nineveh, and there he preaches as he was commanded. (This is where our extract ends.) The Ninevites, from their king downwards, are moved by Jonah's preaching, and they put on sackcloth and ashes and repent. God therefore decides not to destroy them; but now Jonah is angry with him, because he thus appears to derogate from his dignity as a true prophet. He goes off in a huff, and makes himself a little bower of ferns and hay in the hot sunshine outside the city. As he lies asleep in it, God causes a great plant to spring up to shield him from the sun. Jonah is delighted, and wishes he could take it home with him. But the next night as he lies asleep God sends a wind to destroy the plant. This makes Jonah still more offended, and he asks God why he is tormenting him, and why he does not kill him straight away if that is his purpose. God points the moral: Jonah is upset about the destruction of a plant he has done nothing to create, and yet he expects God not to hesitate in destroying a whole city full of penitent people whom he did create. God can be patient; why not Jonah? God's final speech merges at an uncertain point into some brief concluding comments by the narrator, and there the poem ends.

The narrative of *Patience* is taken entirely from the Bible; our concern must be with what the poet makes of that narrative. Perhaps the first thing that strikes one, as one considers the poet's treatment of his story, is its extraordinarily detailed realism. He begins with a rather bare Scriptural account, but his imagination creates from it a complete world, crowded with people, things, actions and voices. The plain 'ship' of the Book of Jonah is not just a ship in the poem, but is crowded with tackle—square-sail, cables, windlass, anchors, bowline, guide-ropes, and so on. The English alliterative poets, from Anglo-Saxon times on, had been fond of descriptions of sea voyages, and the vocabulary at this point is particularly likely to baffle modern landlubbers. When the storm breaks, the sailors do not just throw overboard the unspecified 'wares' mentioned in the Bible, but bags, featherbeds, bright clothes, chests, coffers and casks. Jonah falls asleep not just in 'the inner part of the ship', but on a board near the rudder-band, and he is aroused not by a dignified speech from the master—'Why art thou fast asleep? Rise up, call upon thy God, if so be that God will think upon us, that we may not perish' (Jonah 1.6)—but by a kick and a curse from a steersman:

> The freke him frunt with his foot and bede him ferk up;
> There Ragnel in his rakentes him rere of his dremes! (Pat 127–8)

The events of the poem occupy a fully-imagined three-dimensional space, and one sees how skilfully the poet uses even such small details as changes from direct to indirect speech to create the illusion of this 'poem-space'. When Jonah refuses to obey God's command, his reasons are first given in direct speech: 'If I go to Nineveh and the people there are as bad as God says they are, they'll send me to prison, put me in the stocks, poke out my eyes . . .'. But when he sets off for the port of Joppa, still grumbling, his complaints are turned into reported speech, to give the sense of his moving further away from us into the distance of the poem: 'He wouldn't endure pains like that, not on any account, not he . . .'. It is not until we have had time to follow him into the depths of the poem-space that he reverts to direct speech.

Much of this unusually detailed realism tends to give a comic effect to the story. Medieval realism in literature is not usually neutral, but tends towards the grotesque (as can often be seen in *Piers Plowman*); and in this poem, so far as it is concerned with Jonah, it is entirely appropriate that we should be encouraged to see his behaviour in a comic light. He has set himself up against an all-powerful God, with no sense of his own pettiness and impotence; like Gawain, but to a greater extent, he is in the undignified position of struggling against an un-beatable opponent. He imagines that he can escape from God's notice by taking a ship to another country, even though, as the poet points out, he has often read in the Psalms that God, who created all eyes and ears, must inevitably be able to see and hear everything. Many of his speeches, in particular, have a comic effect. His voice tends to sound like that of a sulky child, a tendency which reaches its peak outside our extract, at the moment when God asks him why he is so bad-tempered about so little a thing as the destruction of a plant, and he answers that it isn't little at all, and anyway he wishes he were dead and buried:

> 'Why art thou so waymot, wye, for so littel?'
> 'Hit is *not* littel,' quoth the lede, 'bot lykker to right;
> I wolde I were of this worlde, wrapped in moldes.'

('Why are you so bad-tempered, man, about so little?' 'It is *not* little,' said the man, 'but more a matter of justice; I wish I were out of this world, buried in the earth.') Some of the most comic suggestions in the poem come in suppositions on the narrator's part about details left unmentioned by the Bible, introduced with an 'I guess' or 'it may well be'. For instance, the poet has stressed Jonah's diminutive size in com-parison with the whale (this goes along with the treatment of him as a sulky child): he floats in through its jaws like a speck of dust going through a cathedral door, 'as mote in at a munster door' (Pat 208). But, small though that speck is, I guess, says the narrator, that it was enough to make the whale feel queasy once it was inside him:

> For that mote in his mawe made him, I trowe,
> Thagh hit littel were him with, to wamel at his hert.   (Pat 239–40)

Then again, when the whale vomits Jonah up, the poet imagines how messy the prophet's clothes must have been, and adds, with a delightful understatement, that it may well be that his cloak was in need of a wash:

> Thenne he swepe to the sonde in sluched clothes;
> Hit may well be that mester were his mantile to washe! (Pat 281–2)

But the poem's realism is by no means entirely comic, and the description of the storm, for example, the poem's directest expression of God's effortless power over the world he has created, is genuinely terrifying, for all the unscriptural realism of the explanation that the whale was near the surface, ready to swallow up Jonah, because the violence of the seas had driven it from the abyss where it usually dwelt. The sea envelops or enfolds Jonah in a way that is both destructive and protective, and its power is coveyed with superb flamboyance through a great battery of liquid sounds—*r*'s and *l*'s—alongside the normal strenuous alliteration:

> The gret flem of thy flood folded me umbe;
> Alle the gotes of thy guferes and groundeless pooles
> And thy strivande stremes of strindes so mony
> In on dashande dam drives me over. (Pat 249–52)

Flamboyant perhaps, but never losing touch with sense or the senses. If any medieval poetry is Shakespearian in its orchestrated richness of sound and multiple suggestion, this is.

As a whole, the meaning of the story is not in any way limited by the materialistic tendency of the realism with which the poet imagines it. Its meaning is moral and spiritual, as well as realistic, and we must now say more about how the poet conveys those two kinds of meaning through his narrative. The prologue makes it clear that this is to be a poem (unlike, say, *Sir Orfeo*) in which the story will be given a meaning or set of meanings carefully defined by the poet as lying within certain limits. The prologue begins to build up the opposing meanings of patience and impatience through what in modern English one might see as a series of puns or half-puns on words such as suffering, long-suffering, endurance, and patience itself. The narrator will be patient in his poverty, because once Dame Poverty comes to one, she endures and therefore has to be endured. This is not merely a matter of playing with words, but of using verbal links and transitions to give a more substantial presence to ideas. Once the story itself begins, Jonah is seen first as a type of impatience, unwillingness to endure the will of God even after one has been forcibly brought to see the impossibility of doing otherwise. The paradox stated in the prologue, that by seeking to avoid the trouble of putting up with what is ordained for one, one only brings worse trouble upon oneself, is fully demonstrated in the case of Jonah, who, as a result of trying to avoid the danger of preaching God's word to the Ninevites, finds himself in the even worse danger (and discomfort and indignity too) of lurching around in a storm inside the unsavoury stomach of a whale. As the poet puts it, 'Ther was bilded his bowr that will no bale suffer' (Pat 216)—*that* was the bower (the place of safety and delight) prepared for the man who wanted to avoid suffering harm. But Jonah does not fully learn even this lesson, and so he has to proceed to a further bower, this time a literal one, outside Nineveh: 'Ther he busked him [made himself] a bowr, the best that he might'. That bower, like the whale's stomach, is a place both of protection and of danger: in each case, God shows his irresistible power, the final unanswerable argument for human patience, by both threatening and protecting Jonah. And then, if we look back over the poem from this point, we see that it was not only about man's impatience but about God's patience. At the beginning, God said that he could not be patient, he could not abide, or suffer, the evil of the Ninevites:

> . . . her malis is so much, I may not abide,
> Bot venge me on her vilanye and venim bilive.   (Pat 10–11)

But however wicked the Ninevites were, once they had repented God was patient, and did not destroy them as he had threatened. Similarly he was patient with his wayward prophet Jonah, setting up a most elaborate series of demonstrations to bring him to see through experience that patience was the only way for him. He might so easily have drowned Jonah in the storm, and chosen himself another prophet, or let him die of sunstroke outside Nineveh once he had served his purpose and failed to take the second chance that was offered him; just as he might have destroyed Nineveh if he had wished. But the God of this poem is a universal creator and father, who tells Jonah about the Ninevites that 'I made hem of matteres myn one [out of my own substance]', and he loves his creation and cannot bring himself to destroy it. God is patient of human pride and weakness; man must be patient of God's will.

We have been giving a sketch of the poem's moral significance, though inevitably a very rough one, compared with the fineness of the poem itself. But, as we have said, the story is also given a spiritual significance. The poet conveys spiritual meaning through symbolism, but it is not a kind of symbolism that contradicts or replaces the realism of his poem. The combination of realism with symbolism is common enough in medieval art: for example, in many representations of the Virgin and Child, the infant Christ is carrying a ball or apple—on the realistic level a suitable plaything for a baby, and at the same time on the symbolic level an emblem, like the royal orb which is often carried by the adult Christ in glory, of kingly power over the globe of the world. In *Patience*, one example of this combination of realism and symbolism can be found in Jonah's sleep in the boat. It is described, with grotesque realism, as particularly repulsive and animal-like: 'slobberande he routes' (Pat 126). At the same time, it represents metaphorically his state of spiritual ignorance or blindness: he is oblivious in his sleep of the unmistakable manifestation of God's power in the storm, and even the heathen sailors are shocked that he should sleep rather than pray. The curse with which he is awakened—'There Ragnel in his rakentes him rere of his dremes!' (Pat 128)—is fully appropriate to this spiritual meaning, for he is indeed in jeopardy of being roused by the devil and finding himself in hell. Since the whale is a common symbol of hell or the devil, this symbolic meaning is continued in the narrative. And Jonah's second sleep, beneath the plant which God causes to grow, is similarly a metaphor for the spiritual unawareness into which he once more lapses.

But the story of Jonah has a more fundamental spiritual meaning than this, and one which existed independently of this particular poem. The story of Jonah was seen as being an Old Testament pre-figuration, or foreshadowing, of the story of Christ, in two respects in particular, both having the authority of the New Testament behind them. In Luke 11.30 we read that Jonah as a prophet of God's word was a type of Christ: 'For as Jonas was a sign to the Ninivites, so shall the Son of man also be to this generation.' And in Matthew 12.40 we read that Jonah's three days in the whale were a type of Christ's descent into hell after the crucifixion: 'For, as Jonas was in the whale's belly three days and three nights, so shall the Son of man be in the heart of the earth three days and three nights.' These figural meanings of the story of Jonah were extremely well known in the Middle Ages, and probably no educated medieval audience, hearing the story retold, could have failed to have them in mind. They are present in *Patience*; but, once more, not in a way that contradicts its realism, but as part of its realism. Jonah as prophet is not required to be simultaneously a type of Christ and an all-too-human man: the point the poem makes is that he is not fit to be the type of Christ that we cannot help expecting him to be. This is perhaps brought out most clearly when he is imagining the horrid things that are likely to happen to him if he preaches God's word in Nineveh. 'Our Lord', he says, 'sits on his throne on high, in his shining glory, and it worries him very little though I should be seized in Nineveh and stripped naked, miserably torn to pieces on a cross by many ruffians'—

> 'Oure Sire sittes,' he says, 'on sege so highe
> In His glowande glorye, and gloumbes full littel
> Thagh I be nummen in Ninive and naked dispoiled,
> On roode ruly torent with ribaudes mony.' (Pat 33–6)

The figural allusion to the crucifixion is present only as part of Jonah's realistic forebodings, and its presence serves only to make us aware of Jonah's inadequacy to play the part he foreshadows.

The stay in the whale is full of reminiscences of the traditional figural meaning, and these also collaborate with the comic realism of the poet's treatment. A well-established tradition about hell is that it stinks; one can plausibly suppose that a whale's stomach is also smelly, and so the two meanings are combined in what seem at first sight like casual oaths—the stomach 'stank as the devel' (Pat 214), and, in the very next line, it was full of grease and filth that 'savoured as helle'. Later Jonah describes himself as praying to God 'out of the hole . . . of hellen wombe' (Pat 246). Yet at the same time, in a simile we have already mentioned, Jonah has been described as entering the whale's jaws like a speck of dust going through a cathedral door. This simile serves simultaneously to evoke on the material level Jonah's smallness compared with the whale, and to suggest on the spiritual level that the whale will be not only a place of punishment but, like a cathedral, a place of prayer, protected by God. The recognition of God's power and mercy which leads Jonah to pray even when he is inside the whale also has the effect of disclosing something new in the very nature of the place where he is imprisoned. When he first finds himself in the whale's belly, he looks in vain for a place of rest and recovery, but once he has begun to pray to God he finds a refuge. 'With that', we are told ('that' being his first prayer), 'he came upon a nook and stationed himself within it, where no stain of impurity was close to him; there he sat as safely—save only for the darkness—as he had previously slept in the hold of the boat':

> With that he hitte to a hirne and helde him therinne,
> There no defoule of no filthe was fest him aboute;
> There he sete also sounde, saf for merk one,
> As in the bulk of the bote there he bifore sleeped. (Pat 229–32)

His refuge is at once material and spiritual: the safe and clean place he has found in the darkness is the objective correlative to his newly-acquired trust in God. The *filthe* from which he is now safe, at least for the moment, is spiritual as well as material uncleanness; and he owes his safety to the 'sweetness' of God ('sweet' also meaning pure, as in 'sweet water'), which in line 220 is so tellingly contrasted with the muck of the whale's belly.

Suggestions for further reading

Edition of the complete poem by J. J. Anderson (Manchester University Press, 1969)

A. C. Spearing, *The Gawain-Poet: A Critical Study* (Cambridge University Press, 1970)

Patience

Hit bitidde sumtime in the termes of Jude,
Jonas joyned was therinne gentile prophete;
Goddes glam to him glod, that him unglad made,
With a roghlich rurd rowned in his ere.
'Rys radly,' He says, 'and rayke forth even;   5
Nym the way to Ninive withouten other speeche,
And in that ceté my sawes sowe alle aboute,
That in that place, at the point, I put in thy hert.
For iwisse hit arn so wikke that in that won dowelles,
And her malis is so much, I may not abide,   10
Bot venge me on her vilanye and venim bilive.
Now sweghe me thider swiftly and say me this erende.'
    When that steven was stint that stunned his minde,
All he wrathed in his wit, and witherly he thoght,
'If I bowe to His bode and bring hem this tale,   15
And I be nummen in Ninive, my nyes beginnes.
He telles me those traitoures arn tipped shrewes;
I com with those tithinges, they ta me bilive,
Pinnes me in a prisoun, put me in stokkes,
Writhe me in a warlok, wrast out myn yyen.   20
This is a mervail message a man for to preche
Amonge enmies so mony and mansed fendes!—
Bot if my gainlich God such gref to me wolde,
For desert of sum sake, that I slain were.
At alle periles,' quoth the prophete, 'I approche hit no nerre; 25
I will me sum other waye that He ne waite after;
I shall tee into Tarce and tarry there a while,
And lightly when I am lest He letes me alone.'
    Thenne he rises radly and raykes bilive,
Jonas toward port Japh, ay janglande for tene   30
That he nolde thole for no thing non of those pines,
Thagh the Fader that him formed were fale of his hele.
    'Oure Sire sittes,' he says, 'on sege so highe
In His glowande glorye, and gloumbes full littel
Thagh I be nummen in Ninive and naked dispoiled,   35
On roode ruly torent with ribaudes mony.'
Thus he passes to that port his passage to seeche,

1	Once upon a time, within the borders of Judea, it happened (that)
2	*joyned* appointed *gentile prophete* prophet to the gentiles
3	*glam* word *glod* came *that* i.e. and it *unglad* unhappy
4	*roghlich rurd* harsh clamour *rowned* (it) breathed
5	*Rys radly* rise quickly *rayke* go *even* directly
6	*Nym* take
7	*ceté* city *sawes* decrees *sowe* spread
8	*That* i.e. *sawes at the point* when the time comes *put* shall put
9	For indeed those who dwell in that city are so wicked
10	*malis* evil *much* great *abide* endure (it)
11	*venge me* avenge myself *venim* wickedness *bilive* at once
10–11	In these lines God is expressing his own impatience, which later gives way to longsuffering, or patience.
12	*sweghe me* hasten for me *erende* message
13	*steven* voice *stint* ceased
14	*wrathed* grew angry *wit* mind *witherly* rebelliously
15	*bowe* give way *bode* bidding
16	*And ... nummen* if I should be captured *nyes* troubles
17	*tipped shrewes* consummate villains
18	*I com* if I come *tithinges* tidings *ta* (will) take, seize
19	*pinnes* (will) confine
20	*Writhe* torture *warlok* foot-shackle *wrast* pluck
	yyen eyes
22	*mansed fendes* accursed evil-doers
23–4	Unless my gracious God wishes me such harm, in punishment for some offence, that I should be slain
25	*At alle periles* whatever the consequences (There is dramatic irony in this phrase, for Jonah, to avoid peril, is thrusting himself into even greater peril.) *approche ... nerre* will approach no nearer to it
26	*will me* will (take) myself (omission of verb of motion)
	ne waite after does not watch over
27	*tee* go *Tarce* Tarshish
28	*lightly* perhaps *lest* lost *letes* will let
29	Compare with line 5; Jonah is exactly obeying God's command, but in the wrong direction.
30	*port Japh* the port of Joppa *ay ... tene* always grumbling in annoyance
31	*nolde thole* would not suffer *pines* torments
32	*Thagh* though *formed* created
	fale ... hele unconcerned about his safety
33	*Sire* Lord *on sege* in His seat, enthroned
34	*glowande* shining *gloumbes* worries
35	*dispoiled* stripped
36	Miserably torn to pieces on a cross by many ruffians

Findes he a fair ship to the fare redy,
Maches him with the marineres, makes her paye
For to towe him into Tarce as tid as they might.   40
   Then he tron on tho tres, and they her tramme ruchen,
Cachen up the crossail, cables they fasten;
Wight at the windas weghen her ankres,
Spinde spak to the sprete the spare bawe-line;
Gederen to the gide-ropes, the grete cloth falles,   45
They laiden in on ladde-borde and the lofe winnes.
The blithe brethe at her bak the bosum he findes,
He swenges me this sweete ship swift fro the haven.
Was never so joyful a Jue as Jonas was thenne,
That the daunger of Drightin so derfly ascaped;   50
He wende well that that Wye that all the world planted
Hade no might in that mere no man for to greve.
Lo, the witless wreche, for he wolde noght suffer,
Now has he put him in plyt of peril well more!
Hit was a wening unwar that welt in his minde,   55
Thagh he were soght fro Samarye, that God segh no fyrre.
Yis, He blushed full brode, that burde him be sure;
That ofte kid him the carpe that king saide,
Digne David on des, that deemed this speeche
In a psalme that he set the sauter withinne: 60
'O fooles in folk, feeles otherwile
And understondes umbestounde, thagh ye be stape foole!
Hope ye that He heres not that eres alle made?
Hit may not be that He is blinde that bigged uche yye.'
Bot he dredes no dint that dotes for elde,   65
For he was fer in the flood foundande to Tarce;
Bot I trow full tid overtan that he were,
So that shomely too short he shot of his ame.
   For the Welder of wit that wot alle thinges,
That ay wakes and waites, at wille has He slightes.   70
He calde on that ilk crafte He carf with His hondes;
They wakened well the wrotheloker, for wrothely He cleped:
'Eurus and Aquiloun that on est sittes,
Blowes bothe at my bode upon blo watteres.'
Thenne was no tom there bitweene His tale and her deede,   75
So bain were they bothe two His bone for to wyrk.
Anon out of the north-est the nois biginnes,
When bothe brethes con blowe upon blo watteres;

38   *fare* journey
38   *Maches him* settles   *her paye* their payment
40   *towe* take   *tid* swiftly
41–6   Then he stepped onto the (deck-)boards, and they get their gear ready, hoist the square-sail, and fasten the cables; they swiftly weigh anchor at the windlass, smartly fasten the spare bowline to the bowsprit; they heave at the guy-ropes, and the mainsail comes down; they laid in (oars) on the port side and gain the luff (i.e. a position close to the wind).
47   *breth* wind   *the bosum he findes* finds the belly of the sail
48   *swenges me* swings (*me* is an 'ethic dative', indicating the narrator's personal involvement in the story, but untranslatable)
50   Who had so boldly escaped from the power of the Lord
51   *wende well* fully believed   *Wye* Being   *planted* established
52   *mere* sea   *greve* harm
53   *for* because
54   *plyt ... more* a state of much greater danger
55   *wening unwar* foolish supposition   *welt* revolved
56–9   That, though he had gone from Samaria, God saw no further (than that). Yes, He looked with eyes wide open; he (Jonah) ought to have been sure of that; he had often been shown that by (literally, 'that often showed him') the words which that king spoke, noble David on his throne, who uttered this speech
60   *sauter* psalter (see Psalm 93, 8–9 : 'Understand, ye senseless among the people; and, you fools, be wise at last. He that planted the ear, shall he not hear? Or he that formed the eye, doth he not consider?')
61   *feeles otherwhile* perceive now and then
62   *umbestounde* occasionally   *stape fole* quite mad]
63   *Hope ye* do you believe
64   *bigged uche yye* made every eye
65   But he (Jonah), who was foolish with old age, fears no blow
66   *fer ... foundande* far out to sea, hastening
67–8   But I believe that he was very swiftly overtaken, so that his shot fell shamefully short of his target
69   *Welder of wit* Master of wisdom (i.e. God)   *that wot* who knows
70   *waites* watches   *wille* command   *slightes* devices
71   He called upon that very power (i.e. the winds) (that) He made with his hands
72   *wrotheloker* more fiercely   *wrothely* fiercely   *cleped* called
73   *Eurus ... Aquiloun* the south-east and north-east winds
74   *bode* command   *blo* dark
75   *tom* delay   *tale* word
76   *bain* willing   *bone* request   *wyrk* carry out
78   *con* (auxiliary verb, indicating past tense)

E

Rogh rakkes there ros with rudning anunder,
The see soughed full sore, gret selly to here.   80
The windes on the wonne water so wrastel togeder
That the wawes full woode waltered so highe
And efte bushed to the abym, that breed fishes
Durst nowhere for rogh arest at the bothem.
　　When the breth and the brook and the bote metten,   85
Hit was a joyless gin that Jonas was inne,
For hit reeled on roun upon the rogh ythes;
The bur ber to hit baft, that braste alle her gere,
Then hurled on a hepe the helme and the sterne;
First tomurte mony rop and the mast after;   90
The sail sweyed on the see; thenne suppe bihoved
The cogge of the colde water, and thenne the cry rises.
Yet corven they the cordes and cest all theroute;
Mony ladde there forth-lep to lave and to cest,
Scoopen out the scathel water, that fain scape wolde,   95
For, be mannes lode never so luther, the lyf is ay sweete.
　　There was busy overborde bale to cest,
Her bagges and her fetherbeddes and her bright weedes,
Her kystes and her cofferes, her caraldes alle,
And all to lighten that lome, yif lethe wolde shape.   100
Bot ever was iliche loud the lot of the windes,
And ever wrother the water and wooder the stremes;
Then tho wery forwroght wist no bote
Bot uchon glewed on his god that gained him beste.
Summe to Vernagu ther vouched avowes solemne,   105
Summe to Diana devout and derf Neptune,
To Mahoun and to Mergot, the moone and the sunne,
And uche lede as he loved and laide had his hert.
　　Thenne bispeke the spakest, dispaired well nere:
'I leve here be sum losinger, sum lawless wrech,   110
That has greved his god and gos here amonge us.
Lo, all sinkes in his sinne and for his sake marres.
I lovye that we lay lotes on ledes uchone,
And whoso limpes the losse, lay him theroute;
And when the gilty is gon, what may gome trawe   115
Bot He that rules the rak may rue on those other?'
This was sette in assent, and sembled they were,
Herried out of uche hyrne to hent that falles;
A lodesman lightly lep under haches,

79	*rakkes* storm-clouds *rudning anunder* redness underneath
80	*soughed* roared *sore* violently *selly* wonder
81	*wonne* dark *wrastel* wrestle, struggle
82	*wawes* waves *woode* mad *waltered* rolled
83	And (so) plunged back into the abyss, that terrified fishes
84	*for rogh* because of the roughness *arest* remain
85	*brook* sea
86	*gin* craft
87	*on roun* round *ythes* waves
88	The onslaught took it abaft, so that all their gear was broken
89	*hurled* crashed *helme* tiller
90	*tomurte* broke
91	*sweyed* collapsed
91–2	*suppe . . . cogge* the boat had to drink
93	*corven* cut *cest all* threw everything
94–5	Many a lad (i.e. man) rushed forward there to bale out and to throw overboard ; those who would willingly escape scooped out the dangerous water
96	*be . . . luther* however wretched a man's burden may be
97	*busy* a bustle *bale* packages
98	*weedes* clothes
99	*kystes* chests *caraldes* casks
100	*lome* vessel *yif . . . shape* in case calm should fall
101	*iliche* just as *lot* roaring
102	*wooder the stremes* the currents more furious
103	Then those (men), weary with overwork, knew no remedy
104	*Bot . . . glewed* except that each one called *gained* suited
105	*Vernagu* (a saracen giant in French epic poems) *vouched* offered
106	*devout* holy *derf* mighty (Diana is the classical goddess of virgins, and of the moon which controls the tides ; Neptune the god of the sea.)
107	*Mahoun* Mahomet *Mergot* (a supposed heathen god)
108	*uche lede as* each man according as
109	*spakest* cleverest
110	*I . . . losinger* I believe there is some traitor here
112	*in* on account of *for . . . marres* perish because of his offence
113	*lovye* propose *lay lotes on* cast lots among
114	And let whoever loses be thrown overboard
115–16	*what . . . Bot* what may one believe but that
116	*rak* storm-cloud *rue* take pity
117	*sette in assent* agreed to *sembled* assembled
118	Driven out of every corner to take whatever comes
119	*lodesman* steersman *lightly lep* swiftly leapt

For to layte mo ledes and hem to lote bring.   120
Bot him failed no freke that he finde might,
Saf Jonas the Jue, that jowked in derne;
He was flowen for ferde of the floode lotes
Into the bothem of the bot, and on a brede lyggede,
Onhelde by the hurrok, for the heven wrache,   125
Slipped upon a slumbe-sleepe, and slobberande he routes.
The freke him frunt with his foot and bede him ferk up;
There Ragnel in his rakentes him rere of his dremes!
By the hasp-hede he hentes him thenne,
And broght him up by the brest and upon borde sette,   130
Arrained him full runishly what resoun he hade
In such slaghtes of sorwe to sleepe so faste.
Soone haf they her sortes sette and serelich deled,
And ay the lote upon laste limped on Jonas.

      Thenne ascried they him skete and asked full loude,   135
'What the devel has thou don, doted wrech?
What seeches thou on see, sinful shrewe,
With thy lastes so luther to lose us uchone?
Has thou, gome, no governour ne god on to calle,
That thou thus slides on sleepe when thou slain worthes?   140
Of what londe art thou lent, what laytes thou here,
Whider in worlde that thou wilt, and what is thyn erende?
Lo, thy doom is thee dight, for thy deedes ille;
Do gif glory to thy godde, er thou glide hens.'

      'I am an Ebru,' quoth he, 'of Israil borne;   145
That Wye I worship, iwisse, that wroght alle thinges,
Alle the worlde with the welkin, the winde and the sternes,
And alle that wones there withinne, at a worde one.
Alle this meschef for me is made at this time,
For I haf greved my God and gilty am founden;   150
Forthy beres me to the borde and bathes me theroute;
Er gete ye no happe, I hope forsoothe.'

      He ossed hem by unninges that they undernomen
That he was flowen fro the face of freelich Drightin;
Thenne such a ferde on hem fell and flayed hem withinne   155
That they ruit hem to rowe and letten the rink one.
Hatheles hied in haste with ores full longe,
Sin her sail was hem aslipped, on sides to rowe,
Hef and hale upon hight to helpen hemselven;
Bot all was needless note, that nolde not bitide.   160

120	To look for more men and bring them to the casting of lots
121	*him failed* he missed *finde might* might have found
122	*Saf* except *jowked* lay sleeping *derne* secret
123	*flowen* fled *ferde* fear *floode lotes* sea's roaring
124	*brede* board *lyggede* lay
125	Huddled up by the rudder-band, for (fear of) the vengeance of heaven
126	*slumbe-sleepe* heavy sleep *slobberande* slobbering
	routes snores
127	*frunt* kicked *ferk up* jump up
128	May Ragnel (a devil) in his chains arouse him from his dreams!
129	*hasp-hede* clasp-head (the body of the brooch fastening his cloak)
	hentes seizes
130	*borde* the deck
131	*Arrained* questioned *runishly* roughly
132	*slaghtes of sorwe* onslaughts of misery
133	*her sortes sette* arranged their lots *serelich deled* separately dealt
	out
134	And always (i.e. each time they cast lots) the lot fell in the end to Jonah
135	*ascried* cried out upon *skete* quickly
136	*doted* stupid
137	*shrewe* villain
138	Ruining us all with thy vices so evil?
139	*gome* man *governour* master *on to calle* to call upon
140	*slain worthes* art about to be slain
141	*lent* come *laytes* seekest
142	*that thou wilt* (is it) that thou desirest (to go) *erende* mission
143	*thee dight* ordained for thee
144	*er . . . hens* before thou pass away
146	*Wye* being (i.e. God) *wroght* made
147	*welkin* sky *sternes* stars
148	*wones* dwells *at . . . one* with a single word
149	*meschef* trouble
151	*borde* side *bathes* plunge
152	Before (that) you will get no good fortune, I truly believe
153	*ossed* showed *unninges* signs *undernomen* understood
154	*was flowen* had fled *freelich* most high *Drightin* (the) Lord
155	*ferde* fear *flayed* terrified *withinne* inwardly
156	*ruit hem* rushed *rink* man *one* alone
157	*Hatheles hied* men (i.e. the sailors) hurried
158	*Sin* since *was hem aslipped* had got away from them
159	*Hef . . . hight* (to) heave and pull energetically
160	But it was all useless activity, it would not work

In bluber of the blo flood bursten her ores;
Thenne hade they noght in her hande that hem help might;
Thenne nas no cumfort to kever, ne counsel non other
Bot Jonas into his juis jugge bilive.
First they prayen to the Prince that prophetes serven   165
That He gef hem the grace to greven Him never
That they in baleless blood there blenden her handes,
Thagh that hathel wer His that they here quelled.
Tid by top and by to they tooken him sinne;
Into that lodliche loghe they luche him soone.   170
He was no titter out-tulde that tempest ne cesed;
The see saghtled therwith as soone as ho moght.
    Thenne thagh her takel were torne that totered on ythes,
Stiffe stremes and streght hem strained a while,
That drof hem drighlich adown the deepe to serve,   175
Till a swetter full swithe hem sweyed to bonk.
Ther was lofing on lofte, when they the londe wonnen,
To oure merciable God, on Moises wise,
With sacrafice upset and solempne vowes,
And graunted Him on to be God and graithly non other.   180
Thagh they be jolef for joye, Jonas yet dredes;
Thagh he nolde suffer no sore, his seele is on aunter;
For whatso worthed of that wye fro he in water dipped,
Hit were a wonder to weene, yif Holy Writ nere.
    Now is Jonas the Jue jugged to drowne;   185
Of that shended ship men shoved him soone.
A wilde walterande whal, as wyrde then shaped,
That was beten fro the abyme, by that bot flotte,
And was war of that wye that the water soghte,
And swiftely swenged him to sweepe and his swolwe opened.   190
The folk yet holdande his feete, the fish him tid hentes;
Withouten touche of any toothe he tult in his throte.
Thenne he swenges and swaives to the see bothem,
By mony rokkes full roghe and ridelande strondes,
With the man in his mawe malskred in drede—   195
As littel wonder hit was, yif he wo dreyed,
For nad the highe Heven-king, thurgh His hande might,
Warded this wrech man in warlowes guttes,
What lede moght leve, by lawe of any kinde,
That any lyf might be lent so longe him withinne?   200
Bot he was socored by that Sire that sittes so highe,

161   *bluber* the seething   *blo* dark   *bursten* shattered
163–4 Then there was no comfort to be obtained, nor any other plan but to consign Jonah to his doom immediately.
166   *gef* should give   *greven* offend
167   *baleless* innocent   *blenden* were steeping
168   *His* i.e. God's   *quelled* were killing
169   *Tid* swiftly   *sinne* then
170   *lodliche loghe* fearsome sea   *luche* pitch
171   He was no sooner (*titter*; compare *Tid* in line 169) thrown out than that tempest ceased
172   *saghtled* became calm   *ho moght* it might
173   Then, though the tackle of the ship, that tossed on the waves, was damaged
174   *stiffe* strong   *streght* compelling   *strained* gripped
175   And drove them relentlessly along to be the slave of the deep
176   *swetter* more favourable (current)   *swithe* swiftly
      sweyed sped   *bonk* shore
177   *lofing on lofte* praising to heaven   *wonnen* gained
178   *on Moises wise* in the manner of Moses (because these men, formerly of various religions, have been convinced by the calming of the storm that Jonah's God is the true one)
179   *upset* raised up
180   *graunted* acknowledged   *on* alone   *graithly* truly
181   *jolef* light-hearted
182   *sore* sorrow   *seele* happiness   *on aunter* in jeopardy
183   *whatso worthed* what became   *fro* after   *dipped* plunged
184   *weene* believe   *yif ... nere* were it not for Holy Writ
185   With this line we are taken back in time, to the moment at which the decision is taken to throw Jonah overboard; previously we saw it from the sailors' point of view, lines 181–4 provide a transition and are seen from the narrator's point of view, and now we see the same events from Jonah's point of view.
186   *shended ship* ship which was about to be destroyed
187   *walterande* wallowing   *wyrde* fate   *shaped* ordained
188   We have been prepared for this in line 83.   *beten* driven
189   *was war of* noticed   *soghte* was going into
190   *swenged him* swung round   *sweepe* swoop   *swolwe* gullet
191   Jonah is frequently shown in this halfway position in medieval pictures (including the one in the *Gawain*-manuscript).   *yet holdande* still holding   *hentes* seizes
192   *tult in* tumbled into
193   *swaives* sweeps
194   *ridelande strondes* surging currents
195   *mawe* belly   *malskred in drede* petrified with fear
196   *wo dreyed* endured misery
197   *nad* had not   *hande might* power of his hands
198   *warded* guarded   *wrech* wretched   *warlowes* the devil's
199–200 What man might believe, by any natural law, that any life could be granted for so long to him inside (the whale)? (A contrast is implied between the laws of nature and the divine grace which causes this miracle despite them.)

Thagh were wanless of wele in wombe of that fishe,
And also driven thurgh the deepe and in derk walteres.
Lord, colde was his cumfort, and his care huge,
For he knew uche a case and kark that him limped,   205
How fro the bot into the bluber was with a best lached,
And thrue in at hit throte withouten thret more,
As mote in at a munster door, so mukel wern his chawles.
He glides in by the gilles thurgh glaimande glette,
Reelande in by a rope, a rode that him thoght,   210
Ay heele over hed hurlande aboute,
Till he blunt in a blok as brod as a halle.
And there he festnes the feete and fathmes aboute,
And stood up in his stomak, that stank as the devel;
There in saim and in sorwe that savoured as helle,   215
There was bilded his bowr that will no bale suffer.
And thenne he lurkes and laytes where was lee best
In uche a nook of his navel, bot nowhere he findes
No rest ne recoverer bot ramel and mire,
In wich gut soever he gos; bot ever is God sweete.   220
    And there he lenged at the last, and to the Lede called:
'Now, Prince, of thy prophete pité Thou have.
Thagh I be fool and fikel and false of my hert,
Devoide now thy vengaunce, thurgh vertu of routhe.
Thagh I be gilty of gile, as gaule of prophetes,   225
Thou art God, and alle goodes are graithely thyn own;
Haf now mercy of thy man and his misdeedes,
And preve Thee lightly a lorde in londe and in water.'
With that he hitte to a hirne and helde him therinne,
There no defoule of no filthe was fest him aboute;   230
There he sete also sounde, saf for merk one,
As in the bulk of the bote there he bifore sleeped.
So in a bowel of that best he bides on live,
Three dayes and three night, ay thenkande on Drightin,
His might and His mercy, His mesure thenne;   235
Now he knowes Him in care that couthe not in sele.
And ever walteres this whal by wildren deepe,
Thurgh mony a regioun full roghe, thurgh ronk of his wille;
For that mote in his mawe made him, I trowe,
Thagh hit littel were him with, to wamel at his hert.   240
And as sailed the segge, ay sikerly he herde
The bigge borne on his bak and bete on his sides;

202	*were ... wele* (he) were without hope of well-being
	wombe belly
203	*in dark walteres* (though he) rolls about in the darkness
204	*care* trouble (chiastic order: adjective–noun, noun–adjective)
205	For he was aware of every misfortune and trouble that had befallen him
206	How (he) was seized by a monster out of the boat into the seething (water)
207	*thrue* sped *hit* its *thret more* more ado
208	*As mote* like a speck of dust *munster* cathedral (with a possible pun on 'monster') *so ... chawles* its jaws were so large
209	*glides* passes *glaimande glette* slimy filth
210	Reeling in by an intestine, which seemed to him (as big as) a road
211	*hurlande* tumbling
212	*blunt* stopped *blok* cavern, cavity
213	*festnes the feete* gets his footing *fathmes* gropes
215	*saim* grease *sorwe* filth *savoured as* smelt like
216	There a bower was built for this man who did not wish to suffer harm (an ironic line, because *bowr* suggests a delightful place, the very opposite of the whale's malodorous inside; and this is the reward Jonah gets for trying to *avoid* trouble!)
217	*lurkes* lies low *laytes* looks to see *lee* shelter
218	*In ... navel* in every corner of its bowels
219	*recoverer* safety *ramel* muck
220	*gut* intestine
221	*lenged* remained *Lede* i.e. God
222	*Thou have* (imperative)
223	*fool* foolish
224	*Devoide* forego *thurgh ... routhe* by the power of (thy) pity
225	*gile* deceit *as gaule* as (being) the scum
226	*goodes* things *graithely* truly
228	*preve Thee lightly* swiftly prove thyself (to be)
229	*hitte ... hirne* came upon a nook *helde him* installed himself
230	*defoule* stain *fest* close
231	There he remained, as safe—except only for the darkness—
232	*bulk* hold *there* where
233	*bides on live* remains alive
234	*ay ... on* always thinking of
235	*mesure* moderation, fairness
236	Now he who could not acknowledge Him in happiness does so in trouble
237	*walteres* rolls about *by ... deepe* amid the angry sea
238	*thurgh ronk* in the pride
239	*trowe* believe
240	*Thagh ... with* though it were little (compared) with him
	wamel feel sick
241	*segge* man *ay sikerly* always in safety
242	*bigge borne* mighty ocean *his* its *bete* beating

Then a prayer full prest the prophete there maked;
On this wise, as I weene, his wordes were mony:
   'Lorde, to Thee haf I cleped in cares full stronge;   245
Out of the hole Thou me herde of hellen wombe;
I calde, and Thou knew myn uncler steven.
Thou diptes me of the deepe see into the dimme hert;
The gret flem of thy flood folded me umbe;
Alle the gotes of thy guferes and groundeless pooles   250
And thy strivande stremes of strindes so mony
In on dashande dam drives me over.
And yet I saide as I sete in the see bothem,
"Careful am I, cest out fro thy cler yyen
And desevered fro thy sight, yet surely I hope   255
Efte to trede on thy temple and teme to Thyselven."
I am wrapped in water to my wo-stoundes;
The abyme bindes the body that I bide inne;
The pure poplande hourle playes on my heved;
To laste mere of uche a mount, man, am I fallen;   260
The barres of uche a bonk full bigly me holdes,
That I may lache no londe, and Thou my lyf weldes.
Thou shall releve me, Renk, while thy right sleepes,
Thurgh might of thy mercy that mukel is to triste.
For when th'access of anguish was hid in my saule,   265
Thenne I remembred me right of my rich Lorde,
Prayande Him for pité His prophete to here,
That into His holy hous myn orisoun moght entre.
I haf meled with thy maistres mony longe day,
Bot now I wot witterly that those unwise ledes   270
That affien hem in vanité and in vaine thinges
For thing that mountes to nought her mercy forsaken.
Bot I devoutly avowe, that verray bes holden,
Soberly to do Thee sacrafice when I shall safe worthe,
And offer Thee for my hele a full hol gifte,   275
And holde goode that Thou me hetes, have here my trauthe.'
   Thenne oure Fader to the fish ferslich biddes
That he him sput spakly upon spare drye.
The whal wendes at His wille and a warthe findes,
And there he brakes up the burne as bede him oure Lorde.   280
Thenne he swepe to the sonde in sluched clothes;
Hit may well be that mester were his mantile to washe!
The bonk that he blushed to and bode him biside

243	*prest* quickly				
244	*his ... mony* he spoke at length				
245	*cleped* called *stronge* great				
246	Thou heardest me (calling) out of the hole of the belly of hell				
247	*knew* recognized *uncler steven* feeble voice				
248	Thou hast plunged me into the dim heart of the deep sea				
249	*flem* flow *umbe* about				
250	*gotes* currents *guferes* whirlpools *groundeless* bottomless				
251	*strivande* restless *stremes* seas *of ... mony* of so many currents				
252	*on ... dam* a single rushing flood				
253	*sete* stayed				
254	*careful* full of care *cest* cast				
255	*desevered* cut off *surely* confidently				
256	To walk again in thy temple and belong to Thyself				
257	*wrapped* enveloped *to ... stoundes* to my innermost anguish				
258	*body* creature (i.e. whale) *bide* dwell				
259	*The ... hourle* the boiling sea-surge itself *heved* head				
260	*laste mere* (literally, 'furthest limit') the lowest depths				
	uche a mount every mountain				
261	*bonk* shore *bigly* strongly (Compare Jonah 2.7: 'the bars of the earth have shut me up for ever'.)				
262	*lache* reach *weldes* controllest				
263	*releve* succour *Renk* i.e. God *right* justice				
264	*mukel* great *triste* be relied on				
265	*access* fit *was hid* occurred inwardly				
266	*right* duly *rich* noble				
269	*meled* spoken *maistres* learned men				
270	*witterly* for certain *ledes* men				
271	*That ... hem* who put their faith				
272	*thing ... nought* something that amounts to nothing *her* their				
273	*that ... holden* (a promise) that will be truly kept				
274	*Soberly* solemnly *worthe* be				
275	*hele* safety *hol* perfect				
276	And hold good what Thou commandest me, take my pledged word				
277	*ferslich biddes* sternly orders				
278	*sput spakly* should spit out quickly *spare drye* bare dry (land)				
279	*wendes* turns *His* i.e. God's *warthe* shore				
280	*brakes* spews *burne* man *bede* ordered				
281	*swepe* swept in *sonde* shore *sluched* filthy				
282	*mester were* there was need				
283	The shore that he looked upon, and which lay close to him				

Was of the regiounes right that he renayed had.
Thenne a winde of Goddes worde efte the wye bruxles: 285
  'Nilt thou never to Ninive by no kinnes wayes?'
  'Yis, Lorde,' quoth the lede, 'lene me thy grace
For to go at thy gree; me gaines non other.'
  'Ris, approche then to prech, lo, the place here!
Lo, my lore is in thee loke, lause hit therinne!'   290
  Thenne the renk radly ros as he might,
And to Ninive that night he neghed full even.

284	*regiounes right*	very regions	*renayed*	renounced

284 *regiounes right* very regions   *renayed* renounced
285 *efte ... bruxles* upbraids the man again
286 Wilt thou never (go) to Nineveh by any kind of way?
287 *lene* grant
288 *gree* pleasure   *me ... other* nothing else profits me
290 *lore* teaching   *loke* locked   *lause* give vent (to)
291 *radly ... might* rose as quickly as he could
292 *neghed full even* approached very close

Langland: Piers Plowman

Introduction

To judge from the survival of over fifty manuscripts, *Piers Plowman* was one of the most popular poems of the age of Chaucer. The manuscripts fall into three groups, each giving a distinct text of the poem; the three texts are called A, B and C. It is highly probable, though not completely certain, that the three texts were written in succession, between about 1370 and 1390, by the same poet, William Langland, who was probably a clerk in minor orders, born in the Malvern area, but living and writing in London. Apart from what can be gleaned from the poem itself, little is known about him. The poem purports to recount a series of dreams, interspersed with partly allegorical accounts of the Dreamer's real life, and we cannot be certain how far these represent the real life of William Langland. If one considers the three texts of the poem together, they give strongly the impression of constituting one man's life-work; not exactly a spiritual autobiography, but certainly a poem in which he attempts, in three successive versions, to make sense of the experience of his own life, as a fourteenth-century Englishman, in the light of the teaching of the Church and his own understanding of the meaning of Christianity. *Piers Plowman* stands with other late fourteenth-century phenomena such as the flowering of devotional writing (as in the works of Walter Hilton and the author of *The Cloud of Unknowing*), the Wycliffite movement, and even certain aspects of the Peasants' Revolt, as evidence of a more personal, critical and questioning kind of religion. Langland, like the devotional writers, but unlike Wycliffe and his followers, was anxious to keep within the bounds of orthodox Catholicism, but his work has an imaginative freedom and a dreamlike inconsequentiality and even at times obscurity which cannot be fully reconciled with the precision of medieval scholastic theology. A leading motive in his work is a sense of personal pain, bewilderment and indignation at the contrast between the simplicity of the Christian message and the chaotic corruption of the Christian society in which he lived.

The extract we print is from the B-text, which has altogether over 7200 lines. It comes from the first of the two large sections into which the poem is divided, the *Visio* (vision) and the *Vita* (life). The poem is further divided into *passus* (steps or chapters), and our extract consists of Passus V, lines 63–468. It is extremely difficult to give a meaningful summary of such a lengthy work, which has no single allegorical narrative structure and which is divided into a series of semi-independent dreams; but very roughly the course of the poem is as follows. In the early stages, the Dreamer's vision is of the social, political and economic world of his own time, and of attempts to remedy its corruption. He is offered guidance by Lady Holychurch, watches an enactment of the fable of 'belling the cat', and sees Lady Meed—that is, financial reward—being accused by Conscience and put on trial before the King. Reason, in the garb of a pope, advises that all the estates of society should perform their own functions, and the first stage in the moral reform of the community begins with the confessions of the seven deadly sins to Repentance (this is the passage we print). The whole community, with its sins thus absolved, sets out on a pilgrimage to Truth (which is, among other things, a name of God). But they need a guide to lead them, and at this point Piers Plowman enters the poem for the first time. At this stage he is no more than a literal ploughman, a labourer on whose work the whole of society depends for its sustenance, but he is able to describe the route to Truth, which the people will eventually find in their own hearts. He says he will lead them there if they first help him to plough his half-acre—that is, once material needs have been provided for, then man can turn to his spiritual needs. The half-acre is a microcosm of medieval society, in which each class, as Reason recommended, has its own work to do; but the experiment eventually collapses into a cycle of excess and famine like that which Langland saw in the contemporary world around him. Truth himself hears of Piers's efforts, and offers him a pardon; but it turns out to be only a promise that the good will be saved and the evil damned. In anger, Piers tears the pardon, and vows to give up material concerns and turn his plough to prayers and penance. This is the end of the *Visio*.

The *Vita* begins with a quest for Dowell, Dobetter and Dobest, three categories deriving from the pardon's promise that those who do well shall be saved. The Dreamer meets first two friars, then a whole series of personifications such as Thought, Wit, Study, Learning and Scripture; then Trajan, a type of the good pagan; Reason returns; the Dreamer acquires the company of Patience and Conscience; and lastly he is shown by Free Will an obscure vision in which the devil steals human souls in the form of apples from the Tree of Charity, and the remedy for his theft takes the form of the birth of Christ. This is the point at which the divine entered into human history, and it marks a clarification in the poem, as the centre the Dreamer has been vainly searching for proves to be the Incarnation. He sees Faith, in the form of Abraham, Hope, in the form of Moses, and Charity, in the form of the Good Samaritan, and then, at the poem's emotional climax, he has a moving vision of the Crucifixion and Harrowing of Hell, in which Christ is imagined as a knight wearing Piers Plowman's armour— human flesh. This might make a triumphant conclusion to the poem, but it is a sign of its strength that it does not end there. The Dreamer is returned to the world of his own day, where Christ's bequest to man, the Church, imagined as a barn called Unity belonging to Piers (whose name, which means Peter, suggests St Peter and the papacy), is under siege by the deadly sins, who are as vigorous as before their confessions. At the same time the Dreamer himself is being attacked by Old Age and Death. Defeat seems imminent; but the poem ends with the pro- mise of a further quest, when Conscience vows to go in search of Piers Plowman till the end of the world. It is only outside time and history that perfect satisfaction can be found; but the human quest for this satisfaction will continue till the end of time.

In the rest of these introductory remarks, we shall make no attempt to offer any general interpretation of *Piers Plowman* as a whole, but shall simply comment on the section concerning the seven deadly sins. The allegorical narrative which provides the framework of this section is that of the confession of the sins to their 'priest', Repentance. It is a common non-realistic device in medieval literature for a wicked charac- ter to give us a detailed account of his own wickedness; this is done, for example, in the *Roman de la Rose* by characters such as Hypocrisy and the Old Woman. In Chaucer such confessions are given a more realistic air of loquaciousness or rash boastfulness in the cases of the Pardoner and the Wife of Bath. But in Langland the traditional device is handled in a different way, by making use of the real-life practice of spoken confession to a priest. In 1215 the Lateran Council had made it obliga- tory upon all Catholics to confess themselves at least once a year to their parish priests; and this insistence on the necessity of confession had given an impetus towards moral education in the later Middle Ages, because it was obviously necessary, if confessions were to be carried out effectively, for both priests and their parishioners to under- stand what acts and thoughts were sinful, what were the different cate- gories and aspects of sin, how people were led into sin, and what they must do, through repentance and restitution, to obtain absolution of their sins. A close and subtle analysis of the moral life was thereby encouraged, and this undoubtedly had its effects on literature, not only in the production of many manuals on the sins for priests or (like Chaucer's *Parson's Tale*) for laymen, but also perhaps in leading to a subtler treatment of moral issues in literature generally. In *The Friar's Tale* it is taken for granted that even a devil, if not a summoner, will understand the importance of intention or 'disposition', rather than mere words, in making a statement valid. The question of the validity or invalidity of a confession also comes up in *Sir Gawain and the Green*

Knight (at a later stage of the poem than the extract in this book), when Gawain confesses himself to a priest after promising to keep and conceal the green girdle but apparently does not mention his promise, and then is later offered a form of confession and absolution by the Green Knight. The framework of Gower's *Confessio Amantis* is provided by a secular parody of confession, in which the Lover is systematically questioned as to his sins against the religion of love by Genius, the priest of Venus.

One of the most striking things about our extract from *Piers Plowman* is its detailed knowledge and subtle understanding of the multifarious and interconnected ways in which human sinfulness operates in the everyday world of Langland's time. The conceptual scheme he uses, that of the seven deadly sins, had been established long before the fourteenth century. It claims comprehensiveness: every variety of sin can be included under one or other of the seven categories; and this is its great advantage as a tool for moral analysis. Its disadvantage is a tendency to rigidity and abstraction, because it may isolate the seven concepts from each other and from the complex experience of real life which gives them meaning and importance. In literature, this disadvantage might have been intensified by the personification-allegory which Langland uses, a literary device which could and sometimes did lead to bloodless conceptualization. But in fact Langland triumphed over these possible disadvantages, to produce a remarkable combination of inclusiveness with individual life, in ways we shall now examine.

Firstly, Langland's whole conception of the sins is not as emblematic representations of ideas but as individual sinners. The emblematic approach can be seen in, for example, Spenser's treatment of the sins in *The Faerie Queene*, Book I, canto iv, where each sin has exactly 27 lines, each rides on an appropriate beast (Gluttony on a swine, Lechery on a goat, and so on), in an appropriate posture, carrying appropriate symbolic attributes, and none has a life-history or any possibility of merging into the lives of other human beings. (There is a similar treatment in the fourteenth century by John Gower, in his French poem, the *Mirour de l'Omme*.) Langland, by contrast, gives his sins names such as Peronelle and Hervy, and, by means of the framework of confession, lets them tell the stories of their lives. Their many social contacts are used to illustrate the ramifications of sin, and in narrating them Langland goes into extraordinary detail about such matters as the sharp practice of drapers and brewers, the ignorance of priests, and the malice of nuns. The minutest aspects of the low life of his time seem to have come under his searching eye; and yet his conception is not one that leads to mere satire or mere despair. If the sins are individual sinners, they must be capable not only of confession but of repentance; and Langland can express in this way a hope of reform which does not mean abandoning the whole allegorical structure. Spenser's sins could not repent without ceasing to exist. Further, the repentance of any of Langland's sinners, even if we are convinced of its sincerity, does not imply the disappearance of that sin from the world he depicts in his poem. Sinfulness comes into *Piers Plowman* not only in the form of confessing sinners, but in many other forms; for example, in the form of stains on the cloak of Hawkin, the representative of the active life at its lowest level, or, near the end of the poem, in the form of the army besieging Unity. It is characteristic of Langland's poetic thought that no mere *form* should be final: none of his allegories is anything more than a single crystallization out of the changing flux of life itself. This may sometimes be confusing, but it helps to give his poem the flexible and protean quality of life as we really experience it.

In his treatment of the sins, there are many ways in which Langland avoids mere formalism or schematism. The sections devoted to each sin are of very variable lengths, ranging from four lines (Lechery) to 115 lines (Avarice). This is part of the poem's realism, for real-life confessions would not be of equal length; but the variation is not merely random. It is not by accident that, in a part of the poem concerned above all with the economic aspect of society (as in the trial of Lady Meed), greatest attention should be given to Avarice, and that Avarice should be shown at work particularly among tradesmen and financiers. The warning from Repentance that gains made by unjust dealing cannot be sanctified simply by being devoted to religious purposes was one with a particular relevance for the fourteenth century, when an economic system based on money as opposed to the customary exchange of services was beginning to make a bewildering impact on moral thought. Again, the confessions are variable in method as well as in length. Obviously enough, the longer the confession the more opportunity it gives for detail from the sinner and for questioning by Repentance; but there is also the case of Gluttony, most of whose section is not a confession at all, but a hilarious account of how his very sin intervened when he was on the way to confess himself. The nicely-observed smugness of his good intention, when he answers the alewife's question where he is going with

> To holy cherche, . . . for to here masse,
> And sithen I will be shriven and sinne namore,   (PP 245–6)

quickly gives way as he succumbs to temptation, abandons himself to yet another squalid bout of drinking, and only turns to Repentance when his wife takes advantage of his massive hangover to reproach him for his sin. The tavern-scene is a splendid example of medieval realism, full of energy and detail, and of telling incongruities—the prostitute and the parish-clerk side by side on the tavern bench, or repentance being mentioned only in the context of a session of the gambling game of 'newe faire' (see line 278). There is variation once more in what we are led to guess of the efficacy of the confessions. We are not implausibly assured that each of the sinners repented and never sinned again. Some of them sound modestly determined to keep their good resolutions, as with Envy's 'I will amende this, yif I may, thorw mighte of God almighty' (PP 71); but others give us less confidence. Gluttony ends by saying that he will never eat even fish on Fridays unless his aunt Abstinence gives him leave, 'And yet have I hated hir all my lyf-time' (PP 327)'. He is already beginning to waver, which is perhaps what we might have expected after the sentimental excess of his confession: 'And thanne gan Glotoun grete and gret doel to make . . .' (PP 322). No doubt his wife and daughter have heard it all before. With Avarice, too, the final emphasis is not hopeful. He cannot be absolved till he has made restitution, and, despite the insistence on God's mercy and on the means of making restitution even when it is impossible to do so directly, we are given no assurance that Avarice will in fact follow Repentance's advice rather than giving way to despair and suicide.

Then, there is even variation in the traditional order of the list of sins. It is usual to begin, as Langland does, with Pride, considered the head of all the other sins, but to end with Sloth is unusual. However, it is part of the realism of the extract that this sin should come lagging behind all the others. Lastly, it is no mere carelessness on Langland's part that leads him to include in the section devoted to one sin suggestions of behaviour that might seem more appropriate to a different sin. Wrath, for instance, is paradoxically shown to arise in some cases from 'low speeche' (i.e. false humility) (PP 77), and is then associated with gluttony (he does not like living with monks because they make him fast, and Repentance enjoins him to 'drinke noughte over-delicatly ne too deepe noither' (PP 122)). And Sloth is linked with wrath, when he admits that he tells his beads only in anger (PP 343), and with avarice when he explains how he neglects to pay his workmen, which also leads to anger: 'So with wikked wille and wrathe my werkmen I paye' (371). There are many such links among the sins, and their effect is to keep it in our minds that even these seven very solidly-conceived sinners do not represent a final categorization of the universal experience of human sinfulness. Though *Piers Plowman* makes much use of lists and categories, as essential tools for the analysis of human life, and even divides doing well into Dowell, Dobetter and Dobest, its fundamental effort is directed against the tendency to treat categories as final realities. This tendency was very powerful in the theological and philosophical thought of the fourteenth century, with its attempt to contain universal experience in a net of rational divisions and subdivisions; but Langland saw that experience was really a continuum, that there was no single way in which it could properly be categorized, and that true understanding could come only in moments of vision, such as that in which his Dreamer sees on the cross a figure who is at once Christ and Piers Plowman.

In our General Introduction we have already said something of Langland's use of allegory. Here we wish only to add a reminder that his allegory is as much an imaginative as a rational achievement, that we must allow it to affect our imaginations as we read it, and that we cannot hope to 'de-allegorize' his narrative and be left with a satisfactory literal equivalent. Allegory, for example, serves to compress rather than to decorate his thought. In line 385 of our extract Sloth falls into a faint, 'Till *Vigilate* the veille fette water at his eyen'. The personification *Vigilate*, a character who exists, like many others in Langland, only for a few lines, comes from a Scriptural text, either Mark 13.37 ('And what I say to you I say to all: watch') or Matthew 26.41 ('Watch ye; and pray that ye enter not into temptation'). He is thus a kind of embodiment of watchfulness, and watchfulness produces tears from Sloth's eyes, and tears of contrition. Yet at the same time, as is indicated by the next line—'And flatte it on his face and faste on him criede . . .'—this water is not only tears but the water that is thrown on someone in a faint in order to revive him. No laborious exposition such as this can hope to convey the compressed multiple suggestiveness of the lines as Langland wrote them. And analysis helps one to see that in Langland allegory is not merely a conception conveyed by his language, but a quality of his language itself. Thus Wrath tells us that, as soup-cook to the convent, he fed the sisters on vegetables consisting of wicked words, 'Till "Thou lixte" and "Thou lixte" lopen oute at ones' (PP 101). Here, even a colloquial phrase such as 'You're a liar' becomes momentarily a personification with enough life to 'leap out'; and indeed in the C-text version of these lines—'Till "thou lixt" and "thou lixt" be lady over hem alle'—it becomes mother superior of the convent.

For all his use of Latin quotations, which his learned audience would understand and see the point of, while the less learned would put up with them as they were accustomed to do in hearing sermons, Langland's treatment of the sins is permeated with life and energy, often of a gross enough kind. Sloth is summed up, in all his graceless irreverence, by the belch which interrupts the beginning of his confession (PP 333), and the swaying drunkard's walk of Gluttony is directly imitated in the rhythm and structure, as well as the content, of the lines in which it is described:

> And thanne gan he to go liche a glewmannes biche,
> Somme time aside and somme time arere,
> As whoso layth lines forto lache fowles.   (PP 289–91)

Piers Plowman is perhaps the most demanding of the texts included in this volume, but it is also one that will reward the effort a modern reader has to put into it with an incomparably penetrating insight into the experience of being alive in England in the fourteenth century.

Suggestions for further reading

Editions of the poem:
> all three texts parallel, ed. W. W. Skeat (Oxford University Press, 1886, and many reprints)
>
> selections from the C-text, ed. Elizabeth Salter and Derek Pearsall (London, Edward Arnold, York Medieval Texts, 1967)
>
> B-text, newly annotated, ed. J. A. W. Bennett (Oxford, Clarendon Press, vol. 1 1972, vol. 2 forthcoming)

John Lawlor, *Piers Plowman: An Essay in Criticism* (London, Edward Arnold, 1962)

Elizabeth Salter, *Piers Plowman: An Introduction* (Oxford, Basil Blackwell, 1962)

Introduction to Salter and Pearsall edition, as above

Piers Plowman

Superbia

Peronelle proude-herte platte hir to the erthe,
And lay long er she looked and 'Lorde, mercy!' cried,
And bihighte to Him that us alle made
She shulde unsowen hir serke and sette there an haire
To affaiten hire fleshe that fierce was to sinne;   5
'Shall nevere heighe herte me hente, but holde me lowe
And suffre to be missaide—and so did I nevere.
But now will I meeke me and mercy biseeche,
For all this I have hated in mine herte.'

Luxuria

Thanne Lechoure saide 'Allas!' and on Oure Lady he cried,
To make mercy for his misdeedes bitweene God and his soule,
With that he shulde the Saterday sevene yere thereafter   12
Drinke but mid the doke and dine but ones.

Invidia

Envye with hevy herte asked after shrifte,
And carefullich *mea culpa* he comsed to shewe.   15
He was as pale as a pellet, in the palsye he seemed,
And clothed in a caurimaury, I couthe it noughte discreve;
In kirtel and courteby and a knyf by his side;
Of a freres frokke were the forsleeves.
And as a leeke hadde ylaye longe in the sonne,   20
So looked he, with lene cheekes, louringe foule.
His body was tobolle for wrathe, that he bote his lippes,
And wringinge he yede with the fiste, to wreke himself he
    thoughte
With werkes or with wordes whan he seighe his time.
Eche a worde that he warpe was of an addres tonge;   25
Of chidinge and of challanginge was his chief liflode,
With bakbitinge and bismer and bering of false witnesse;
This was all his curteisye where that evere he shewed him.
    'I wolde been yshrive,' quod this shrewe, 'and I for shame
        durst.
I wolde be gladder, by God, that Gybbe had meschaunce   30

Superbia Pride

1   *Peronelle*   a woman's name, often applied to someone showily dressed
         platte hir   threw herself flat (an appropriate posture for confession)
2   *looked*   looked up
3   *bihighte*   promised
4   *unsowen*   pick open   *serke*   shirt, smock
         sette ... *haire*   fasten a hair-shirt inside it (the wearing of a hair-shirt
         was a common form of self-mortification)
5   *affaiten*   tame   *fierce*   eagerly given
6   Pride of heart shall never grip me, but I shall keep myself humble
7   *suffre* ... *missaide*   put up with being slandered   *nevere*   never before
8   *meeke me*   humble myself
9   *all this*   i.e. humility and endurance of slander

Luxuria Lechery

10   *Oure Lady*   i.e. the Blessed Virgin, as mediator between God and man,
         and as specially associated with chastity
12   *With*   on condition   *the Saterday*   on Saturdays (dedicated to Our
         Lady)
13   *but mid the doke*   only with the duck (i.e. on water) (Excessive eating
         and drinking are regularly associated with lechery in the Middle Ages.)

Invidia Envy

14   *asked* ... *shrifte*   requested confession
15   And sorrowfully he began to reveal (his sins by saying) 'my fault' (*Mea
         culpa* is a phrase from the beginning of the *Confiteor*, the prescribed
         form of confession.)
16   *pellet*   (white) stone ball (used as a missile)
         palsy   paralysis, or (as here) condition producing constant trembling
17   *caurimaury*   rough material   *couthe*   could   *discreve*   describe
18   *kirtel*   under-jacket   *courteby*   short jacket
19   The half-sleeves were those of a friar's habit (suggesting that friars were
         especially given to envy).
20   *as*   as if   *ylaye*   lain
21   *louringe foule*   frowning hideously
22   *tobolle*   swollen up   *that he bote*   so that he bit
23   And he went about clenching his fist, intending to avenge himself
24   *werkes*   deeds   *seighe*   saw
25   *Eche a*   every   *warpe*   uttered
         of   (as poisonous as if it came) from
26   His main sustenance consisted of complaining and fault-finding
27   *bismer*   reproach(es)
28   *him*   himself
29   *been yshrive*   be shriven (i.e. confessed)   *shrewe*   villain   *and*   if
30   *Gybbe*   (short for Gilbert)   *meschaunce*   misfortune

Than thoughe I had this woke ywonne a weye of Essex cheese.
I have a neighbore neighe me; I have ennuyed him ofte
And lowen on him to lordes to don him lese his silver,
And made his frendes been his foon thorw my false tonge;
His grace and his good happes greveth me full sore.   35
Bitweene many and many I make debate ofte,
That bothe lyf and lime is lost thorw my speeche.
And whan I meete him in market that I moste hate,
I hailse him hendeliche as I his frende were:
For he is doughtier than I, I dar do non other.   40
Ac hadde I maistrye and mighte, God wot my wille!

    And whan I come to the kirke and sholde kneele to the roode,
And praye for the poeple as the prest techeth,
For pilgrimes and for palmers, for alle the poeple after,
Thanne I crye on my knees that Criste yif hem sorwe   45
That baren away my bolle and my broke shete.
Away fro the auter thanne turne I myn eyen,
And biholde how Elaine hath a newe cote;
I wishe thanne it were mine, and all the webbe after.

    And of mennes lesinge I laughe; that liketh myn herte;   50
And for her winninge I weepe and waille the time,
And deeme that hi don ille there I do well worse;
Whoso undernimeth me hereof, I hate him dedly after.

    I wolde that uche a wight were my knave,
For whoso hath more than I, that angreth me sore.   55
And thus I live loveless, like a luther dogge,
That all my body bolneth for bitter of my galle.
I mighte noughte eet many yeres as a man oughte,
For envye and ivel wille is ivel to defye.
May no sugre ne sweete thinge assuage my swellinge,   60
Ne no *diapenidion* drive it fro mine herte,
Ne noither shrifte ne shame, but whoso shrape my mawe?'

    'Yus, redily,' quod Repentaunce, and radde him to the beste:
'Sorwe of sinnes is savacioun of soules.'

    'I am sorry,' quod that segge, 'I am but selde other,   65
And that maketh me thus megre, for I ne may me venge.
Amonges burgeises have I be dwellinge at Londoun,
And gert Bakbitinge be a brokoure to blame mennes ware.
Whan he solde and I noughte, thanne was I redy
To lie and to loure on my neighboure and to lakke his chaffare.
I will amende this, yif I may, thorw mighte of God almighty.'

31 *thoughe* if *woke* week *weye* weight (Essex cheeses were especially heavy, and weighed three hundredweight.)
32 *neighe* near *ennuyed* annoyed
33 *lowen on* told lies against *don* make *lese* lose
34 *foon* foes
35 *grace* luck *happes* fortunes
36 *debate* disagreement
38 *that* whom
39 *hailse* greet *hendeliche* courteously *as* as if
40 *For* because *doughtier* more powerful
41 *maistrye* dominance *my wille* what I would do
42 *kirke* church *roode* cross
44 *palmers* pilgrims who had been to the Holy Land
45 *yif* may give
46 Who carried off my bowl and my torn sheet (i.e. instead of praying, he nurses his resentment against people who have stolen even such trifles.)
47 *auter* altar
49 *all ... after* the whole piece of cloth (from which it was cut) as well
50 *of* at *lesinge* losses *liketh* pleases
51 *her winninge* their gains
52 And judge that they are acting badly (i.e. making their gains dishonestly), when I am acting worse (by envying their gains)
53 *Whoso undernimeth* if anyone reproves
54 I wish that every man were my servant
56 *luther* bad
57 So that my whole body is swollen with the bitterness of my anger
59 *ivel to defye* hard to digest
61 *diapenidion* barley-sugar (used as an expectorant)
26 *but ... mawe* or will someone (have to) scrape my stomach
63 *redily* easily *radde ... beste* advised him what was best to do
64 *Sorwe* contrition (but Envy takes *sorwe* to mean 'unhappiness')
65 *segge* man *but selde other* only rarely anything else
66 *megre* thin *me venge* take vengeance
67 *burgeises* citizens *be* been
68 *gert* made (if one 'translates' it out of allegory, 'I made Backbiting a broker' means 'I employed backbiting'.)
to ... ware to depreciate what people were selling
70 *lie ... loure* tell lies about and frown at
lakke his chaffare find fault with his goods (or his trading methods)

Ira

Now awaketh Wrath with two white eyen,   72
And nivelinge with the nose, and his nekke hanginge.
'I am Wrath,' quod he, 'I was sumtime a frere,
And the coventes gardiner for to graffe impes;   75
On limitoures and listres lesinges I imped,
Till they bere leves of low speeche lordes to plese,
And sithen they blosmed obrode in bowre to here shriftes.
And now is fallen therof a frute, that folke han well levere
Shewen her shriftes to hem than shrive hem to her persones. 80
And now persones han parceived that freres parte with hem,
Thise possessioneres preche and deprave freres,
And freres findeth hem in defaute, as folke bereth witness,
That whan they preche the poeple in many place aboute,
I, Wrath, walke with hem and wisse hem of my bookes.   85
Thus they speken of spiritualté, that either despiseth other,
Till they be bothe beggers and by my spiritualté libben,
Or elles alle riche and riden aboute.
I, Wrath, rest nevere, that I ne moste folwe
This wikked folke, for suche is my grace.   90
    I have an aunte to nonne, and an abbesse bothe;
Hir were levere swowe or swelte than suffre any paine.
I have be cook in hir kichin and the covent served,
Many monthes with hem and with monkes bothe.
I was the priouresses potagere, and other poure ladies,   95
And made hem joutes of jangelinge—that Johanne was a
        bastard,
And dame Clarice a knightes doughter, ac a kokewolde was
        hire sire,
And dame Peronelle a prestes file; priouresse worth she nevere,
For she had childe in chirrytime, all oure chapitere it wiste.
Of wikked wordes I, Wrath, here wortes imade,   100
Till "Thou lixte" and "Thou lixte" lopen oute at ones,
And either hitte other under the cheeke;
Hadde they had knives, by Crist, her either had killed other.
Saint Gregorie was a goode pope and had a goode forwit,
That no priouresse were prest for that he ordaigned.   105

Ira Anger, Wrath

72	*white eyen* eyes rolling so that only the whites showed
73	*nivelinge* snivelling
74	*sumtime a frere* at one time a friar
75	*coventes* convent's (a 'convent' could be of monks or friars)
	for... impes in order to graft shoots (the allegory or running metaphor which follows is based on the idea that Wrath plants shoots of anger where they would not naturally grow, until they spring up into anger itself)
76–80	I grafted (the habit of) lying on limitors (i.e. friars assigned a specific district in which to beg) and lecturers (i.e. preaching friars), until they bore leaves of humble words with which to flatter lords, and then they flowered far and wide, hearing confessions in ladies' chambers. And now from this has dropped the fruit, that people would much prefer to reveal (their sins in) confession to them (i.e. the friars) than to confess themselves to their parish priests. (The antagonism between friars and parish priests, based on the friars' claim to hear confessions, was notorious. The friar who tells Chaucer's *Friar's Tale* is a 'limitor', and we learn in the *General Prologue* of his skill as a beggar, and how he receives cash payments as a sign of penitence from sinners.)
81	*parte with hem* take a share in the profits (of hearing confessions)
82	*possessioneres* clergy with benefices *deprave* slander
83	*findeth... defaute* claim that *they* are at fault
84	*That... preche* so that when they preach to
85	*wisse hem of* teach them from
86	*spiritualté* (in two senses: spiritual matters, of which they ought to be speaking, and ecclesiastical properties, about which they are actually arguing) *that... other* so that each side expresses contempt fo the other
87	*bothe beggers* (i.e. the priests go about begging like the friars.) *by... libben* live on the endowment (a third sense of *spiritualté*) which I provide (i.e. anger, which they express towards each other)
88	i.e. the friars get rich enough to buy horses and ride about like priests (lines 87–8 imply the paradox that it doesn't matter whether you think of them as rich or as beggars: both parties are both.)
89	*that... folwe* from following
90	*grace* luck (with a pun on the sense 'divine grace', which is certainly *not* involved)
91	*to... bothe* who is a nun and, moreover, an abbess
92	*Hir... swelte* she would rather faint or die
95	*potagere* stew-maker
96	*joutes of jangelinge* stews of gossip *Johanne* Joanna
97	*ac... sire* but her father was a cuckold (i.e. she wasn't really his daughter)
98	*file* mistress *worth* will be
99	*chirrytime* the cherry season *chapitere* chapter (i.e. members)
100	*here wortes imade* made their vegetable-soup (pun on *wordes* and *wortes*)
101	*lopen* leapt (i.e. both shouted 'You're a liar' at the same time.)
103	*her either* each of them
104–6	A parenthetical comment by the author
104	*forwit* foresight
105	Because he ordained that no prioress should be a priest (i.e. have the right to hear confessions)

They had thanne been *infamis* the firste day, they can so ivel
   hele conseille.
  Amonge monkes I mighte be, ac many time I shonye:
For there been many felle frekes my feres to aspye,
Bothe prioure and supprioure and oure *pater abbas*;
And if I telle any tales they taken hem togideres,   110
And do me faste Fridayes to bred and to water,
And am challanged in the chapitelhous as I a childe were,
And baleised on the bare ers, and no breeche bitweene.
Forthy have I no liking with tho leodes to wonye.
I ete there unthende fishe and fieble ale drinke;   115
Ac other while, whan wyn cometh whan I drinke wyn at eve,
I have a fluxe of a foule mouthe well five dayes after.
All the wikkednesse that I wot by any of oure bretheren,
I couth it in oure cloistre that all oure covent wot it.'
  'Now repent thee,' quod Repentaunce, 'and reherse thou
   nevere   120
Conseille that thou knowest, by contenaunce ne by righte;
And drinke noughte over-delicatly ne too deepe noither,
That thy wille by cause therof to wrath mighte torne.
Esto sobrius,' he saide, and assoiled me after,
And bad me wilne to weepe, my wikkednesse to amende. 125

Avaricia

  And thanne cam Coveitise. Can I him noughte descrive,
So hungriliche and holwe sire Hervy him looked.
He was bitelbrowed and baberlipped also,
With two blered eyen as a blinde hagge;
And as a letheren purs lolled his cheekes,   130
Well sidder than his chin they chiveled for elde;
And as a bondman of his bacoun his berde was bidraveled;
With an hoode on his hed, a lousy hatte above,
And in a tawny tabarde of twelve winter age,
All totorne and bawdy and full of lys creepinge;   135
But if that a lous couthe have lopen the bettre,
She sholde noughte have walked on that welche, so was it
   thredebare.
  'I have been coveitouse,' quod this caitive, 'I biknowe it
   here;
For some time I served Simme-atte-stile,
And was his prentis yplighte his profit to waite.   140

106	*infamis* disgraced (i.e. by revealing things confessed to them)			
	they...conseille they (i.e. women) are so bad at concealing confidences			
107	*shonye* avoid (them)			
108	*felle ... aspye* fierce men on the lookout for my comrades (i.e. those who are given to anger)			
109	*supprioure* sub-prior	*pater abbas* father abbot		
110	*taken hem* meet			
111	*do* make	*to* on		
112	*challanged* accused	*chapitelhouse* chapter-house	*as* as if	
113	*baleised* beaten	*ers* arse		
114	*Forthy* therefore	*with... wonye* to dwell with those men		
115	*unthende* poor			
116	*whan I* and I			
117	*fluxe* discharge			
118	*wot by* know concerning			
119	*couth* make known	*that* so that		
120	*reherse* repeat			
121	*Conseille* anything secret	*contenaunce* favour	*by righte* (i.e. because you have a right to know it)	
122	*over-delicatly* too self-indulgently			
123	*That* lest			
124	*Esto sobrius* be sober	*me* Surely this should be Wrath? But in the dream-world of *Piers Plowman* characters have a habit of merging into one another.		
125	*wilne* desire (i.e. try)			

Avaricia Avarice, covetousness

126	*descrive* describe		
127	*hungriliche* hungry	*sire ... looked* Master Harvey appeared	
128	*baberlipped* thick-lipped		
131	*sidder* lower	*chiveled* trembled	*elde* old age
132	And, like a labourer, his beard was greasy from his bacon		
134	*tawny* dull yellow	*tabard* loose coat	
135	*totorne* ragged	*bawdy* dirty	*lys* lice
136	*couthe ... bettre* had been better at running away		
137	*welche* flannel		
138	*caitive* wretch	*biknowe* confess	
139	*Simme-atte-stile* Simon at the stile (an imaginary dishonest tradesman)		
140	*yplighte* pledged	*waite* look after	

First I lerned to lie a leef other twaine,
Wikkedlich to weigh was my first lessoun.
To Wye and to Winchestre I went to the faire
With many mannere marchandise as my maistre me highte;
Ne had the grace of gile ygo amonge my ware,   145
It had be unsolde this sevene yere, so me God helpe!
    Thanne drowe I me amonges draperes my donet to lerne,
To drawe the lyser alonge, the lenger it seemed;
Amonge the riche rayes I rendred a lessoun
To broche hem with a pakneedle, and plaited hem togideres 150
And put hem in a presse and pinned hem therinne
Till ten yerdes or twelve tolled out threteene.
    My wyf was a webbe and wollen cloth made;
She spak to spinnesteres to spinnen it oute.
Ac the pounde that she payed by poised a quarteroun more 155
Than mine owne auncere, whoso weighed treuthe.
    I boughte hir barly malte; she brewe it to selle;
Penny-ale and podding-ale she poured togideres
For laboreres and for low folke; that lay by himselve.
The best ale lay in my bowre or in my bedchambre,   160
And whoso bummed therof boughte it therafter,
A galloun for a grote, God wot, no lesse;
And yit it cam in cupmeel; this craft my wyf used.
Rose the regratere was hir righte name;
She hath holden hokkerye all hire lyftime.   165
    Ac I swere now, so thee ik, that sinne will I lete,
And nevere wikkedliche weighe ne wikke chaffare use,
But wenden to Walsingham, and my wyf als,
And bidde the roode of Bromeholme bringe me oute of dette.'
    'Repentedestow thee evere,' quod Repentaunce, 'ne
        restitucioun madest?'   170
    'Yus, ones I was herberwed,' quod he, 'with an heep of
        chapmen;
I ros whan they were a-rest and yrifled here males.'
    'That was no restitucioun,' quod Repentaunce, 'but a
        robberes thefte;
Thou haddest be better worthy be hanged therfore
Than for all that that thou hast here shewed.'   175
    'I wende riflinge were restitucioun,' quod he, 'for I lerned
        nevere rede on booke,

141   *leef other twaine*   page or two (alluding to the metaphorical book from which he learnt; cf. *lessoun* in 142 and *donet* in 147)

142   *Wikkedlich*   dishonestly

143   *Wye*   Weyhill (in Hampshire). Both towns had famous fairs.

144   *mannere*   kinds of   *highte*   ordered

145   Had not the grace of guile passed among my wares (cf. the grace of God, and line 90)

147   *drowe I me*   I betook myself   *donet*   grammatical primer (and thus, metaphorically, the basic elements of any subject)

148   To draw out the edge of the cloth, so that it seemed longer

149   *rayes*   striped cloths   *rendred*   memorized

150   *broche hem*   piece them together   *plaited*   joined

152   *tolled out threetene*   stretched out to thirteen (i.e. he made a large piece of cloth by joining together and stretching several smaller pieces)

153   *webbe*   weaver

154   *spinnesteres*   (female) spinners   *spinnen it oute*   make it go as far as possible (a phrase now used only metaphorically, but here literally)

155   *pounde ... by*   i.e. pound-weight that she used for weighing the yarn the spinners brought her   *poised*   weighed   *quarteroun*   quarter (of a pound)

156   *auncere*   weighing machine   *whoso ... treuthe*   if one weighed accurately

157   *brewe*   brewed (beer from)

158   *penny-ale*   thin, weak ale   *podding-ale*   the thick dregs

159   *that ... himselve*   this mixture was kept separately

161   *bummed*   tasted   *therafter*   at an appropriate price

162   *grote*   fourpence

163   *in cupmeel*   by cupfuls (which would give better opportunities for profiteering than larger measures)

164   *regratere*   retailer

165   *holden hokkerye*   kept up retailing

166   *so thee ik*   as I may prosper   *lete*   give up

167   *ne ... use*   nor trade dishonestly

168   *Walsingham*   (a famous shrine in Norfolk, dedicated to the Blessed Virgin)

169   *roode of Bromeholme*   (Bromholm was another famous shrine, very near Walsingham, and possessed a piece of the true Cross)   *dette*   sin (a normal sense of the word, but Avarice is obviously thinking in mercenary terms)

171   *herberwed*   lodged   *chapmen*   merchants

172   *males*   bags

175   *shewed*   confessed

176   *wende ... restitucioun*   thought the word 'restitution' meant stealing

And I can no Frenche in faith but of the ferthest ende of
  Norfolke.'
  'Usedestow evere usurie,' quod Repentaunce, 'in alle thy
    lyftime?'
  'Nay, soothly,' he saide, 'save in my youthe.
I lerned amonge Lumbardes and Jewes a lessoun,   180
To weigh pens with a peys and pare the hevyest,
And lene it for love of the crosse, to legge a wedde and lese it;
Suche dedes I did write yif he his day breke,
I have no maneres thorw rerages than thorw *miseretur et
  comodat.*
I have lent lordes and ladies my chaffare,   185
And been her brokour after and boughte it myself.
Eschaunges and chevesaunces, with suche chaffare I dele,
And lene folke that lese wol a lippe at every noble.
And with Lumbardes lettres I ladde golde to Rome,
And tooke it by taille here and tolde hem there lasse.'   190
  'Lentestow evere lordes for love of her maintenaunce?'
  'Ye, I have lent lordes, loved me nevere after,
And have ymade many a knighte bothe mercere and drapere
That payed nevere for his prentishode noughte a paire gloves.'
  'Hastow pité on poore men that mote needes borwe?'   195
  'I have as moche pité of poore men as pedlere hath of cattes,
That wolde kille hem, if he cache hem mighte, for coveitise of
    here skinnes.'
  'Artow manlyche amonge thy neighbores of thy mete and
    drinke?'
  'I am holden,' quod he, 'as hende as hounde is in kichine,
Amonges my neighbores namelich, such a name ich have.'   200
  'Now God leve nevere,' quod Repentaunce, 'but thou repent
    the rather,
The grace on this grounde thy good well to bisette,
Ne thine issue after thee have joye of that thou winnest,
Ne thy executours well bisett the silver that thou hem levest;
And that was wonne with wronge with wikked men be
    despended.   205
For were I frere of that hous there goode faith and charité is,
I nolde cope us with thy catel ne oure kirke amende,
Ne have a penny to my pitaunce of thine, by my soule hele,
For the best booke in oure hous, theighe brent golde were the
    leves,

180   Usury was forbidden by the medieval church, but Lombards and Jews were well known as money-lenders.

181   *pens* pence   *peys* weight (i.e. on scales)

182   And lend the pared coin for love of the cross, so that the borrower should lose the pledge he had laid down (literally, 'lay down a pledge and lose it'). (Avarice was acting as a pawnbroker, and would prefer to keep the valuable pledge which he had received from the borrower, rather than have the debt repaid. He lent money not for love of Christ's cross, i.e. in Christian charity, but for love of the cross on the reverse of the coin, i.e. for love of money.)

183–4   I had such deeds drawn up in case my debtor did not pay up in time that I have acquired more manors through arrears than through being kind and lending (the Latin is from Psalm 112.5).

185   *chaffare* goods

186   *been ... after* afterwards acted as their broker (i.e. he lent in the form of goods, which he afterwards bought back at a higher price, in order to conceal the taking of interest)

187   *Eschaunges and chevesaunces* (probably euphemisms for usury)
            with ... dele that's the kind of merchandise I deal in

188   And lend to people who are willing to lose a fraction of every coin

189–90   And I transmitted gold to Rome by means of bills of exchange, and kept an accurate account of what I received here, and paid out less to them there

191   Didst thou ever lend money to lords for the sake of their support?

192   *loved* who loved

193–4   And have made many a knight into a dealer in silk and cloth, who never paid a pair of gloves for his apprenticeship. (The knights became mercers and drapers by having to sell their rich clothes in order to pay their debts. A pair of gloves was a customary present when a boy was apprenticed to a trade; the implication is that the knights had to pay much more dearly for their initiation.)

195   *mote needes* must necessarily

198   *manlyche* generous

199   *hende* kind (used ironically; the dog would be greedily snatching food for itself)

200   *namelich* especially

201–2   'Now,' said Repentance, 'unless thou repent at once, may God never grant thee the grace to employ thy possessions well on this earth ...'

205   *that* may that which   *with* by

206   *frere* friar   *there* where

207   I would not provide us with copes or improve our church with thy money

208   *soule hele* soul's salvation

209   *For* for the sake of   *hous* religious house   *theighe* though *brent* burnished

And I wist witterly thou were such as thou tellest: 210
Servus es alterius cum fercula pinguia queris,
Pane tuo pocius vescere, liber eris.

Thou art an unkinde creature, I can thee noughte assoille
Till thou make restitucioun and rekne with hem alle,
And sithen that Resoun rolle it in the registre of hevene   215
That thou hast made uche man good, I may thee noughte
    assoille:
    Non dimittitur peccatum, donec restituatur ablatum, etc.
For alle that have of thy good, have God my trouthe!
Been holden at the heighe doome to helpe thee to restitue.
And whoso leveth noughte this be sooth, looke in the sauter
    glose,
In *miserere mei deus*, where I mene treuthe: 220
    Ecce enim veritatem dilexisti, etc.
Shall nevere werkman in this worlde thrive with that thou
    winnest:
Cum sancto sanctus eris—construe me that on Englishe!'
Thanne wex that shrewe in wanhope and wolde have hanged
    himself
Ne hadde Repentaunce the rather reconforted him in this
    mannere:
'Have mercye in thy minde and with thy mouth biseeche
    it,
                                     225
For Goddes mercye is more than alle his other werkes:
    Misericordia eius super omnia opera eius, etc.
And all the wikkednesse in this worlde that man mighte worche
    or thinke
Ne is no more to the mercye of God than in the see a glede:
    Omnis iniquitas quantum ad misericordiam dei, est sintilla in
        medio maris.
Forthy have mercy in thy minde, and marchandise, leve it,
For thou hast no good grounde to gete thee with a wastel,   230
But if it were with thy tonge or elles with thy two hondes.
For the good that thou hast getten bigan all with falsehede,
And as longe as thou livest therwith thou yeldest noughte, but
    borwest.
And if thou wite nevere to whiche ne whom to restitue,
Bere it to the bishop and bidde him, of his grace,   235
Bisette it himselve as best is for thy soule.
For he shall answere for thee at the heigh doome,

210   *And ... witterly* if I knew for certain

211–12 Thou art the slave of another if thou seekest after dainty dishes; rather feed upon thine own bread, and thou shalt be free. (Source unknown)

213   *unkinde* unnatural   *assoille* absolve

214   *rekne ... alle* settle with all those you have wronged

215   *sithen that* until   *rolle* enter

216   *made ... good* made good your debts to each man

         The sin is not remitted unless restitution be made (Augustine, *Epistles*)

217–20 For I swear to God that all who have received any of thy possessions will be expected at the day of Judgment to have helped thee to make restitution. And if anyone does not believe this to be true, let him look in the commentary on the psalter, in 'Have mercy upon me, O God' (i.e. Psalm 51); I refer to (the verse) where truth is mentioned: 'Behold thou desirest truth, etc.' (i.e. verse 8). (The standard medieval commentary, the *Glossa Ordinaria*, quotes St Augustine: 'He giveth indeed His mercies yet in such a way that He may satisfy justice; that the sins of him whom He pardoneth may not go unpunished.')

222   The Latin is from Psalm 18.26, addressed to God: 'With the pure Thou wilt show thyself pure.' It continues: 'and with the froward Thou wilt show thyself froward.'

223   *wex ... wanhope* that wretch fell into despair

224   *Ne hadde* had not   *the rather* at once

225   *Have ... minde* think of mercy

226   The Latin is slightly misquoted from Psalm 145.9: 'His tender mercies are over all his works.'

228   *to* compared to   *in ... glede* a spark in the sea

         The Latin, which is similar to a statement of St Augustine's, means: 'Compared with the mercy of God, all evil is like a spark in the midst of the sea.'

229   *Forthy* therefore

230   For thou hast no means of earning thyself enough to buy a loaf of bread

231   *But ... were* except

233   And as long as you are living on that, you are not repaying but borrowing

234   *wite never* dost not know   *whiche* what

236   *Bisette* employ

237   *at ... doome* at the day of Judgment

For thee and for many mo that man shall yif a rekeninge,
What he lerned you in Lente (leve thou none other),
And what he lent you of oure Lordes good to lette you fro
    sinne.'   240

Gula

Now biginneth Glotoun for to go to shrifte,
And kaires him to kirke-ward his coupe to shewe.
Ac Beton the brewestere bad him good morwe
And axed of him with that whiderward he wolde.
    'To holy cherche,' quod he, 'for to here masse,   245
And sithen I will be shriven and sinne namore.'
    'I have goode ale, gossib,' quod she, 'Glotoun, wiltow assaye?'
    'Hastow aughte in thy purs—any hote spices?'
    'I have pepper and pionés,' quod she, 'and a pounde of
    garlike,
A ferthingworth of fennel-seed for fastingdayes.'   250
    Thanne goth Glotoun in, and Grete Othes after;
Cesse the souteresse sat on the benche,
Watte the warner and his wyf bothe,
Timme the tinkere and twaine of his prentis,
Hikke the hakeneyman and Hughe the needeler,   255
Clarice of Cokkeslane and the clerke of the cherche,
Dawe the dykere and a dozeine other;
Sire Piers of Pridie and Peronelle of Flaundres,
A ribibour, a ratonere, a rakier of Chepe,
A ropere, a redingking and Rose the disheress,   260
Godfrey of Garlikehithe and Griffin the walshe;
And upholderes an hepe erly by the morwe
Geven Glotoun with glad chere good ale to hansel.
    Clement the cobbelere cast of his cloke,
And atte newe faire he nempned it to selle;   265
Hikke the hakeneyman hitte his hood after,
And badde Bette the bochere been on his side.
There were chapmen ychose this chaffare to preise;
Whoso haveth the hood shuld have amendes of the cloke.
Two risen up in rape and rouned togideres,   270
And preised these pennyworthes apart by hemselve;
They couth noughte by her conscience accorden in treuthe,
Till Robin the ropere arise they bisoughte,
And nempned him for a noumpere, that no debate nere.

238   *that man* (i.e. the bishop)   *yif* give

239   For what he taught you in Lent (do not believe otherwise)

240   *oure Lordes good* the grace of God (the idea of lending now being applied to the bishop, who 'lends' God's spiritual wealth to sinners and who, like the money-lender, will be called to account at the Last Judgment) *lette* keep

Gula Gluttony

242   And sets off to church to confess his sin(s).

243   *Beton* Betty

244   *axed ... that* in doing so asked him

247   *gossib* chum   *wiltow assaye* would you like to try it?

248   *spices* (to nibble, like highly-flavoured cocktail-snacks)

249   *pionés* peony seeds

251   *Grete Othes* (an allegorical character; the point of the allegory is that swearing was usually associated with drinking in the tavern, as in Chaucer's *Pardoner's Tale*)

252   *Cesse the souteresse* Cis (Cicely) the shoemaker

253   *Watte the warner* Walter the warrener (gamekeeper)

254   *twaine* two

255   *hakeneyman* hirer out of horses   *needeler* needle-seller

256   *Clarice* Clarissa   *Cokkeslane* Cock's Lane in London was a red-light district, and Clarice was no doubt a prostitute.

257   *Dawe the dykere* Dave the ditcher

258   *Sire Piers* (Peter) would be a priest; *Pridie* might be a corrupt form of *prie-dieu*, a kneeling desk; and *Peronelle of Flaundres* is probably a prostitute (London prostitutes were often Flemish).

259   *ribibour* player of the rubible (a stringed instrument)   *ratonere* rat-catcher   *rakier of Chepe* street-sweeper of Cheapside

260   *ropere* rope-maker   *redingking* (?) horse-soldier   *disheress* (female) dish-seller

261   *walshe* Welshman

262   *upholderes* second-hand dealers   *by the morwe* in the morning

263   *to hansel* as a treat (i.e. they greeted Glutton by saying, 'Have one on us!')

264   *of* off

265   And he offered it for sale at 'new market' (a game in which each of the two contestants offers one of his possessions for exchange with the other, referees are appointed to determine their respective values, and the difference is made up with a drink or round of drinks)

266   *hitte* threw down

267   *Bette* Bat (Bartholomew)

268–9   Merchants were appointed to value this merchandise (and they agreed that) he who had the hood should have compensation for the cloak

270   *rape* a hurry   *rouned* whispered

271   *pennyworthes* i.e. the cloak and hood

273   *arise ... bisoughte* they begged to stand up

274   And appointed him as an umpire, so that there should be no quarrelling

Hikke the hostellere hadde the cloke   275
In covenaunte that Clement shulde the cuppe fille
And have Hikkes hoode hostellere and holde him yserved;
And whoso repented rathest shulde arise after
And greete sire Glotoun with a galloun ale.
    There was laughing and louring and 'Let go the cuppe!'   280
And seten so till evensonge and songen umwhile
Till Glotoun had yglobbed a galloun and a gille.
His guttis gunne to godly as two greedy sowes;
He pissed a potel in a paternoster-while,
And blew his rounde ruwet at his rigge-bon ende,   285
That all that herde that horne held her nose after,
And wisheden it had be wexed with a wispe of furses.
He mighte neither steppe ne stonde er he his staffe hadde;
And thanne gan he go liche a glewmannes biche,
Somme time aside and somme time arere,   290
As whoso layth lines forto lache fowles.
And whan he drow to the doore thanne dimmed his eyen,
He thrumbled on the threshewolde and threwe to the erthe.
Clement the cobbelere caughte him by the middle
For to lifte him alofte, and laide him on his knowes;   295
Ac Glotoun was a grete cherle and a grim in the liftinge,
And coughed up a caudel in Clementes lappe;
Is non so hungry hounde in Hertfordshire
Durst lappe of the levinges, so unlovely they smaughte.
    With all the wo of this worlde his wyf and his wenche   300
Baren him home to his bedde and broughte him therinne.
And after all this excesse he had an accidie,
That he sleepe Saterday and Sonday till sonne yede to reste.
Thanne waked he of his winking and wiped his eyen;
The firste worde that he warpe was, 'Where is the bolle?'   305
His wyf gan edwite him tho how wikkedlich he lived,
And Repentaunce righte so rebuked him that time:
    'As thou with wordes and werkes hast wrought ivel in thy
        live,
Shrive thee and be shamed therof and shewe it with thy mouth.'
    'I, Glotoun,' quod the gome, 'gilty me yelde,   310
That I have trespassed with my tonge I can noughte telle how
        ofte,
Sworen "Goddes soule" and "So God me help and halidom"
There no neede ne was, nine hundred times;

275	*hostellere* stableman (the same man as the horse-hirer)
276	*In covenaunte* on condition
277	And have the hood of Hick the stableman and hold himself content
278	*whoso ... rathest* whichever of them soonest repented (i.e. wished to go back on the exchange). (A penalty usually had to be paid for returning a purchase.)
280	*louringe* frowning *Let go* pass
281	*seten* they sat *umwhile* from time to time
282	*yglobbed* gulped down
283	*gunne to godly* began to rumble
284	*potel* half-gallon *paternoster-while* as long as it took to say the Lord's Prayer (The whole of this highly secular episode is timed in religious terms.)
285	*ruwet* horn *his ... ende* the base of his backbone
287	*be wexed* been stopped up *furses* furse
289	*glewmannes biche* entertainer's dog (either a blind minstrel's guide-dog, or one trained to walk on its hind legs)
290	*aside* sideways *arere* backwards
291	Like someone laying lines criss-cross to trap birds (and therefore moving in a criss-cross way)
293	*thrumbled* stumbled *threshewolde* threshold *threwe* fell
295	*knowes* knees
296	*gret cherl* big fellow *grim* heavy
297	*caudel* mess
298	There is no dog in Hertfordshire so hungry (that it)
299	*smaughte* tasted
300	*wenche* daughter, maid-servant
301	*Baren* carried
302	*accidie* attack of sleepiness
303	*yede* went (This line indicates that Gluttony's *excesse* took place on Friday, a fast-day.)
304	*winking* nap (ironic understatement)
305	*warpe* uttered *bolle* bowl, cup (of drink)
306	*edwite* reproach
307	*righte so* similarly
308	*werkes* deeds
309	*Shrive thee* confess *shewe* admit
310	*gome* man *gilty me yelde* admit that I am guilty
312	*So ... halidom* May God and the relics help me (with this line compare 251 and note)

And overseye me at my soppere and some time at noones,
That I, Glotoun, girt it up er I hadde gone a mile,   315
And yspilt that mighte be spared and spended on somme
       hungry;
Overdelicatly on fasting-dayes drunken and eten bothe,
And sat some time so longe there that I sleepe and ete at ones.
For love of tales, in tavernes, to drinke the more, I dined,
And hied to the mete er noone whan fasting-dayes were.'   320
    'This shewing shrifte,' quod Repentaunce, 'shall be merite to
       thee.'
    And thanne gan Glotoun grete and gret doel to make
For his lither lyf that he lived hadde,
And avowed to fast: 'For hunger or for thurst
Shall never fishe on the Fridaye defien in my wombe,   325
Till Abstinence myn aunte have yive me leve;
And yit have I hated hir all my lyf-time.'

Accidia

    Thanne come Sleuthe, all bislabbered, with two slimy eyen;
'I most sitte,' saide the segge, 'or elles shulde I nappe;
I may noughte stonde ne stoupe ne withoute a stoole kneele;
Were I broughte abedde, but if my taille-ende it made,   331
Sholde no ringinge do me rise er I were ripe to dine.'
He bigan *benedicite* with a bolke, and his brest knocked,
And roxed and rored, and rutte atte laste.
    'What, awake, renke!' quod Repentaunce, 'and rape thee to
       shrifte.'   335
    'If I shulde deie by this day, me liste noughte to looke;
I can noughte perfitly my pater-noster as the prest it singeth,
But I can rimes of Robin Hood and Randolf erle of Chestre,
Ac neither of oure Lorde ne of oure Lady the leste that evere
       was made.
I have made vowes fourty and foryete hem on the morne;   340
I parfourned never penaunce as the prest me highte,
Ne righte sorry for my sinnes yet was I nevere.
And yif I bidde any bedes, but if it be in wrath,
That I telle with my tonge is two mile fro mine herte.
I am occupied eche day, haliday and other,   345
With idel tales atte ale and otherwhile in cherches;
Goddes paine and his passioun full selde thinke I thereon.
I visited nevere fieble men ne fettered folke in puttes;

314	*overseye me* (have) forgotten myself (lines 311–18 are all in the perfect tense)	
315	*girt* vomited	
316	*yspilt ... spared* wasted what might have been saved	
317	*overdelicatly* over-luxuriously	
318	*at ones* at the same time	
319	In order to hear gossip, and to drink more, I ate in taverns	
320	*hied* hastened *mete* food	
321	*shewing* revealing	
322	*grete* weep *doel* lamentation	
323	*lither* evil	
324	*For* despite	
325	*defien in my wombe* be digested in my stomach	
326	*have yive* shall have given (i.e. he will not eat even fish on Fridays until Abstinence agrees that he has fasted long enough.)	

Accidia Sloth

328	*bislabbered* besmeared (with dirt)
329	*shulde I nappe* I shall fall asleep
331	*but ... made* unless I had to go to the lavatory
332	*do* make *ripe* ready
333	*benedicite* Bless (me) (the opening formula of confession)
	bolke belch *knocked* beat
334	*roxed* stretched *rored* groaned *rutte* snored
335	*renke* man *rape thee* hasten
336	If I were to die today, I could not bring myself to open my eyes
337	*can* know
339	*leste ... made* shortest piece ever composed
340	*foryete* forgotten *morne* morrow, next day
341	*highte* directed
343	*bidde any bedes* ever say my rosary
344	*That I telle* what I say
345	*haliday* holy day
346	*atte ale* at the alehouse
348	*fieble* sick *puttes* dungeons (This line mentions the first two of the seven corporal works of mercy.)

I have levere here an harlotry or a sommer-game of souteres,
Or lesinges to laughe at and belie my neighbore,   350
Than all that evere Marke made, Matthew, John, and Lucas.
And vigilies and fasting-dayes, alle thise late I passe,
And ligge abedde in Lenten and my lemman in myn armes,
Till matines and masse be do, and thanne go to the freres;
Come I to *ite, missa est*, I holde me yserved.   355
I nam noughte shriven some time, but if seknesse it make,
Nought tweies in two yere, and thanne up gesse I shrive me.
   I have be prest and persoun passinge thretty winter,
Yete can I neither solfe ne singe ne saintes lives rede;
But I can finde in a felde or in a fourlonge an hare,   360
Better than in *beatus vir* or in *beati omnes*
Construe oon clause well and kenne it to my parochienes.
I can holde lovedayes and here a reeves rekeninge,
Ac in canoun ne in the decretales I can noughte rede a line.
   Yif I bigge and borwe it, but yif it be ytailled,   365
I foryete it as yerne; and yif men it axe,
Six sithes or sevene I forsake it with othes,
And thus tene I trewe men ten hundreth times.
And my servaunts some time her salarye is bihinde,
Reuthe is to here the rekeninge whan we shall rede accomptes;
So with wikked wille and wrathe my werkmen I paye.   371
   Yif any man doth me a benfait or helpeth me at neede,
I am unkinde ayain his curteisye and can noughte understonde
      it;
For I have and have hadde some dele hawkes manneres:
I nam noughte lured with love, but there ligge aughte under
      the thombe.   375
The kindeness that mine evene-cristene kidde me fernyere,
Sixty sithes I, Sleuthe, have foryete it sith;
In speeche and in sparinge of speeche yspilte many a time
Bothe fleshe and fishe and many other vitailles;
Both bred and ale, butter, melke, and cheese   380
Forsleuthed in my servise till it mighte serve noman.
   I ran aboute in youthe and yaf me noughte to lerne,
And evere sith have be beggere for my foule sleuthe;
Heu michi, quod sterilem vitam duxi juvenilem!'
   'Repentedestow thee naughte?' quod Repentaunce; and righte
      with that he swowned   385
Till *Vigilate* the veille fette water at his eyen,

349 I would rather hear a dirty joke or a cobblers' midsummer game
350 *lesinges* lies
351 *made* composed
352 *vigilies* vigils (eves of holy days, when devotional watches were kept)
353 *ligge* lie *lemman* mistress
354 *do* done *freres* friars (instead of to his parish church; for the competition between friars and parish priests, see lines 76–80 and note)
355 If I arrive at *Ite, missa est* (near the end of the mass), I hold myself content
356–7 *nam noughte . . . Nought* am not (triple negative)
356 *But . . . make* unless sickness brings it about (by frightening him into confession)
357 *up gesse* by guesswork
358 *solfe* (i.e. *sol, fa*) sing scales
360 *fourlonge* space between ploughed areas
361 *beatus vir* Psalm 1 or 112 *beati omnes* Psalm 128
362 *construe* (I can) interpret *kenne* explain
     parochienes parishioners
363 *lovedayes* meetings of the manorial court
     here . . . rekeninge audit a steward's accounts
364 *canoun* canon (i.e. ecclesiastical) law *decretales* collection of popes' edicts and decrees of ecclesiastical councils
365 If I buy on credit, unless it is set down on a tally
366 *as yerne* as soon (as I have bought it) *it axe* ask for payment
367 *sithes* times *forsake* deny
368 *tene* injure
370 *Reuthe is* it is pitiful *shall rede accomptes* must go through the accounts
373 *ayain* in response to
374 *some . . . manneres* somewhat of the habits of a hawk
375 *but . . . thombe* unless something (eatable) is held in the hand
376 *mine . . . fernyere* my fellow-Christians formerly showed me
377 *foryete* forgotten *sith* since
378 *In speeche . . . yspilte* both by speaking and by remaining silent (I have) wasted (i.e. both deliberately and by not bothering)
381 *Forsleuthed* wasted by laziness
384 'Alas, what a barren youth I have spent!' (source unknown)
386 Until *Vigilate* the watcher produced water from his eyes (i.e., by paying attention to Christ's injunction, 'Watch (and pray)' (Matthew 26.41), he achieves tears of contrition, which arouse him from despair, in the same way that sprinkling water on someone who has fainted can bring him round.)

And flatte it on his face and faste on him criede,
And saide, 'Ware thee fram wanhope wolde thee bitraye.
"I am sorry for my sinnes," say so to thyselve,
And bete thyselve on the breste and bidde Him of grace;   390
For is no gult here so grete that his goodnesse nis more.'
    Thanne sat Sleuthe up and seyned him swithe,
And made avowe tofore God for his foule sleuthe:
'Shall no Sondaye be this sevene yere, but sikenesse it lette,
That I ne shall do me er day to the dere cherche,   395
And heren matines and masse as I a monke were.
Shall none ale after mete holde me thennes
Till I have evensonge herde, I behote to the roode.
And yete will I yelde ayain, if I so moche have,
All that I wikkedly wan sithen I witte hadde.   400
And though my liflode lakke, leten I nelle,
That eche man ne shall have his er I hennes wende;
And with the residue and the remenaunt, by the roode of
    Chestre,
I shall seeke Treuthe arst er I see Rome!'

387   *flatte* dashed   *faste* quickly
388   *Ware ... wolde* beware of despair which would
390   *bidde ... grace* beg God for his grace
391   *gult* sin   *nis more* is not greater
392   *seyned him swithe* crossed himself quickly
393   *tofore* before   *for* about
394   Unless sickness prevents me, there shall not be a Sunday for the next seven years
395   *ne ... me* shall not go   *dere* beloved
396   *as* as if
397   *holde me thennes* keep me away
398   *behote ... roode* vow before the cross
399–402 And furthermore, if I possess enough, I will repay all that I gained dishonestly since I was old enough to understand. And though I lack means of life, I will not give up until each man has what belongs to him before I pass away.
403   *roode of Chestre* (There was a famous cross at Chester, which was the object of many pilgrimages.)
404   *arst er* before (i.e. his will be a spiritual pilgrimage towards Truth, which in Langland is one of the names of God, rather than a physical one to Rome.)

Chaucer: The Friar's Tale

Introduction

We have more information about Geoffrey Chaucer than about any of the other poets whose work is represented in this book. Although in his lifetime he had a considerable reputation as a poet, in France as well as in England, and was by far the most important influence on English poetry in the century after his death, we owe our knowledge of his life chiefly to the fact that he was also a courtier, civil servant and diplomat of some importance. He was born in the early 1340s, the son of a prosperous London wine-merchant. He entered the service of Prince Lionel and his wife, the Countess of Ulster, and later, in the 1360s, that of King Edward III, for whom he undertook several diplomatic missions to France and Italy. The visits to Italy in particular were of importance to his writing, because they brought him a knowledge of the works of three great contemporary Italian writers, Dante, Boccaccio and Petrarch, who were otherwise almost unknown in England. In 1374 he became a high customs official, an office in which he was confirmed when Richard II became king in 1377, but which he relinquished in 1386. In 1389, when Richard II came of age and took over power, Chaucer was made Clerk of the King's Works. After 1391 he held less important offices, but received a royal annuity which was continued in 1399, after Richard II had been deposed and Henry IV crowned. He died in 1400.

Among Chaucer's more important works are: *The Book of the Duchess* and *The House of Fame* (from the 1370s); *The Parliament of Fowls*, *Troilus and Criseyde* and *The Legend of Good Women* (1380–86); and, from the later years of his life, *The Canterbury Tales*. In this introduction, we shall say a little about *The Canterbury Tales* before passing on to *The Friar's Tale*; for studies of Chaucer's literary career as a whole, we refer readers to some of the books listed as suggestions for further reading.

The Canterbury Tales is a large collection of stories of very different kinds, which Chaucer left incomplete at his death. It was not Chaucer's first attempt at a collection—the unfinished *Legend of Good Women* is a group of stories of women who suffered in love, mostly taken from Ovid—and there are several other large-scale fourteenth-century collections of tales, for example Boccaccio's *Decameron* (which Chaucer probably did not know) and the *Confessio Amantis* of Chaucer's friend

John Gower. Chaucer's collection contains a greater variety of kinds of tale than most, and it is justified by a fictional framework (the agreement of a group of pilgrims of various social classes and professions, travelling from Southwark to the shrine of St Thomas Becket at Canterbury, to pass the time by telling stories as they ride along) which gives the possibility of an additional, dramatic interest to the stories. This possibility is not always fulfilled: some of the tales are merely appropriate in a general way to the pilgrims who tell them, as when the Knight tells a courtly romance and the Nun's Priest a highly entertaining beast-fable. But in other cases, the tale has a special association with its teller, as when the domineering Wife of Bath, who has had five husbands, tells a story of how an old woman gained a young husband and the mastery over him. And in some cases, a tale told by one pilgrim is taken as having some personal reference by another, who immediately retaliates. This happens especially among the pilgrims of lower social class, whose tales are normally *fabliaux*—comic and frequently dirty stories of lower- and middle-class life. Thus the Miller tells a tale about how a foolish and gullible old carpenter with a beautiful young wife was cuckolded in a particularly ridiculous way; and the Reeve, who is himself a carpenter by trade, takes offence and tells a story of how a grasping dishonest miller was also cuckolded, and outwitted in other ways, by two Cambridge students. So it is with the Summoner and the Friar, whose tales form one of the most closely interlinked pairs in the whole collection. We are told that the Friar as he rode along kept on glaring at the Summoner, and that, after the Wife of Bath had told her tale, he announced that he intended to tell one against summoners, assuring the other pilgrims as he did so that

> Pardee, ye may well knowe by the name
> That of a somnour may no good be said.

The Summoner promises in advance that he will give as good as he gets, and after the Friar has finished he tells a story of how a flattering friar, who was always on the lookout for gifts, received one of a most unsavoury kind.

In the *General Prologue* to the *Canterbury Tales*, Chaucer describes most of his pilgrims in some detail. Though in some cases the descriptions may have included allusions to real persons known to Chaucer's audience, the pilgrims are largely characterized not as specific individuals but by means of their professions, most of which (like the callings, let us say, of commercial traveller or model in our own time) had their own firmly-outlined traditional reputations, whether justified or not. The Friar is described, in accordance with a long tradition of cynicism about the worldliness of clerics, as well nourished and easy-going, familiarly acquainted with landowners and rich merchants, and with innkeepers and barmaids, but not with the poor and sick, and highly accomplished at persuading even a poor widow to part with her last farthing. (Friars were supposed not to own property, but to live by begging.) He is a man of great charm and plausibility, dressed as well as a pope, accomplished in 'daliaunce and fair langage', and one whose eyes twinkled like stars on a frosty night. In our time he would probably be in public relations; his gifts and his charm are certainly totally inappropriate to the order to which he belongs, vowed in theory to complete poverty, to the imitation of Christ, and to spreading Christ's message among all classes of society. The portrait of the Summoner forms a striking contrast. A summoner was an official of the diocesan court (which in the Middle Ages had powers over spiritual offenders almost as great as those of the secular courts over people who broke the king's laws), whose task it was to summon offenders to appear before the archdeacon, who presided over the court. Summoners were traditionally abused as oppressors of the poor and receivers of bribes, especially from sexual offenders; they are seen in this way in *Piers Plowman,* and there is a lively dramatization of a brutal and corrupt summoner at work in a scene in one of the great medieval cycles of religious drama, the *Trial of Joseph and Mary* in the *Ludus Coventriae.* Chaucer describes his Summoner in similar terms, adding that his face was so knobbed and spotted that children were afraid of it, and that he was fond, when drunk, of repeating a few fragments of Latin which he did not understand. This coarse and ugly figure would naturally be repellent to the well-heeled Friar, and the imaginary summoner in the Friar's tale is shown up again and again as not only brutal and totally unprincipled, but stupid, a ready victim to the devil, in whose smooth plausibility there is something Friar-like. It is the devil who is the hero of the Friar's story, and this, in its turn, throws an interesting light on the storyteller.

There are many ways in which the dramatic setting adds a new dimension to the tale. For example, the Friar's skill in getting widows to part with their money by sheer persuasiveness helps us to recognize his contempt for the crudeness of approach of the summoner in the story. It is not that the Friar has anything against getting money out of widows; but let it be done delicately, with sweet talk, not with the bullying tactics of the summoner, which only arouse the widow to turn on him and curse him. Throughout the tale, we find implied an attitude towards the summoner which is not one of hatred for an equal, but of contempt for an inferior and for the whole professional group to which the inferior belongs. The summoner is 'a theef, and eek a somnour, and a bawde' (FT 54)—a line which implies that the very word 'summoner' is as much a term of abuse as 'thief' and 'bawd'. The summoner is naturally ashamed of telling his new companion what his real

calling is, 'for verray filthe and shame' (FT 93): the word 'summoner'
could only arouse contempt in any chance acquaintance, so he calls
himself a *bailly*. It is natural enough that such a being should find it so
easy to make friends with a devil, and, moreover, that he should show
not the least horror, but only idle and ill-informed curiosity, when he
learns who his companion is. *The Friar's Tale* can perfectly well stand by
itself as a finely plotted and proportioned comic story, nor can it be
said that every detail in it relates to the pilgrim-Friar and the pilgrim-
Summoner; but it gains a new layer of interest when one recognizes
how ingeniously it is meshed into its context in the Canterbury pil-
grimage.

We remarked in our General Introduction that the typical *fabliau* is
farcical and coarse; but *The Friar's Tale*, as befits its teller, is an alto-
gether finer article, which gains its effect, to borrow the devil's distinc-
tion (FT 131) by *sleighte* rather than by *violence*. There is none of the
thickly-detailed setting in bourgeois life that we find in *The Miller's
Tale* or *The Reeve's Tale*, with their cat-doors and cradles, but only a
few necessary indications of scene—'under a forest side' (FT 80) or
'right at the entring of the townes ende' (237). The only physical vio-
lence in it is that of the carter, vainly trying to get his horses to pull
harder, and there the point is that, for all the violence of his language,
he does not really mean what he says. There is bullying language from
the summoner himself, as he tries to bluster a bribe out of the widow,
but it is quite ineffective, and even if he were not carried off to hell he
would have to be content with the widow's pan rather than with the
large sum (in medieval times) of twelve pence which he demands from
her. A medieval audience would probably have expected violent,
boisterous comedy in the depiction of the devil. There is nothing deli-
cate or witty about most medieval devils, whether in literature or in the
other arts. This is how a typical one speaks, bellowing vigorously as
he finds himself freed from his chains in the York play of the Last
Judgment:

> Out, harrow, out, out! Harken to this horn!
> I was never in dowte ere now at this morn;   *fear*
> So sturdy a shout sin that I was born
> Heard I never hereabout in earnest ne in scorn—
>   A wonder!
>   I was bound full fast
>   In irons for to last,
>   But my bands they brast,   *burst*
>   And shook all in sunder.

In *The Friar's Tale* there is none of this boisterousness, and the devil is
not 'blak and rough of hewe' (FT 322), as in the widow's conventional

description of him. There is the slightly odd touch, it is true, of the black fringe on his hat; but apart from that his disguise is perfect, and nothing in his behaviour calls attention to his supernatural status. When the summoner asks where he comes from, 'This yeman him answerde in softe speeche' (FT 112). When he finally discloses who he is, it is equally quietly and unemphatically, and with a smile which is all the more sinister for being so slight:

> In this meene while
> This yeman gan a littel for to smile.
> 'Brother,' quod he, 'wiltow that I thee telle?
> I am a feend; my dwelling is in helle.' (FT 145–8)

This is the story's first major turning-point; its culmination comes when the devil carries the summoner off to hell with him forever (thereby disclosing the full implication of that soothing word, *brother*), and that is handled with equal restraint. There are no threats, no protests, no firecrackers, just quiet statements of undeniable facts:

> 'Now, brother,' quod the devel, 'be nat wroth;
> Thy body and this panne been mine by right.
> Thou shalt with me to helle yet tonight,
> Where thou shalt knowen of oure privetee
> More than a maister of divinitee.'
> And with that word this foule feend him hente;
> Body and soule he with the devel wente
> Where as that somnours han hir heritage. (FT 334–41)

It is typical of the devil's calm restraint that he should remember to claim the pan, which the widow has also committed to him, and that he should treat it as a prize exactly on a level with the summoner's body. As usual, the devil's calmness seems to express the Friar's effortless superiority: there is no reason for excitement because there has been no difficulty in trapping the summoner, and there is nothing unusual in the outcome—just another summoner going the way they can all be expected to go, 'where as that somnours han hir heritage'.

But for all the coolness of its surface, *The Friar's Tale* is animated by a powerful energy, which expresses itself in irony. The poem's irony depends on the existence of different levels of awareness among the characters and the audience, and in order to include the audience in it Chaucer does something which for him is unusual. Normally Chaucer, like Shakespeare, takes his audience into his confidence and thus frequently puts them in a position of superiority to some or all of his characters. But in *The Friar's Tale*, on a first hearing, we do not know that the yeoman whom the summoner meets is really a devil: we simply hear the summoner disclosing his own conscienceless rapacity with surprising openness once he meets an apparently congenial companion. The openness we can easily put down to boastful stupidity, and in that way it becomes part of the Friar's satire against the pilgrim-Summoner, though no doubt it also has its roots in the non-realistic literary convention of self-confession, which underlies the confessions of the sins in *Piers Plowman*. But on a second hearing, we shall recognize a further satirical point. The companion with whom the summoner feels so much at home is a devil, and this is natural enough, because summoners and devils are much the same kind of thing, at least by intention—in practice, as we see, devils are more skilful at carrying out their evil intentions than summoners are. We shall also recognize a double meaning in many of the supposed yeoman's remarks, in which the summoner sees only one meaning. Thus we shall grasp the sinister implication of the yeoman's assertion that he lives 'fer in the north contree' (FT 113), since it was generally held that the devil lived in the north. And we shall see the full point of the yeoman's assurance that

> Er we departe, I shall thee so well wisse
> That of myn hous ne shaltow nevere misse,   (FT 115–16)

and of his reference to his 'hard . . . and daungerous' lord (in whom we shall recognize Satan himself).

It might be expected that once the 'yeoman' had disclosed his true identity to the summoner, irony of this kind would disappear, with a consequent anticlimax. In fact, it is replaced by a different kind of irony, because the summoner is still at a disadvantage, in failing to grasp the crucial fact that the prey the devil is after is himself. This failure of understanding on the part of the summoner in the story is of course peculiarly insulting to the pilgrim-Summoner against whom it is directed. For example, the devil can expound his methods quite openly, and can explain that devils take on such shapes 'As most able is oure preyes for to take' (FT 172), without the least fear that the summoner will wonder why on this occasion the devil has taken the shape of a yeoman-bailiff. He can even assure the summoner that his curiosity about diabolic disguises will be fully satisfied because

> Thou shalt herafterward, my brother deere,
> Come there thee needeth nat of me to leere,   (FT 215–16)

and still the complacent victim will not have the wit to wonder what he really means. Finally, irony goes so far that the summoner himself starts making remarks with double meanings, without in the least realizing that he is doing so. For example, when the devil promises to keep company with him 'Till it be so that *thou* forsake *me*' (FT 222), the summoner is quick to reassure him: '"Nay," quod this somnour, "that shall nat bitide!"' (223). And when the summoner demands money from the poor widow, and insists,

> I shall no profit han therby but lite;
> My maister hath the profit, and nat I,   (FT 300–01)

he again speaks more truly than he knows, because he has put himself so far in the power of evil that his master is now not, as he supposes, the archdeacon, but Satan, who will indeed allow him little profit on the deal. The summoner has gradually become enmeshed in a situation which he totally fails to understand (so totally that he does not realize that he does not understand it), and over which he has no control. Thus the comedy of *The Friar's Tale* lies, beneath its naturalness, vigour and ease of narration and dialogue, almost entirely on the intellectual plane, on which different levels of consciousness give different meanings to the same words.

Suggestions for further reading

There is no separate edition of *The Friar's Tale*, but the standard edition of Chaucer's work is *The Works of Geoffrey Chaucer*, ed. F. N. Robinson (Oxford University Press, 2nd edn, 1957). Anyone who had read the texts included in this collection would be able to read most of *The Canterbury Tales* without great difficulty.

There has been little sustained comment on *The Friar's Tale* in book form, but there is a useful chapter in T. W. Craik, *The Comic Tales of Chaucer* (London, Methuen, 1964). Those to whom the periodical *Mediaeval Studies* is available will find in vol. XXI (1959), pp. 17–35, an excellent article by Earle Birney, '"After his Ymage": The Central Ironies of *The Friar's Tale*'. Of the many general studies of Chaucer, the following seem to us among the best:

Nevill Coghill, *The Poet Chaucer* (Oxford University Press, 1949)
John Lawlor, *Chaucer* (London, Hutchinson, 1968)
Charles Muscatine, *Chaucer and the French Tradition* (Berkeley, University of California Press, 1957)

The Friar's Tale

Whilom ther was dwellinge in my contree
An erchedeken, a man of heigh degree,
That boldely dide execucioun
In punishinge of fornicacioun,
Of wicchecraft, and eek of bawderye,   5
Of diffamacioun, and avowtrye,
Of chirche reves, and of testaments,
Of contractes and of lakke of sacraments,
Of usure, and of simonye also.
But certes, lechours dide he grettest wo—   10
They sholde singen if that they were hent—
And smalle titheres weren foule yshent,
If any persoun wolde upon hem plaine.
There mighte asterte him no pecunial paine.
For smalle tithes and for small offringe   15
He made the peple pitously to singe.
For er the bishop caughte hem with his hook,
They weren in the erchedeknes book.
Thanne hadde he, thurgh his jurisdiccioun,
Power to don on hem correccioun.   20
He hadde a somnour redy to his hond;
A slyer boye nas non in Engelond;
For subtilly he hadde his espiaille,
That taughte him well wher that him mighte availle.
He coude spare of lechours on or two,   25
To techen him to foure and twenty mo.
For thogh this somnour wood were as an hare,
To telle his harlotry I wol nat spare;
For we been out of his correccioun;
They han of us no jurisdiccioun,   30
Ne nevere shullen, terme of alle hir lives.
    'Peter! so been the women of the stives,'
Quod the Somnour, 'yput out of oure cure!'
    'Pees! with mischance and with misaventure!'
Thus saide oure Host, 'and lat him telle his tale.   35
Now telleth forth, though that the Somnour gale;
Ne spareth nat, myn owne maister deere.'

1	*Whilom* once *my contree* my parts
2	*erchedeken* archdeacon (who presided over the local ecclesiastical court)
3	*dide execucioun* executed judgment
6	*diffamacioun* slander *avowtrye* adultery
7	*chirche reves* robberies from churches
7–8	*testaments . . . contractes* (In these cases, the archdeacon executes judgment, but this does not imply punishment.)
8	*lakke of* failure to take
9	*simonye* buying or selling ecclesiastical preferment
11	*singen* i.e. cry out in pain *hent* caught
12	And those who paid insufficient tithes were severely punished
13	*persoun* parson *upon hem plaine* lay a complaint against them
14	No fine could ever escape him
15	*smalle . . . small* i.e. too small
17	*hook* i.e. the hooked end of his crozier
21	*somnour* summoner (who summoned delinquents to appear before the ecclesiastical court)
22	*nas* there was not
23	For he skilfully kept a gang of spies
24	*taughte* showed *that . . . availle* there was advantage for him
25–6	i.e. he could afford to let off one or two lechers on condition that they would act as informers
26	*techen* direct
27	*this somnour* i.e. the pilgrim-summoner *wood* mad
28	*harlotry* villainy
29	*we* i.e. friars *out . . . correccioun* outside his power
31	*terme . . . lives* as long as they live
32	*stives* stews (i.e. brothels)
33	*cure* supervision
34	*mischance . . . misaventure* Both words mean 'bad luck'.
36	*telleth forth* get on with your storytelling *gale* cries out

This false theef, this somnour, quod the Frere,
Hadde alway bawdes redy to his hond
As any hawk to lure in Engelond,   40
That tolde him all the secree that they knewe;
For hire acqueyntaunce was nat come of newe.
They weren his approwours prively.
He took himself a greet profit therby;
His maister knew nat alway what he wan.   45
Withouten mandement a lewed man
He coude somne, on paine of Cristes curs,
And they were glade for to fille his purs,
And make him grete feestes atte nale.
And right as Judas hadde purses smalle,   50
And was a theef, right swich a theef was he;
His maister hadde but half his duetee.
He was, if I shall yeven him his laude,
A theef, and eek a somnour, and a bawde.
He hadde eek wenches at his retenue,   55
That, wheither that sir Robert or sir Huwe,
Or Jakke, or Rauf, or whoso that it were
That lay by hem, they tolde it in his ere.
Thus was the wenche and he of oon assent;
And he wolde fecche a feined mandement,   60
And somne hem to chapitre bothe two,
And pile the man, and lete the wenche go.
Thanne wolde he seye, 'Frend, I shall for thy sake
Do striken hire out of oure lettres blake;
Thee thar namoore as in this cas travaille.   65
I am thy frend, there I thee may availle.'
Certain he knew of briberies mo
Than possible is to telle in yeres two.
For in this world nis dogge for the bowe
That can an hurt deer from an hool yknowe   70
Bet than this somnour knew a sly lechour,
Or an avowtier, or a paramour.
And for that was the fruit of all his rente,
Therfore on it he sette all his entente.
    And so bifell that ones on a day   75
This somnour, evere waiting on his prey,
Rood for to somne an old widwe, a ribibe,
Feininge a cause, for he wolde bribe.

39	*bawdes redy* procurers (as) ready
40	*lure* device used by the falconer to recall a hawk
41	*secree* secret things
42	*come of newe* newly made
43	*approwours* agents *prively* secretly
45	*wan* gained, made
46	*mandement* summons *lewed* ignorant
47	*coude somne* knew how to summon
49	*atte nale* (i.e. *atten ale*) at the alehouse
52	*his duetee* what was due to him
53	*yeven him his laude* praise him as he deserves
55	*at his retenue* who were retained by him
56	*sir* The title implies that they were priests.
57	*Rauf* Ralph *whoso ... were* whoever it might be
58	*lay by* slept with
59	*of oon assent* in agreement
60	*feined mandement* false summons
61	*chapitre* court
62	*pile* plunder
64	Have her struck out of our records
65	You need trouble no more over this case
66	*there ... availle* where I can be of use to you
69	*nis ... bowe* there is not a hunting-dog
70	That can tell a wounded deer from an unwounded one
71	*Bet* better
72	*avowtier* adulterer *paramour* concubine
73	And because that was the main part of his whole income
74	*entente* attention
76	*waiting on* on the watch for
77	*ribibe* old bag (slang term for old woman, literally 'fiddle')
78	*Feininge* pretending *wolde bribe* wished to be bribed

And happed that he saugh bifore him ride
A gay yeman, under a forest side.   80
A bowe he bar, and arwes brighte and keene;
He hadde upon a courtepy of greene,
An hat upon his heed with frenges blake.
    'Sire,' quod this somnour, 'hail, and well atake!'
'Welcome,' quod he, 'and every good felawe!   85
Wher ridestow, under this greenewoode shawe?'
Saide this yeman, 'wiltow fer today?'
    This somnour him answerde and seyde, 'Nay;
Here faste by,' quod he, 'is myn entente
To riden, for to raisen up a rente   90
That longeth to my lordes duetee.'
    'Artow thanne a bailly?' 'Ye,' quod he.
(He durste nat, for verray filthe and shame
Saye that he was a somnour, for the name.)
    'Depardieux,' quod this yeman, 'deere brother,   95
Thou art a bailly, and I am another.
I am unknowen as in this contree;
Of thyn aquaintaunce I wolde praye thee,
And eek of bretherhede, if that you leste.
I have gold and silver in my cheste;   100
If that thee happe to comen in oure shire,
All shall be thyn, right as thou wolt desire.'
    'Grantmercy,' quod this somnour, 'by my faith!'
Everich in otheres hand his trouthe laith,
For to be sworne bretheren till they deye.   105
In daliaunce they riden forth and playe.
    This somnour, which that was as full of jangles
As full of venim been thise waryangles,
And evere enquering upon every thing,
'Brother,' quod he, 'where is now youre dwelling,   110
Another day if that I sholde you seeche?'
    This yeman him answerde in softe speeche:
'Brother,' quod he, 'fer in the north contree,
Whereas I hope som time I shall thee see.
Er we departe, I shall thee so well wisse   115
That of myn hous ne shaltow nevere misse.'
    'Now, brother,' quod this somnour, 'I you praye,
Teche me, whil that we riden by the waye,
Sin that ye been a baillif as am I,

80	*yeman* yeoman (small independent landowner)
	under ... side alongside a forest
82	*courtepy* short coat
83	*frenges* fringes
84	*atake* overtaken
85	*felawe* companion
86	*greenewoode shawe* leafy wood
87	*wiltow fer* do you intend to go far
90–1	*raisen ... duetee* collect some revenue that is owing to my lord
92	*bailly* steward
93	*filthe* disgrace
94	*for the name* because of their reputation
95	*Depardieux* in God's name
97	*as ... contree* so far as these parts are concerned
98–9	I would be glad to become acquainted with you, and also to enter into alliance, if you please. (Note that in *you leste* he momentarily uses the deferential plural form.)
103	*Grantmercy* many thanks
104	Each of them pledges his faith to the other by shaking hands
106	Chatting together, they ride on and amuse themselves
107	*jangles* chatter
108	As shrikes (butcher birds) are full of venom
109	*enquering upon* poking into
111	*seeche* seek
113	The devil was generally understood to live in the north (see Isaiah 14.13, where Lucifer says 'I will sit ... in the sides of the north'), and this is the first hint, except perhaps for the black fringes on his hat, of the 'yeoman's' true identity.
115	*departe* part *thee ... wisse* give you such good directions
116	That thou shalt never fail to reach my house
119	*Sin that* since

Som subtiltee, and tell me faithfully   120
In myn office how that I may most winne;
And spareth nat for conscience ne sinne,
But as my brother tell me, how do ye.'
  'Now, by my trouthe, brother deere,' saide he,
'As I shall tellen thee a faithful tale,   125
My wages been full streite and full smalle.
My lorde is hard to me and daungerous,
And myn office is full laborous,
And therfore by extorcions I live.
For soothe, I take all that men wol me yive.   130
Algate, by sleighte or by violence,
Fro yeer to yeer I winne all my dispence.
I can no bettre telle, faithfully.'
  'Now certes,' quod this somnour, 'so fare I.
I spare nat to taken, God it wot,   135
But if it be too hevy or too hot.
What I may get in conseil prively,
No manner conscience of that have I;
Nere myn extorcioun, I mighte nat liven.
Ne of swiche japes wol I nat be shriven;   140
Stomak ne conscience ne knowe I noon;
I shrewe thise shrifte-fadres everychoon.
Well be we met, by God and by Saint Jame!
But, leeve brother, tell me thanne thy name,'
Quod this somnour. In this meene while   145
This yeman gan a littel for to smile.
  'Brother,' quod he, 'wiltow that I thee telle?
I am a feend; my dwelling is in helle,
And here I ride aboute my purchasing,
To wit wher men wol yeve me any thing.   150
My purchas is th'effect of all my rente.
Looke how thou ridest for the same entente,
To winne good, thou rekkest nevere how,
Right so fare I, for ride wolde I now
Unto the worldes ende for a preye.'   155
  'A!' quod this somnour, 'benedicite! what say ye?
I wende ye were a yeman trewely.
Ye han a mannes shap as well as I;
Han ye a figure thanne determinat
In helle, ther ye been in youre estat?'   160

120	*subtiltee* trick
121	*office* employment *winne* gain, make
122	*sinne* i.e. fear of sin
123	*how do ye* how you behave
124	*trouthe* honour
125	*faithful* reliable
126	*streite* scanty
127	*daungerous* grudging
130	*yive* give
131	*Algate* at any rate *sleighte* cunning
132	*dispence* money I need to spend
135	*spare* refrain
136	A proverbial expression.
137	*conseil* secret
138	*manner* kind of
139	*Nere* were it not for
140	*swiche japes* such tricks *shriven* confessed
141	*Stomak* compassion
142	I curse every one of those priests who hold confessions
144	*leeve* dear
149	*aboute my purchasing* acquiring what I can
150	*wit wher* find out where (or possibly 'whether')
151	What I pick up amounts to my whole income
152	*Looke how* just as *entente* purpose
153	*winne good* acquire wealth *rekkest* carest
154	*ride ... now* at this moment I would be willing to ride
156	*benedicite* (pronounced 'ben'dis'tee') bless you (The plural forms in this speech show a proper respect for the diabolic.)
157	*wende* supposed
159	*figure thanne determinat* fixed appearance then
160	*ther* where *estat* proper state

'Nay, certainly,' quod he, 'there have we noon;
But whan us liketh, we can take us oon,
Or elles make you seeme we been shape
Somtime lyk a man, or lyk an ape—
Or lyk an angel can I ride or go.   165
It is no wonder thing though it be so;
A lousy jogelour can deceive thee,
And pardee, yet can I more craft than he.'
    'Why,' quod this somnour, 'ride ye thanne or goon
In sondry shap, and nat alway in oon?'   170
    'For we,' quod he, 'wol us swiche formes make
As most able is oure preyes for to take.'
    'What maketh you to han all this labour?'
    'Full many a cause, leeve sire somnour,'
Saide this feend, 'but alle thing hath time.   175
The day is short, and it is passed prime,
And yet ne wan I nothing in this day.
I wol entende to winning, if I may,
And nat entende oure wittes to declare.
For, brother myn, thy wit is all too bare   180
To understonde, although I tolde hem thee.
But, for thou axest why labouren we:
For somtime we been Goddes instruments,
And meenes to doon his comandements,
Whan that him list, upon his creatures,   185
In diverse art and in diverse figures.
Withouten him we have no might, certain,
If that him list to stonden theragain.
And somtime, at oure prayere, han we leve
Only the body and nat the soule to greve;   190
Witnesse on Job, whom that we diden wo.
And somtime han we might of bothe two,
This is to sayn, of soule and body eke.
And somtime be we suffred for to seeke
Upon a man, and doon his soule unreste,   195
And nat his body, and all is for the beste.
Whan he withstandeth oure temptacioun,
It is a cause of his savacioun,
All be it that it was nat oure entente
He sholde be sauf, but that we wolde him hente.   200
And somtime be we servant unto man,

161 The devil takes the deferential form to be a genuine plural, and to apply to devils generally.

162 *us liketh* it pleases us *us oon* one (shape) for ourselves

163 *you seeme* it appear to you *shape* shaped

165 Devils were supposed to be able to take on any appearance they chose to human eyes, even that of an angel. *go* walk

167 *lousy jogelour* filthy juggler (as in modern slang, *lousy* could mean contemptible in a general sense, as well as lice-infested)

168 *can . . . craft* I possess greater skill

169 *Why* (introducing a question, not an exclamation)

goon walk (*ride or go* is a formula, as in line 165)

170 *sondry shap* various shapes

171 *For* because *wol . . . make* wish to make such forms for ourselves

172 *take* capture

174–5 The devil's reticence no doubt conceals the answer, 'In order to capture for hell human souls such as yours'.

176 *prime* early morning (6–9 a.m.)

177 *ne . . . nothing* I have not made anything

178 *entende* attend

179 *oure . . . declare* expressing our (i.e. the devils') thoughts

180 *wit* intelligence *bare* scanty

182 *axest* askest

183 *For* because

184 And means by which his commandments are performed

185 *Whan . . . list* when it pleases him

186 By various skills and in various appearances

187 *might* power

188 If it pleases him to oppose our intentions

189 *han we leve* we have permission

190 *greve* harm

191 *whom . . . wo* to whom we caused misery

194 *suffred* permitted

194–5 *seeke/Upon* attack

195 *doon* cause

198 *savacioun* salvation

200 *sauf* saved *hente* seize

201–3 There are medieval legends of how devils served St Dunstan and various apostles.

As to the erchebishop Saint Dunstan,
And to the apostles servant eek was I.'
    'Yet tell me,' quod the somnour, 'faithfully,
Make ye you newe bodies thus alway   205
Of elements?' The feend answerde, 'Nay.
Somtime we feine, and somtime we arise
With dede bodies, in full sondry wise,
And speke as renably and faire and well
As to the Phitonissa dide Samuel.   210
(And yet wol som men saye it was nat he;
I do no fors of youre divinitee.)
But o thing warne I thee, I wol nat jape:
Thou wolt algates wite how we been shape?
Thou shalt herafterward, my brother deere,   215
Come there thee needeth nat of me to leere.
For thou shalt, by thyn owne experience,
Conne in a chaier rede of this sentence
Bet than Virgile, while he was on live,
Or Dant also. Now let us ride blive,   220
For I wole holde compaignye with thee
Till it be so that thou forsake me.'
    'Nay,' quod this somnour, 'that shall nat bitide!
I am a yeman, knowen is full wide;
My trouthe wol I holde, as in this cas.   225
For though thou were the devel Sathanas,
My trouthe wol I holde to my brother,
As I am sworn, and ech of us till other,
For to be trewe brother in this cas;
And bothe we goon abouten oure purchas.   230
Tak thou thy part, what that men wol thee yive,
And I shall myn; thus may we bothe live.
And if that any of us have more than other,
Lat him be trewe, and parte it with his brother.'
    'I graunte,' quod the devel, 'by my fay.'   235
And with that word they riden forth hir way.
And right at the entring of the townes ende
To which this somnour shoop him for to wende,
They saw a cart that charged was with hay,
Which that a cartere drof forth in his way.   240
Deep was the way, for which the carte stood.
The cartere smot, and cride as he were wood,

205	*you* for yourselves
206	*Of elements* i.e. out of the four elements, the basic components of matter according to medieval physics
207	*feine* i.e. deceive men's eyes into seeing what is not there at all
208	*full sondry wise* a whole variety of ways
209	*renably* fluently *faire* clearly
210	*Phitonissa* the witch of Endor, who at Saul's request raised up the spirit of Samuel (see I Samuel 28.7 ff.)
211	(Some medieval scholars took the view that it was not really Samuel's spirit, but a diabolic impersonation.)
212	*do ... of* do not care about (The devil, amusingly, is in a position to despise mere human speculation about such matters.)
213	*jape* jest
214	You wish to know completely how we get our shapes?
216	*thee needeth nat* it will be unnecessary for you *leere* learn
218	Be capable of giving lectures on this subject from a professorial chair
219	*Bet* better
219–20	Virgil wrote about the other world in *Aeneid*, Book VI, and Dante in the *Divine Comedy*.
220	*blive* quickly
222	*forsake* abandon (with a pun on the slightly different sense, 'renounce': it is never going to come about that the summoner will renounce the devil)
224	*knowen is* it is known
225	*trouthe* pledged word *as ... cas* (perhaps implying, 'for this once')
228	*till other* to the other
230	*abouten oure purchas* picking up what we can
231–4	(He is proposing that each of them should collect what he can, and that they should then share the proceeds equally between them.)
231	*what that* whatever
234	*parte* share
235	*graunte* agree *fay* faith
237	*townes ende* edge of the town
238	*shoop ... wende* was intending to make his way
239	*charged* loaded
240	*drof ... way* was driving forward on the way he had to go
241	The road was bad (i.e. deeply marked with ruts and stones), for which reason the cart had come to a halt
242	*smot* lashed out (at the horses) *as* as if *wood* mad

'Hayt, Brok! hayt, Scot! what spare ye for the stones?
The feend,' quod he, 'you feche, body and bones,
As ferforthly as evere were ye foled,   245
So muche wo as I have with you tholed!
The devel have all, bothe hors and cart and hay!'
      This somnour saide, 'Heere shall we have a play.'
And neer the feend he drow, as noght ne were,
Full prively, and rowned in his ere: 250
'Herkne, my brother, herkne, by thy faith!
Herestow nat how that the cartere saith?
Hent it anon, for he hath yeve it thee,
Bothe hay and cart, and eek his caples three.'
      'Nay,' quod the devel, 'Got wot, never a deel!   255
It is nat his entente, trust me weell.
Axe him thyself, if thou nat trowest me;
Or elles stint a while, and thou shalt see.'
      This cartere thakketh his hors upon the croupe,
And they bigonne to drawen and to stoupe.   260
'Hayt! now,' quod he, 'ther Jhesu Crist you blesse,
And all his handwerk, bothe more and lesse!
That was well twight, myn owene lyard boy.
I pray God save thee, and Sainte Loy!
Now is my cart out of the slough, pardee!'   265
      'Lo, brother,' quod the feend, 'what tolde I thee?
Here may ye see, myn owne deere brother,
The carl spak o thing, but he thoughte another.
Lat us go forth abouten oure viage;
Here winne I nothing upon cariage.'   270
      Whan that they comen somwhat out of towne,
This somnour to his brother gan to rowne:
'Brother,' quod he, 'here woneth an old rebekke,
That hadde almost as lief to lese hire nekke
As for to yeve a penny of hir good.   275
I wole han twelf pens, though that she be wood,
Or I wol sompne hire unto oure office;
And yet, God wot, of hire knowe I no vice.
But for thou canst nat, as in this contree,
Winne thy cost, tak here ensample of me.'   280
      This somnour clappeth at the widwes gate.
'Com out,' quod he, 'thou olde viritrate!
I trowe thou hast som frere or preest with thee.'

243	*Hayt* gee-up! *Brok ... Scot* (common horses' names)
	what ... for why do you stop because of
244	*feche* (like *have* in line 247, this expresses a wish.)
245	As complete as you came into the world
246	*tholed* suffered
248	*a play* entertainment
249	*as ... were* as if nothing were happening
250	*rowned* whispered
253	*Hent it anon* seize it at once *yeve* given
254	*caples* cart-horses
255	*never a deel* not a bit
256	*his entente* what he intends
257	*thou nat trowest* you do not believe
258	*stint* stop
259	*thakketh* pats *croupe* rump
260	*drawen* pull *stoupe* lean forward
262	*handwerk* work of his hands
263	*twight* pulled *lyard* grey (This is presumably the leading horse in the team of three; *Brok*, mentioned first in line 243, meaning 'badger', was a name given to grey horses.)
264	*Loy* Eligius, patron saint of carriers
265	*pardee* by God
268	*carl* fellow
269	*viage* journey
270	*upon cariage* out of carting
272	*rowne* whisper
273	*rebekke* old woman (like *ribibe* in line 77, a slang term, meaning literally 'fiddle')
274	*lief ... nekke* soon lose her life (literally 'neck')
275	*good* money, possessions
276	*though ... wood* even if it drives her mad
277	*sompne* summon
279	*as ... contree* in these parts
280	Cover your expenses, follow my example
281	*clappeth* knocks
282	*viritrate* hag
283	(He implies, for immoral purposes.)

'Who clappeth?' saide this wyf, 'benedicitee!
God save you, sire, what is youre sweete wille?'   285
      'I have,' quod he, 'of somonse here a bille;
Up paine of cursing, looke that thou be
Tomorn bifore the erchedeknes knee,
T'answere to the court of certain thinges.'
      'Now, Lord,' quod she, 'Crist Jhesu, king of kinges,   290
So wisly helpe me, as I ne may.
I have been sik, and that full many a day.
I may nat go so fer,' quod she, 'ne ride,
But I be deed, so priketh it in my side.
May I nat axe a libel, sire somnour,   295
And answere there by my procuratour
To swich thing as men wole opposen me?'
      'Yis,' quod this somnour, 'pay anon, lat see,
Twelf pens to me, and I wol thee acquite.
I shall no profit han therby but lite;   300
My maister hath the profit, and nat I.
Com of, and lat me riden hastily;
Yif me twelf pens, I may no lenger tarrye.'
      'Twelf pens!' quod she, 'now, lady Sainte Marye
So wisly help me out of care and sinne,   305
This wide world though that I sholde winne,
Ne have I nat twelf pens withinne myn hold.
Ye knowen well that I am povre and old;
Kithe youre almesse on me, povre wreche.'
      'Nay thanne,' quod he, 'the foule feend me feche   310
If I th'excuse, though thou shull be spilt!'
      'Allas!' quod she, 'Got wot, I have no gilt.'
      'Pay me,' quod he, 'or by the sweete Sainte Anne,
As I wol bere away thy newe panne
For dette which thou owest me of old.   315
Whan that thou madest thyn housbonde cokewold,
I paide at hom for thy correccioun.'
      'Thou lixt!' quod she, 'by my savacioun,
Ne was I nevere er now, widwe ne wyf,
Somoned unto youre court in all my lyf;   320
Ne nevere I nas but of my bodye trewe!
Unto the devel blak and rough of hewe
Yeve I thy body and my panne also!'
      And whan the devel herde hire cursen so

286   *bille* writ
287   *Up ... cursing* on pain of being cursed (by the church)
291   As sure as I hope (Jesus) may help me, I am unable (to be there)
293   *go* walk (cf. line 169 and note)
294   Or it will kill me, I have such a pain in my side
295   *axe a libel* request a copy (of the indictment)
296   *procuratour* legal representative
297   *opposen me* accuse me of
299   *thee acquite* get you off
300   *no ... but lite* no more than a little
302   *Com of* i.e. hand it over
305   *So wisly help* as sure as I hope (Mary) may help
307   *hold* possession
308   *povre* poor
309   *Kithe* bestow (literally, 'show')   *almesse* alms
311   If I excuse you, even though you should be ruined
312   *have no gilt* am guiltless
316   *cokewold* cuckold
317   *at hom* back at the court (?)   *correccioun* fine
318   *lixt* liest
321   Nor was I ever anything but chaste
322   *hewe* complexion

Upon hir knees, he saide in this mannere,   325
'Now, Mabely, myn owne moder deere,
Is this youre will in ernest that ye saye?'
　　'The devel,' quod she, 'so feche him er he deye,
And panne and all, bot he wol him repente!'
　　'Nay, olde stot, that is nat myn entente,'   330
Quod this somnour, 'for to repente me
For any thing that I have had of thee.
I wolde I hadde thy smok and every cloth!'
　　'Now, brother,' quod the devel, 'be nat wroth;
Thy body and this panne been mine by right.   335
Thou shalt with me to helle yet tonight,
Where thou shalt knowen of oure privetee
More than a maister of divinitee.'
And with that word this foule feend him hente;
Body and soule he with the devel wente   340
Where as that somnours han hir heritage.
And God, that maked after his image
Mankinde, save and gide us, alle and some,
And leve thise somnours goode men bicome!

328	*so feche*	may (he) fetch
329	*bot ... repente*	unless he is willing to repent
330	*stot*	(literally, 'horse')
333	*every cloth*	every one of your clothes
336	*yet tonight*	this very night
337	*privetee*	secrets
344	*leve*	grant

Short Poems

Some comments on these poems have already been made in the General Introduction (pp. 32–3). Here, before proceeding to a brief consideration of each poem separately, we wish to underline our earlier point that one cannot expect to find direct expressions of personal experience in medieval short poems; they are not 'lyrics' in the Romantic and post-Romantic sense of the word. A distinguished scholar has written of medieval poetry generally that 'in interpreting a poem, we must ask, not on what "experience" it was based, but what theme the poet set himself to treat'.[1] One consequence of this is a sense of monotony if one reads a large collection of medieval short poems. In retrospect, it becomes difficult to distinguish one poem on the Joys of the Blessed Virgin, or one appeal from the Cross, from another, because poems of this kind were created to serve the devotional purposes of other people, not usually to express the author's own religious emotions, Further, the fact that the style of medieval poetry is generally somewhat diffuse means that it tends to appear at its best in longer poems, where the poet has more room for manœuvre, and where the larger shapes of narrative can carry meaning and emotion. Hence the merit of the average short poem, considered as an isolated piece of literature—a way in which, in most cases, it was never originally intended to be considered—is disappointingly low. In spite of this, there are at least a few dozen short English poems of Chaucer's age which are of lasting literary value, and in this small collection we have tried to choose among them, balancing merit with as wide a typicality as possible.

1 Lullaby

This poem survives in a single manuscript version, dating probably from the first half of the fourteenth century. It is the earliest existing example of the lullaby in English, but it seems plain that the genre must already have been firmly established, for what we have in this poem is an ironic rehandling of the lullaby pure and simple. (One advantage

---

[1] E. R. Curtius, *European Literature and the Latin Middle Ages* (New York, Pantheon, 1953), p. 158.

of a situation in which literary genres have firm boundaries, as in the Middle Ages, is that it gives such opportunities for parody or for other kinds of oblique treatment.) The ordinary lullaby is intended to soothe the crying baby and send it to sleep; this 'lullaby' makes clear from its second line on that the child, considered as a representative of the human race in general, has much cause for weeping and that there is little comfort to be offered. The underlying assumption of the poem is that the child, like all human beings, is descended from Adam, and has therefore inherited from him the taint of original sin, long before it is of an age to commit any sins of its own. This assumption is made more and more explicit as the poem proceeds, through the references to the child's ancestors in line 4 and to Adam in lines 10, 28 and 29, until it is brought completely into the open with the painfully simple statement of the final couplet. From Adam the child has inherited not only a life of sorrow (as God ordained in Genesis 3.17–19) but also the ultimate terror of death (which God had established in Genesis 2.17 as the penalty for eating the fruit of the forbidden tree). As the second stanza points out, the condition of man is worse than that of all the other species of Creation. They can all 'do themselves some good' in this world, and only man is doomed to 'care'—a sad thought which was commonly expressed in the Middle Ages. The poem reaches its imaginative height in the evocation of death coming 'with a blast out of a well dim horre' (line 27). The terror of death became an increasingly frequent theme of literature and art in the later Middle Ages; here it is all the more potent because it is left vague, not spelled out in all the details of worms and corruption that are found in many late medieval poems. What the controlled pessimism of this poem leaves out of account, of course, is the possibility of salvation opened up by the life and death of Christ. If this is taken into account, then, contrary to what line 31 says, man *can* be a pilgrim in this world, with the hope of achieving a heavenly goal at the end of his pilgrimage. It is not to be supposed that the poet has forgotten this or would wish to deny it; it is rather that his poem is intended to stir up in its users a full sense of the wretchedness of human life as a prelude to further meditations on the greatness of what God has done for man in sacrificing his son.

2 Lenten is Come

This is a poem from the most famous and probably the best manuscript collection of Middle English short poems, the 'Harley lyrics', found in the British Museum manuscript Harley 2253, and dating from the early fourteenth century. Its strongly-marked dancing rhythm, underlined by much alliteration and carried forward by repeated rhymes, gives it a delightful sense of gaiety and vitality. It is one of an enormous number of medieval poems which celebrate the coming of spring and associate it with the rebirth of love. Springtime love is enough of a cliché, perhaps, to make it difficult for us to enter imaginatively into the meaning of the return of spring for a society far less securely protected than our own against the elements and hunger. After a winter with no central heating, few glazed windows and little fresh food, spring must have come as the fulfilment of an unbearable need. There is also the consideration that in the Middle Ages, when most of the life in a castle or a cottage, eating, sleeping and entertainment, all took place in a single public room, the return of fine weather must have given young people a welcome chance of privacy in the woods or fields for their lovemaking. In this poem, as in many, human love is seen as part of the seasonal rhythm, one with the singing of birds and blossoming of flowers; but also nature is humanized, as the rose is seen as adorning her face and the moon as sending forth her *bleo*, a word which is frequently used in love-poems to mean not only 'radiance' but 'radiant complexion'. Spring as evoked in this poem appeals more fully to the senses than is often the case in medieval poetry. There is little generalization, but much detail—a remarkable sense of the proliferation of nature, not only in the familiar nightingales and roses, but also in thrushes and drakes, woodruff and wild thyme. Spring is not only pretty, it is full of noise and fragrance. In the midst of all this joy is the unhappiness of human lovers, because here, as in the *Lullaby*, human beings are set apart from the rest of creation, in that love comes to them as pain. Here the pain is not very deeply felt; it is absorbed into the lightness of the poem's rhythm, and if the speaker does fail to get his desire of his beloved, and flees like Sir Orfeo into the woods, he will find springtime there too. There is nothing naive or primitive in the poem's identification of love and spring; the speaker keeps at a certain sardonic distance from all this blooming and chattering, silently juxtaposing the pride of women with the wooing of serpents.

3 For Women

The handwriting of the only manuscript version of this poem is later than our period, but the poem itself need not be so late. As its opening line suggests, it is an answer to the dispraise of women which is common enough in the Middle Ages to form a distinct genre of the short poem. The first stanza offers two traditional arguments for seeing this misogynism as shameful: we are all born of women, and the reputation of all women has been cleansed of the blot cast on it by Eve, by the existence of the Blessed Virgin, through whose son mankind was redeemed. But the poem then passes on to a charmingly literal defence of women in their (unliberated) everyday life. What would we do without women to sing us asleep when we are babies, and to do our washing, then and later? Women serve men dutifully, and yet their lot is hard. The poem's rhythm is cheerful, however, and does not suggest either depression or incipient revolt. Perhaps it was written by a man.

4 Quia Amore Langueo

The large number of manuscript versions of this poem, often differing in detail one from another, indicate that it was widely read. It dates from about 1400, and brings together several sets of conventions to create a powerful emotional effect. It belongs to the central movement of medieval Christian devotion, which goes back to St Anselm and St Bernard in the early Middle Ages, and aims to bring men to Christianity by emotional means. The love of God is treated as human love, mediated through the human nature of Christ and through Christ's mother, and demanding human love in return.

The outer framework of the poem is that of dream or vision. The speaker is 'musing' by night when, in spiritual vision, the statue of the Blessed Virgin in a niche seems to come to life and to address a *complaint* (line 5) to mankind in general. The *complaint*, or lamentation, is itself a traditional poetic genre, in which the speaker is frequently either the Virgin or Christ on the cross, appealing to man to turn away from his worldly concerns and passions and to respond to God's love with love of his own. In this poem the Virgin states from the beginning her double relationship to man, as his sister (since she is herself human) and as his mother (by being the mother of Christ, who took on human nature). Thus the emotional appeal is intensified. Her appeal as mother is particularly strong, and in an age which took it for granted that children should revere their parents, a line such as 'Bid me, my childe, and I shall go' (22) would be especially moving, in its implication of a reversal of the norm—a mother humbly obeying her rebellious son (as shocking perhaps as the scene in *King Lear* in which the old king kneels to his daughters). And as sister, she is no more than man's vulnerable equal. A further aspect of her appeal is the thought of all that her son suffered, and that she suffered through him, for the sake of mankind; and at lines 49–55 and 65–7 she turns from mankind to address Christ himself—though the shift is not abrupt, in a context in which she is mother of both. Mary's appeal to man can be more unqualified even than Christ's, because whereas Christ is judge as well as redeemer, she is simply mediatrix, begging her son, with a mother's irresistible pathos, to show mercy rather than justice towards mankind. The poem concludes with a further daring shift in the complex of family relationships, calling on man to enter soon into the royal inheritance which is legally entailed upon him, and to 'Take me for thy wife'. To a modern reader this may even seem to carry shocking implications of incest, but it has been implied from the beginning by the refrain line, 'Quia amore langueo'. This is taken from the Song of Songs (or Song of Solomon), a love-poem in the Old Testament which had long been interpreted as being addressed by God to the Church or to the individual soul, and in which the beloved is addressed as both sister and spouse. The language and the emotions of secular love poetry—'Looke on thy love thus languishing' (90)—are drawn into the service of religion, as so often in medieval literature, and in a way parallel to the use of religious language in secular poetry (mocked by Chaucer in *To Rosemounde*). The resulting effect is piquant and poignant, and it is justified by the assumption that Christ's love for mankind subsumes and purifies all forms of human passion. A poem such as this, with its direct human appeal and its daring intellectual conceits, helps one to realize how much the seventeenth-century devotional poets, such as Donne and Herbert, owe to medieval traditions of thought and feeling.

5   Chaucer: Balade de Bon Conseyl

This poem of Chaucer's survives in over twenty manuscript copies, more than any of his other short poems. Only one of them, however, includes the 'Envoy', which may therefore have been added later, and is conceivably not by Chaucer at all. The *balade* was a metrical form taken over by Chaucer from the French court poets of the fourteenth century, and it demanded considerable virtuosity to keep up the same pair of rhyme-sounds not only through one stanza but through three, and here through a fourth also, in the 'Envoy' addressing the poem to a specific friend or patron. Lines 6 and 13, parallel in syntax and meaning, indicate that the poem was addressed to a man set in authority over others—one of the courtiers for whom Chaucer wrote most of his work. In the 'Envoy' the recipient is identified as Sir Philip de la Vache, a member of the court circle with whom Chaucer was associated. The undignified pun on his name, identifying him personally as the 'beast' which is urged in line 18 to leave its stall, suggests that the relationship was friendly, as between equals. It has been suggested that the poem, or at least the 'Envoy', may date from the late 1380s, when Vache seems to have been out of favour at court, and might have welcomed this call from earthly to heavenly values as a consolation.

The poem explores and defines one of the fundamental values in the ethic of Chaucer and other poets of his time: *trouthe*. Gawain is much concerned with his truth, in the sense of integrity and reliability, and in *Piers Plowman* Truth is one of the names of God. This second meaning is probably implied, along with the first, in the refrain-line of Chaucer's poem, which derives from John 8.32: 'And you shall know the truth;

and the truth shall make you free.' It is not only that the man who follows the poem's injunctions will be liberated from bondage to 'this world', but that his own integrity will draw down the help of Christ, who is Truth, and bring him to salvation. The first two stanzas of the poem express with terse weightiness a kind of pessimistic conservatism, which is partly derived from Chaucer's favourite philosophical writer, the late Roman Boethius, but is also part of the received wisdom of the Middle Ages. The poem sees the world as dominated by the goddess Fortuna, the personified image of transitoriness and instability, with her constantly-turning wheel. Its emphasis is not only on doing what you ought but on not trying to do too much. 'Tempest thee noght all crooked to redresse' (8), it advises, because to be over-ambitious in doing right is itself to put oneself in the power of the world and to court destruction. This doctrine is made particularly appealing by the homely images of the awl, which will pierce anyone who tries to prick it, and the jug, which inevitably loses its quarrel with the wall. The third stanza moves from this counsel of submissiveness or patience (the same lesson that Jonah had to learn in the poem *Patience*—'That thee is sent, receive in buxumnesse' (15)) to a more optimistic and dynamic doctrine, which is also more expressly religious: turn from this world, which is not your true homeland, to the next, which is. In the 'Envoy' the religious note becomes still more explicit, as Vache is enjoined to pray to God for himself and others, that they may gain a heavenly reward; that will be the liberation to which *trouthe* will finally lead them.

6 Chaucer: Balade to Rosemounde

Unlike the preceding *balade*, with its direct moral appeal, this courtly parody exists in only one manuscript, which dates from the later fifteenth century and also includes a text of *Troilus and Criseyde*. The attribution to Chaucer is generally accepted, but cannot be regarded as quite certain. It begins with an apparently serious commitment to the extreme of romantic devotion: the beloved Lady is presented in religious terms as a shrine of beauty for the whole known world, and her lover is dedicated to her service for ever, despite her total unresponsiveness—she will not even give him the pleasure of conversation. His attitude is very similar to that expressed in *The Parliament of Fowls* by the turtle-dove, who is shocked at the vulgar goose's suggestion that a lover who gets no response from the object of his love should simply turn elsewhere:

> 'Nay, God forbede a lovere shulde chaunge!'
> The turtle saide, and wex for shame all red,
> 'Though that his lady everemore be straunge,
> Yit lat him serve hire ever, till he be ded.'

In the *Parliament* this attitude is seen as noble, though it has just the touch of absurdity which comes from the idea of a mere bird expressing such a view, and blushing as it does so. In this *balade*, it is the absurdity of the lover's posture which is emphasized, and its absurdity is brought out especially by elements of excess in the poem's imagery. Already in the first stanza there is something a little ridiculous about the round cheeks as red as a ruby attributed to Rosemounde. It is usually lips, not cheeks, that are compared to rubies, and if her cheeks are round as well as shiny red she must be more like a country girl than a courtly lady. In the second stanza comes the further uncourtliness of the lover weeping a whole tubful of tears, and the suggestions of affectation and squeakiness in the 'out-twining' of the Lady's voice. Uncourtliness reaches its culmination in the ludicrous image at the beginning of the third stanza of the lover being drenched in love like a pike in sauce, and this brings out the gross exaggeration involved in his comparison of himself with Tristram, the tragic lover celebrated in many romances. The poem ends on a note of petulant insistence: he *will* be her slave, even if she does not want him to. Chaucer regularly presents himself in his poetry as one whose interest in love is purely theoretical, and who lacks the experience of reciprocal love which belongs to the truly courtly. Here he takes his ironic self-depreciation a stage further, almost indeed to the extent of farce, as he adopts the postures of romantic love, but with carefully calculated clumsiness.

7 Blacksmiths

This poem survives in a single manuscript, of the early fifteenth century. It could well have been composed earlier, though alliterative verse did go on being written in the traditional style in the fifteenth century. It is a very rare example of a short poem in unrhymed alliterative lines, and shows one aspect of alliterative poetry at its best: violence, vigour, and onomatopoeia. Perhaps more than any other poem in this book, it demands to be read aloud, since so many of its words are intended simply to imitate the clamour of smiths and their work. It expresses, with enormous relish, both their noise and the fury of the speaker who is kept awake by it. No-one who has read it can suppose that industrial noise is only a modern problem.

Suggestions for further reading

Larger selections of medieval short poems can be found in R. T. Davies (ed.) *Medieval English Lyrics* (London, Faber and Faber, 1963) and Theodore Silverstein (ed.), *Medieval English Lyrics* (London, Edward Arnold, York Medieval Texts, 1971).

Peter Dronke, *The Medieval Lyric* (London, Hutchinson, 1968)

George Kane, *Middle English Literature* (London, Methuen, 1951), Part II

Rosemary Woolf, *The English Religious Lyric in the Middle Ages* (Oxford, Clarendon Press, 1968)

1 Lullaby

Lollay, lollay, littil child, why weepestou so sore?
Needes mostou weepe: hit was iyarked thee yore
Ever to lib in sorrow, and sich and mourne therfore
As thine eldren did er this, while hi alives wore.
  Lollay, lollay, littil child, child lollay, lullow,   5
  Into uncouth world icomen so artou!

Bestes and thos fowles, the fisses in the floode,
And euch shef alives, imaked of bone and bloode,
Whan hi cometh to the world hi doth hamsilf sum goode—
All bot the wrech brol that is of Adames bloode.   10
  Lollay, lollay, littil child, to care artou bemette,
  Thou nost noght this worldes wilde bifor thee is isette.

Child, if betideth that thou shalt thrive and thee,
Thench thou wer ifostred up thy moder knee;
Ever hab mund in thy hert of thos thinges three: 15
Whan thou comest, what thou art, and what shall com of thee.
  Lollay, lollay, littil child, child lollay, lollay,
  With sorrow thou com into this world, with sorrow shalt
    wend away.

Ne tristou to this world, hit is thy foul fo.
The rich he maketh pouer, the pouer rich also;   20
Hit turneth wo to well and ek well to wo.
Ne trist no man to this world, while hit turneth so.
  Lollay, lollay, littil child, thy foote is in the wheele;
  Thou nost whoder turne to wo other weele.

Child, thou art a pilgrim in wikedness ibore: 25
Thou wandrest in this fals world; thou looke thee bifore!
Deth shall com with a blast out of a well dim horre,
Adames kin down to cast, himsilf hath ido before.
  Lollay, lollay, littil child, so wo thee worp Adam,
  In the lond of paradis, throgh wikedness of Satan.   30

1   *Lenten* spring   *to towne* among men
2   *blosmen* flowers   *briddes rowne* song of birds
4   Daisies in the valleys
6   Each bird sings its song
7   The thrush keeps on sounding his warning notes
8   Their winter misery has gone
9   *wooderofe* woodruff (a low-growing plant, with white flowers and sweet-scented leaves)
10–11 The birds sing in vast numbers and warble beautifully in their joy
13   *raileth hire rode* displays its blossoms (literally, 'puts on her face')
14   *lighte* bright
15   All grow with a will
16   *mandeth* sends out   *bleo* radiance
17   *lossom* lovely   *seo* see
18   *fille* wild thyme
19–24 The wild drakes woo, the animals please their mates like a stream that flows softly; the passionate man laments, and so do others; I know that I am one of those who are unhappy for love.
26   *seemly* lovely
27   *breme* brightly
28   *donketh the downes* wet the hillsides
29–30 Two very obscure lines, whose meaning no editor has satisfactorily explained; literally, 'animals with their secret cries for giving judgments'.
31   *under cloude* beneath the earth ('clod')
33   It (i.e. spring) becomes them so well
34–6 If I do not get what I want from one (woman), I will abandon this joyful happiness, and quickly become a fugitive in the woods.

3 For Women

To unpraise women it were a shame,
For a woman was thy dame;
Our blessed Lady bereth the name
   Of all women wher that they go.

A woman is a worthy thing: 5
They do the washe and do the wringe;
'Lullay, lullay,' she dothe thee singe,
   And yet she hath but care and woo.

A woman is a worthy wight,
She serveth a man both daye and night,
Therto she putteth all her might,   10
   And yet she hath but care and woo.

1   *unpraise*   dispraise
2   *dame*   mother
3   *bereth the name*   upholds the reputation
4   *wher that*   wherever
5   *worthy thing*   noble creature
8   *wight*   being, creature
10   *putteth*   applies

In a tabernacle of a towre,
As I stoode musing on the moone,
A crowned queene, most of honoure,
Apered in gostly sight full soone.
She made complaint thus by hir one,   5
For mannes soule was wrapped in wo:
'I may nat leve mankinde allone,
    Quia amore langueo.

'I longe for love of man my brother,
I am his vokete to voide his vice;   10
I am his moder—I can none other—
Why shuld I my dere childe dispice?
Yef he me wrathe in diverse wise,
Through fleshes freelté fall me fro,
Yet must we rewe him till he rise,   15
    Quia amore langueo.

'I bid, I bide in grete longing,
I love, I loke when man woll crave,
I plaine for pité of paining;
Wolde he aske mercy, he shuld hit have.   20
Say to me, soule, and I shall save,
Bid me, my childe, and I shall go;
Thou prayde me never but my son forgave,
    Quia amore langueo.

'O wreche in the worlde, I looke on thee,   25
I see thy trespass day by day,
With lechery agains my chastité,
With pride agains my poore array;
My love abideth, thine is away;
My love thee calleth, thou stelest me fro;   30
Sue to me, sinner, I thee pray,
    Quia amore langueo.

1	*tabernacle* niche with a canopy (not where the poet is standing, but where he sees Mary appear, in place of the image)
4	*gostly* spiritual (i.e. the poet is having a religious vision)
5	*complaint* lament *by* on
6	*For* because
8	Because I languish for love (quoted from *Song of Solomon* 2.5 and 5.8)
10	I am his intercessor (cf. 'advocate') to cancel out his sin
11	*can none other* cannot do otherwise
12	*dispice* despise
13	*Yef* if *wrathe* anger, annoy
14	And fall away from me through the weakness of the flesh
15	*rewe* pity
17	*bid* pray *bide* wait
18	*loke ... crave* wait for the time when man will ask (for my help)
19	I lament out of pity for his suffering
21	*Say* speak
22	*Bid* (This combines the senses of 'pray to' and 'tell'; in the latter sense it implies a touching reversal of the normal parent-child relationship as this was understood in the Middle Ages.)
23	*but ... forgave* without my son forgiving
26	*trespass* sin (she goes on to mention two of the deadly sins)
27–8	*agains* against
30	*me fro* from me

'Moder of mercy I was for thee made;
Who needeth hit but thou alone?
To gete thee grace I am more glade   35
Than thou to aske hit; why wilt thou noon?
When said I nay, tell me, till oon?
Forsooth never yet, to frende ne foo;
When thou askest nought, than make I mone,
    Quia amore langueo.   40

'I seeke thee in wele and wrechednesse,
I seeke thee in riches and poverté;
Thou, man, beholde where thy moder is,
Why lovest thou me nat sith I love thee?
Sinful or sorry how evere thou be,   45
So welcome to me there ar no mo;
I am thy suster, right trust on me,
    Quia amore langueo.

'My childe is outlawed for thy sinne,
Mankinde is bette for his trespasse;   50
Yet prikketh mine hert that so ny my kinne
Shuld be diseased, O sone, allasse!
Thou art his brother, his moder I was;
Thou soked my pappe, thou loved man so;
Thou died for him, mine herte he has,   55
    Quia amore langueo.

'Man, leve thy sinne than for my sake;
Why shulde I gif thee that thou nat wolde?
And yet yef thou sinne, some prayere take
Or trust in me as I have tolde.   60
Am nat I thy moder called?
Why shulde I flee thee? I love thee so,
I am thy frende, I helpe beholde,
    Quia amore langueo.

'Now, sone,' she saide, 'wilt thou say nay,   65
Whan man wolde mende him of his miss?
Thou lete me never in vaine yet pray:
Than, sinfull man, see thou to this,
What day thou comest, welcome thou is,

36   *noon*   none (of it)
37   *till oon*   to anyone
39   *make I moon*   I complain
42   *wele*   prosperity
44   *sith*   since
45   *sorry*   wretched
46   There are no others who are so welcome to me
47   *right trust on*   trust directly in
49   *My childe*   (i.e. Jesus)
50   And mankind is punished for its sins
51   *prikketh*   grieves   *so ... kinne*   someone so near akin to me (as mankind)
52   *be diseased*   made to suffer
      O sone   (From here to the end of this stanza, Mary is addressing not man but Jesus.)
54   *soked my pappe*   sucked at my breast
58   *that ... wolde*   something you do not want
59   *yef* if *some prayere take*   repeat a prayer
63   *I helpe beholde*   I am a sign that help is available
66   *mende ... misse*   cure himself of his sin
68   *Than* then *see thou to*   recognize
69   *What* whatever

This hundred yere yef thou were me fro; 70
I take thee full faine, I clippe, I kisse,
    Quia amore langueo.

Now wol I sit and say no more,
Leve, and looke with grete longing;
Whan a man woll calle I wol restore; 75
I love to save him, he is mine hospringe;
No wonder yef mine herte on him hinge,
For he was my neighbore; what may I do?
For him had I this worshipping,
    And therefore *Amore langueo.* 80

'Why was I crowned and made a queene?
Why was I called of mercy the welle?
Why shuld an erthly woman beene
So high in heven above aungelle?
For thee, mankinde, the truthe I telle; 85
Thou aske me helpe, and I shall do
That I was ordained, keepe thee fro helle,
    Quia amore langueo.

'Now, man, have minde of me forever,
Looke on thy love thus languishing; 90
Late us never fro other dissevere,
Mine helpe is thine owne, creepe under my winge;
Thy sister is a queene, thy brother a kinge,
This heritage is tailed, soone come therto,
Take me for thy wife and lerne to singe, 95
    Quia amore langueo.'

70 Even if you were absent from me for a hundred years
71 *take* welcome *full faine* most gladly *clippe* embrace
74 *Leve* cease (speaking)
76 *hospringe* offspring
77 *hinge* hang(s)
78 *For... neighbore* (i.e. because she once lived on earth)
79 *worshipping* (This implies not only worship, but also honour: the supreme position of the Blessed Virgin in medieval Christianity, as expressed in the many images of her such as the one mentioned at the beginning of this poem.)
82 *welle* source, fount
87 *That... ordained* what I was appointed to do
91 *fro other dissevere* be separated from each other
93 *brother* (i.e. Jesus)
94 *tailed* reserved for you (literally, 'entailed', a legal term referring to a possession which is settled on a particular person or sequence of persons, and cannot be bequeathed to anyone else)

5 Balade de Bon Conseyl

Flee fro the prees, and dwelle with sothfastnesse,
Suffice unto thy good, though it be small;
For hord hath hate, and climbing tikelnesse,
Prees hath envye, and wele blent overal;
Savour no more than thee bihove shall;   5
Reule well thyself, that other folk canst rede;
And trouthe thee shall delivere, it is no drede.

Tempest thee noght all crooked to redresse,
In trust of hir that turneth as a ball:
Gret reste stant in littel besinesse;   10
Be war also to sporne ayains an al;
Strive not, as doth the crokke with the wall.
Daunte thyself, that dauntest otheres deede;
And trouthe thee shall delivere, it is no drede.

That thee is sent, receive in buxumnesse;   15
The wrastling for this world axeth a fall.
Her is non hom, her nis but wildernesse:
Forth, pilgrim, forth! Forth, beste, out of thy stall!
Know thy contree, look up, thank God of all;
Hold the heghe way, and lat thy gost thee lede;   20
And trouthe thee shall delivere, it is no drede.

Envoy

Therfore, thou Vache, leve thine old wrechednesse;
Unto the world leve now to be thrall;
Crye Him of mercy, that of his hy goodnesse
Made thee of noght, and in especial   25
Draw unto Him, and pray in general
For thee, and eek for other, hevenlich mede;
And trouthe thee shall delivere, it is no drede.

Bon Conseyl good advice

1   *prees* crowd   *sothfastnesse* truth
2   *Suffice ... good* be content with what you possess
3   For hoarding involves hatred, and climbing involves insecurity
4   *wele blent overal* prosperity blinds (people) completely
5–6 Take pleasure in no more than is necessary for you; you who can advise others, govern yourself well
7   *thee shall delivere* shall set you free   *drede* doubt
8   Do not upset yourself in trying to set straight all that is crooked
9   *In ... hir* trusting in Fortune (alluding to her ever-turning wheel, a favourite medieval image of the changeability of worldly affairs)
10   Serenity depends on having few anxieties
11   *to ... al* of struggling against painful necessities (literally, 'of kicking against an awl', a sharp instrument that will hurt you far more than you will hurt it)
12   *crokke* pot (The allusion is to one of Aesop's fables: if the pot fights against the wall, it will come off worst.)
13   You who get the better of others (literally, 'overcome the deeds of others'), get the better of yourself
15–16 Receive in obedience what is sent to you; if you wrestle for worldly things you are asking for a fall.
17   *nis but* is nothing but
19   *Know thy contree* know which is your true country (i.e. heaven, not earth)
20   *heghe* high (i.e. main road)   *gost* spirit (alluding to St Paul's distinction between the spirit and the flesh)
22   *Vache* A pun, on French *vache* (cow, going back to the address to the reader as a beast in his stall) and on the name of a friend of Chaucer's, Sir Philip de la Vache, for whom the poem may have been written when he was out of favour at court.
23   *thrall* a slave
25   *Made ... noght* created you out of nothing
25–7 *in especial .. mede* draw near to God, so far as you in particular are concerned, and pray for a heavenly reward for mankind in general, including yourself. (There may be a pun on *mede*, which could mean 'meadow'—suitable for a cow—as well as 'reward'.)

6 *Balade to Rosemounde*

Madame, ye been of all beauté shrine
As fer as cercled is the mapemounde,
For as the cristal glorious ye shine,
And like the ruby been your cheekes rounde.
Therwith ye been so merry and so jocounde   5
That at a revel whan that I see you daunce,
It is an oinement unto my wounde,
Though ye to me ne do no daliaunce.

For though I weepe of teres full a tyne,
Yet may that wo mine herte nat confounde;   10
Your semy vois, that ye so small out-twine,
Maketh my thought in joy and bliss habounde.
So curtaisly I go, with love bounde,
That to myself I say, in my penaunce,
'Sufficeth me to love you, Rosemounde,   15
Though ye to me ne do no daliaunce.'

Nas never pyk walwed in galauntine
As I in love am walwed and ywounde,
For which full ofte I of myself devine
That I am trewe Tristam the secounde.   20
My love may not refreyde nor affounde;
I brenne ay in an amorous plesaunce.
Do what you list, I will your thrall be founde,
Though ye to me ne do no daliaunce.

2   As far as the map of the world extends
7   *oinement* ointment   *wounde* (i.e. of love)
8   *ne do no daliaunce* hold no conversation (but *daliaunce* was a vague word, which could imply 'love-making', or at the least 'conversation about love')
9   *full a tyne* a complete tubful
10 *confounde* overcome
11 Your thread of a voice, which you twist out so thinly
12 *habounde* abound
13 I go about so courteously, enchained by love
14 *penaunce* suffering
17 There was never a pike wallowing in sauce
18 *ywounde* entwined
19 *devine* declare
20 *Tristam* Tristan or Tristram, the tragic lover of King Mark's wife Iseult, the hero of many medieval courtly romances
21 *may ... affounde* is not capable of cooling down or becoming deadened
22 *brenne ay* burn continuously
23 Do what you please, I will always be found to be your slave

7 Blacksmiths

Swart smeked smithes smattered with smoke
Drive me to deth with din of her dintes.
Swich nois on nightes ne herd men never:
What knavene cry and clatering of knockes!
The cammede kongons cryen after 'Col, col!'   5
And blowen here bellwes that all her brain brestes.
'Huff, puff,' saith that on, 'Haff, paff,' that other.
They spitten and spraulen and spellen many spelles,
They gnawen and gnachen, they grones togidere,
And holden hem hote with here hard hamers.   10
Of a bole-hide been here barm-felles,
Her shankes been shakeled for the fere-flunderes.
Hevy hameres they han that hard been handled,
Stark strokes they striken on a steled stokke:
'Lus, bus, las, das,' rowten be rowe.   15
Swiche dolful a dreme the Devil it todrive!
The maister longeth a littil and lasheth a lesse,
Twineth hem twain and toucheth a treble:
'Tik, tak, hic, hac, tiket, taket, tik, tak,
Lus, bus, lus, das.' Swich lyf they leden,   20
Alle clothemeres, Crist hem give sorwe!
May no man for brenwateres on night han his rest.

1   Black smoky smiths, begrimed with smoke,
2   Are driving me to death with the noise of their bangs.
3   Such a noise at night-time was never heard by men:
4   Such a shouting of workmen and clatter of knocking!
5   The snub-nosed changelings call out for 'Coal, coal!'
6   And blow their bellows till their brains completely burst.
7   'Huff, puff,' says one, 'Haff, paff,' says another.
8   They spit and lurch around and keep on and on talking
9   They gnaw and gnash their teeth, they groan together,
10   And keep themselves hot by hammering hard.
11   Their leather aprons are made of bull-hide,
12   Their legs are protected against the sparks from the fire.
13   They have heavy hammers that are handled hard,
14   They strike heavy blows on a steel anvil:
15   'Lus, bus, las, das,' they crash down in turn.
16   Such a miserable noise, may the Devil drive it away!
17   The master-smith lengthens a little (piece of iron) and hammers a smaller piece,
18   Twists the two together and strikes a treble note:
19   (Self-explanatory)
20   Such is the life they lead,
21   All horse-outfitters, may Christ give them sorrow!
22   No-one can get his rest at night on account of the water-burners.

Note

Clothemeres and *brenwateres* are both late examples of a characteristic device of alliterative verse, the kenning. This involves substituting a cryptic metaphorical expression for a noun, as 'foamy-necked floater' for ship, or 'gannet's bath' for sea. *Brenwateres* alludes to the steam and hissing when the smiths plunge red-hot iron into water.